Designing with the Body

Design Thinking, Design Theory
Ken Friedman and Erik Stolterman, editors

Designing with the Body

Somaesthetic Interaction Design

Kristina Höök

The MIT Press
Cambridge, Massachusetts
London, England

This book was set in ITC Stone Sans Std and ITC Stone Serif Std by Toppan Best-set Premedia Limited. Printed and bound in the United States of America.

Library of Congress Cataloging-in-Publication Data

Names: Höök, Kristina.
Title: Designing with the body : somaesthetic interaction design / Kristina Höök.
Description: Cambridge, MA : The MIT Press, 2018. | Series: Design thinking, design theory | Includes bibliographical references and index.
Identifiers: LCCN 2018001230 | ISBN 9780262038560 (hardcover : alk. paper)
Subjects: LCSH: Multimodal user interfaces (Computer systems) | Human-machine systems. | Somaesthesia. | Mind and body.
Classification: LCC QA76.9.U83 H64 2018 | DDC 005.4/37--dc23 LC record available at https://lccn.loc.gov/2018001230

10 9 8 7 6 5 4 3 2 1

To my father: missing you

Contents

Series Foreword

As professions go, design is relatively young. The practice of design predates professions. In fact, the practice of design—making things to serve a useful goal, making tools—predates the human race. Making tools is one of the attributes that made us human in the first place.

Design, in the most generic sense of the word, began over 2.5 million years ago when *Homo habilis* manufactured the first tools. Human beings were designing well before we began to walk upright. Four hundred thousand years ago, we began to manufacture spears. By forty thousand years ago, we had moved up to specialized tools.

Urban design and architecture came along ten thousand years ago in Mesopotamia. Interior architecture and furniture design probably emerged with them. It was another five thousand years before graphic design and typography got their start in Sumer with the development of cuneiform. After that, things picked up speed.

All goods and services are designed. The urge to design—to consider a situation, imagine a better situation, and act to create that improved situation—goes back to our prehuman ancestors. Making tools helped us to become what we are; design helped to make us human.

Today, the word *design* means many things. The common factor linking them is service, and designers are engaged in a service profession in which the results of their work meet human needs.

Design is first of all a process. The word *design* entered the English language in the 1500s as a verb, with the first written citation of the verb dated to the year 1548. *Merriam-Webster's Collegiate Dictionary* defines the verb *design* as "to conceive and plan out in the mind; to have as a specific purpose; to devise for a specific function or end." Related to these definitions is the act of drawing, with an emphasis on the nature of the drawing as a plan or map, as well as "to draw plans for; to create, fashion, execute or construct according to plan."

Half a century later, the word began to be used as a noun, with the first cited use of the noun *design* occurring in 1588. *Merriam-Webster's* defines the noun as "a particular purpose held in view by an individual or group; deliberate, purposive planning; a mental project or scheme in which means to an end are laid down." Here, too, purpose and planning toward desired outcomes are central. Among these are "a preliminary sketch or outline showing the main features of something to be executed; an underlying scheme that governs functioning, developing or unfolding; a plan or protocol for carrying out or accomplishing something; the arrangement of elements or details in a product or work of art." Today, we design large, complex processes, systems, and services, and we design organizations and structures to produce them. Design has changed considerably since our remote ancestors made the first stone tools.

At a highly abstract level, Herbert Simon's definition covers nearly all imaginable instances of design. To design, Simon writes, is to "[devise] courses of action aimed at changing existing situations into preferred ones" (Simon, *The Sciences of the Artificial*, 2nd ed. [Cambridge, MA: MIT Press, 1982], 129). Design, properly defined, is the entire process across the full range of domains required for any given outcome.

But the design process is always more than a general, abstract way of working. Design takes concrete form in the work of the service professions that meet human needs, a broad range of making and planning disciplines. These include industrial design, graphic design, textile design, furniture design, information design, process design, product design, interaction design, transportation design, educational design, systems design, urban design, design leadership, and design management, as well as architecture, engineering, information technology, and computer science.

These fields focus on different subjects and objects. They have distinct traditions, methods, and vocabularies, used and put into practice by distinct and often dissimilar professional groups. Although the traditions dividing these groups are distinct, common boundaries sometimes form a border. When this happens, they serve as meeting points, where common concerns build bridges. Today, ten challenges uniting the design professions form such a set of common concerns.

Three performance challenges, four substantive challenges, and three contextual challenges bind the design disciplines and professions together as a common field. The performance challenges arise because all design professions

1. act on the physical world,
2. address human needs, and
3. generate the built environment.

In the past, these common attributes were not sufficient to transcend the boundaries of tradition. Today, objective changes in the larger world give rise to four substantive challenges that are driving convergence in design practice and research. These substantive challenges are

1. increasingly ambiguous boundaries between artifacts, structure, and process;
2. increasingly large-scale social, economic, and industrial frames;
3. an increasingly complex environment of needs, requirements, and constraints; and
4. information content that often exceeds the value of physical substance.

These challenges require new frameworks of theory and research to address contemporary problem areas while solving specific cases and problems. In professional design practice, we often find that solving design problems requires interdisciplinary teams with a transdisciplinary focus. Fifty years ago, a sole practitioner and an assistant or two might have solved most design problems; today, we need groups of people with skills across several disciplines and the additional skills that enable professionals to work with, listen to, and learn from each other as they solve problems.

Three contextual challenges define the nature of many design problems today. Although many design problems function at a simpler level, these issues affect many of the major design problems that challenge us, and these challenges also affect simple design problems linked to complex social, mechanical, or technical systems. These issues are

1. a complex environment in which many projects or products cross the boundaries of several organizations, as well as stakeholder, producer, and user groups;
2. projects or products that must meet the expectations of many organizations, stakeholders, producers, and users; and
3. demands at every level of production, distribution, reception, and control.

These ten challenges require a qualitatively different approach to professional design practice than was the case in earlier times. Past environments were simpler. They made simpler demands. Individual experience and personal development were sufficient for depth and substance in professional practice. Although experience and development are still necessary, they are no longer sufficient. Most of today's design challenges require analytic and synthetic planning skills that cannot be developed through practice alone.

Professional design practice today involves advanced knowledge. This knowledge is not solely a higher level of professional practice. It is also a qualitatively different form of professional practice that emerges in response to the demands of the information society and the knowledge economy to which it gives rise.

In an essay ("Why Design Education Must Change," *Core77* [November 26, 2010]), Donald Norman challenges the premises and practices of the design profession. In the past, designers operated on the belief that talent and a willingness to jump into problems with both feet gives them an edge in solving problems. Norman writes:

> In the early days of industrial design, the work was primarily focused upon physical products. Today, however, designers work on organizational structure and social problems, on interaction, service, and experience design. Many problems involve complex social and political issues. As a result, designers have become applied behavioral scientists, but they are woefully undereducated for the task. Designers often fail to understand the complexity of the issues and the depth of knowledge already known. They claim that fresh eyes can produce novel solutions, but then they wonder why these solutions are seldom implemented, or if implemented, why they fail. Fresh eyes can indeed produce insightful results, but the eyes must also be educated and knowledgeable. Designers often lack the requisite understanding. Design schools do not train students about these complex issues, about the interlocking complexities of human and social behavior, about the behavioral sciences, technology, and business. There is little or no training in science, the scientific method, and experimental design.

This is not industrial design in the sense of designing products, but industry-related design, design as thought and action for solving problems and imagining new futures. This new MIT Press series of books emphasizes strategic design to create value through innovative products and services, and it emphasizes design as service through rigorous creativity, critical inquiry, and an ethics of respectful design. This rests on a sense of understanding, empathy, and appreciation for people, for nature, and for the world we shape through design. Our goal as editors is to develop a series of vital conversations that help designers and researchers to serve business, industry, and the public sector for positive social and economic outcomes.

We will present books that bring a new sense of inquiry to design, helping to shape a more reflective and stable design discipline able to support a stronger profession grounded in empirical research, generative concepts, and the solid theory that gives rise to what W. Edwards Deming described as *profound knowledge* (Deming, *The New Economics for Industry, Government, Education* [Cambridge, MA: MIT, Center for Advanced Engineering Study, 1993]). For Deming, a physicist, engineer, and designer, profound knowledge comprised systems thinking and the understanding of processes embedded in systems; an understanding of variation and the tools we need to understand variation; a theory of knowledge; and a foundation in human psychology. This is the beginning of *deep design*—the union of deep practice with robust intellectual inquiry.

A series on design thinking and theory faces the same challenges that we face as a profession. On one level, design is a general human process that we use to understand and to shape our world. Nevertheless, we cannot address this process or the world in its general, abstract form. Rather, we meet the challenges of design in particular situations, addressing problems or ideas in a situated context. The challenges we face as designers today are as diverse as the problems clients bring us. We are involved in design for economic anchors, economic continuity, and economic growth. We design for urban needs and rural needs, for social development and creative communities. We are involved with environmental sustainability and economic policy, agriculture, competitive crafts for export, competitive products and brands for microenterprises, developing new products for bottom-of-pyramid markets, and redeveloping old products for mature or wealthy markets. Within the framework of design, we are also challenged to design for extreme situations, for biotech, nanotech, and new materials, and to design for social business, as well as to face conceptual challenges for worlds that do not yet exist, such as the world beyond the Kurzweil singularity—and to design for new visions of the world that does exist.

The Design Thinking, Design Theory series from the MIT Press will explore these issues and more—meeting them, examining them, and helping designers to address them.

Join us in this journey.

Ken Friedman   Erik Stolterman
Editors, Design Thinking, Design Theory Series

Preface

Sometimes when I go horseback riding I become "one" with the horse—together, we form a sort of centaur. This transformation requires a complete somatic communication between human and horse and full presence in the moment as our individual movements fold into each other and become one.

One instance of such a "centaur moment" stands out. Years ago, I took a riding lesson with a horse named Liberty. The lesson wasn't easy: Liberty was tense and easily spooked and I struggled for control. Finally, the instructor asked us to move into a canter, one of the faster gaits of the horse, a controlled three-beat gait. The speed and the rhythmic beat of the canter are exhilarating in themselves, and I felt my tensions begin to dissolve. I no longer feared that Liberty would be spooked again and as I relaxed, I also took more control. As our speed increased, our nervous energy was let loose, and the steering became easier. The gait became physically enjoyable.

Liberty's canter was big in its stride and had an expansive, rolling rhythm. Together we moved between canter and rising trot—a slightly slower two-beat gait—back and forth. Both rhythms felt relaxed and beautiful. Liberty became more interested in the dialogue with me. The experience became fun, which in turn made the whole thing work. I only had to think "forwards" or "let's canter" and it happened (see figure 0.1).

For this to occur, true sympathy is required. You have to recognize the otherness and difference in the horse and create a lived experience together. You have to forget about your own human self and instead create a centaur self—consisting of two agents acting together. It is not without risks or wilderness; you might fall, the horse might take off in an unexpected direction. But when the connection and collaboration between the two minds happen, it is inexpressibly joyful. (excerpt based on Höök 2010, 232–233)

This might seem like an odd beginning for a book on interaction design. What does horseback riding have to do with the design of interactive systems? In many ways, of course, they couldn't be more different. And yet, what we strive to achieve in interaction design is very similar to the sense

Figure 0.1
Horseback riding

of oneness I felt with Liberty. A successful interactive tool will invite the user to become a sort of centaur, engaging in a smooth, embodied interaction, creating an intimate correspondence between users' actions and system response. In my research, this has become my guiding ideal: to design interactions that harmonize—aesthetically and somatically.

I decided to write this book for two reasons. First, we are at a watershed moment: our relationship to technology is about to undergo a dramatic and irreversible shift. With the rise of ubiquitous technology, data-driven design, and the Internet of Things, our interactions and our interfaces with technology will look radically different in the years ahead, incorporating changes like full body interaction, shape-changing interfaces, wearables, and body- and movement-tracking apps. At the same time that the elements of this shift have come into place, my own long and winding design journey convinced me that an aesthetically oriented, soma-grounded design approach will render better design processes, far better suited to the development of interaction design right now. I call this approach *soma design*—a process that reincorporates the body and movement into a design regime that has long privileged language and logic.

Claiming that a soma design process will render better design is a bold statement, and it is a statement that needs qualifying: What do I mean by *better*? I will return to this concept throughout the book, but in short, I have come to see the importance of caring for and cultivating my own soma—my subjective way of being in the world, moving, perceiving, engaging, experiencing—and my capacity for aesthetic appreciation, because those somatic engagements will in turn shape me as a designer in profound ways. They will shape me in a literal sense, changing my ways of being in the world, changing my muscles, nervous system reactions, behaviors, experiences, and feelings. They will change my capacity for aesthetic appreciation, which in turn changes my ability to design. At the same time, however, it is crucial to recognize that engaging with my own soma is not a selfish and egocentric undertaking with the goal of developing solely one's own soma and appreciation skills; it is also an empathic, intersubjective engagement, a route to caring about others' somas, however radically they may differ from our own. When we hone and care for aesthetic qualities of the technologies we use to construct our interactions, and when we attend to our own experiences, the designs we bring forth can orchestrate experiences that spur improved aesthetic engagement for our end users.

My second reason for writing this book is that it also became clear to me that the soma design process offers an important alternative to prevailing ways of working in my field—a style I find increasingly oppressive, both in its approach and in the design work it produces. Contemporary design-practice values emphasize fast-moving, aggressive, lean processes intended to arrive at design concepts as quickly as possible. Any novelty in method will only be accepted if it claims to help end users achieve their goals more rapidly, to reduce friction, to get users hooked in fast feedback loops, or to arrive at a working design through the rapid generation of semi-finished design elements (such as wireframes). The prevailing brainstorming methods focus on getting ideas out there rapidly by relaxing your reflective, critical mind. The drawback of this approach is a narrowness of design and a potential lack of aesthetic enjoyment on the part of the user. Soma design, on the other hand, provides an alternative to this aggressive, goal-oriented design process; it offers a slower, more thoughtful approach. Although a high-pressured industry will certainly resist such change, such a process would yield better products and create healthier and more sustainable companies in every sense. Delivering better experiences and better products for users who engage with interactive technologies on an everyday basis would, in the end, benefit both these businesses and their customers.

My hope is that this book will be the beginnings of a new approach, appealing both to professional designers and to academics teaching or learning how to design with interactive technologies. Hopefully, we can spread tacit knowledge about how to engage fully, with our whole beings, in design: aesthetically, bodily, intellectually, and with our values.

In fact, while writing this book, I have come to believe that engaging somatically and aesthetically in the design process is fundamental to *all* interaction design. I no longer regard soma design as relevant solely for designing bodily engagement. Somatic awareness is not only a matter of being aware of your body—muscles, nervous system, emotions, or organs. Somatics acknowledges that there is no separation between mind and body and connects the self with all of these processes, as well as with empathic engagements with others. Ultimately, this means better design processes—and better design overall.

My Journey to Soma Design

When I started working on designing interactive applications for body-based interaction in 2000, I fumbled around, looking for design ideals, methods, and examples of interesting systems. At the time, in my lab, we were building games and life-logging reflection tools, using sensors and movement models (Paiva et al. 2002; Ståhl et al. 2009). I will describe some of these early efforts later in the book. I'm still very proud of this work, but I also have to admit: that was a frustrating time. My colleagues and I were exploring the design space in an unstructured, uninformed manner, without any clear theory or design practice to build on. Something was missing. While I wanted to engage with the aesthetics of body-based designs, we had no theory, no strategy, no sense of what aesthetics we could be striving for. The designs we worked on, such as SenToy (Paiva et al. 2002), Affective Diary (Ståhl et al. 2009), Affective Health (Sanches et al. 2010), and eMoto (Fagerberg, Ståhl, and Höök 2004), inadvertently exposed our language-oriented, symbolic, hypothesis-rationalization-driven assumptions—beliefs we did not even realize that we held at the time. It was hard to liberate ourselves from the strong focus on symbolic interaction and visualizations. At the same time, it was clear that our end users engaged with our systems for all sorts of reasons, not only as a rational language-oriented process pursuing well-defined, preset goals. They looked for playful interactions, for mystery, for artful experiences of their own somatics, and for ways of making meaning out of the chaotic randomness of everyday events in their lives.

These user encounters reminded us of the richness in how people make sense of their everyday, subjective lives. But the design work also pointed to the problematic issues around *representation* of bodily, subjective engagements. In particular, as soon as we created a representation of some movement or emotional engagement and mirrored it back to our users, the representation would, of course, only highlight certain somatic engagements and not others. As the representation became available for scrutiny and comparison with our users' inner experience of themselves, it sometimes enriched their view of themselves, but at other times it felt reductionist to them. For example, when building the Affective Diary system (Ståhl et al. 2009)—a system that collects mobile data (text messages, Bluetooth encounters, phone calls) and biosensor data, then visualizes the result as a "blobby" character on the screen (see figure 0.2)—we discovered that the image distanced users from their subjective experience of their own bodies. The body portrayed on the screen sometimes had a life of its own—a strange organism with its own emotional and social processes. For users to respond to the image and use it in their own practices, they had to consciously work to engage themselves with it. This made the interaction less seamless and intuitive than was intended.

Although this was a frustrating period, as I mentioned, it was also a very fertile incubation period. We experimented, engaged with new ideas, observed people using our designs, and developed the basis for theories. Later, this allowed us to form the design research program (Redström 2017) presented in this book. Without this experimentation and the freedom to pursue our design ideas, we would not have known what to look for or understood when we finally found it.

Embodied Interaction, Emotion, and User Experience

When we were conducting our early experiments, interaction design researchers had recently turned toward three concepts as a path to understanding and designing for richer interactions: theories of *embodied interaction*, models of *emotion*, and new ways of engaging with *user experience*. Let me make a brief detour into those three areas to explain why they helped us—and also why they failed to provide us with all the guidance we sought.

Embodied interaction was introduced in 2001 by Dourish in his book *Where the Action Is*. *Embodiment* is a term used in phenomenological theories to denote our subjective selves—the ways we perceive the world through our bodily and social presence. By using the term *embodiment*, Merleau-Ponty and others aimed to emphasize the difference between our subjective, bodily ways of being in the world and the (literally) *objective* perspective, in which the body is considered an object, separated from the world. The latter is a useful perspective in some situations, such as medical scientific studies, because it allows us to study certain affordances of the

Figure 0.2
The interface of the Affective Diary system, displaying mobile data alongside "blob-by" characters portraying biosensor data over time

human body—but this perspective cannot fully explain human behavior and experience. Embodiment speaks of how we are always in the world, with our bodies, sociality, and practices—that we are inseparable from the world. The way our perception and knowing works is entangled deeply, inseparably, with our surroundings. We are shaping and being shaped by our social and physical contexts. There is no way of understanding our perception and cognition without engaging with those contexts.

Dourish saw an opportunity to connect this understanding of what it means to be an embodied subject in the world, immersed in our physical and social settings, to contemporary developments in social and tangible computing. *Tangible computing* refers to ways of moving interfaces off the screen and into tangible forms, allowing us to interact through objects, rather than symbols on a screen. Tangible computing made it even clearer that our bodily ways of being in the world had to be considered in our design processes. At the time, sociological studies of how people incorporated digital tools into their practices had made headway into the field of human-computer interaction. Social computing was a recognition of how "meaning is something that users create through the ways in which they interact with technology and with each other" (Dourish 2001, 128). Embodied interaction put a spotlight on how we need to design with a keen eye on social practices and how they emerge, as well as on our bodily ways of being in the world. This way of looking at the human condition and interaction design helped me see how design processes could never start from some abstract idea of a "human being" in her "natural habitat." Nor do we function as predictable machines that, given certain input stimuli, always respond in certain predictable ways. Instead, any system we build has to be made part of our lifeworld because this is where our perception, actions, and practices are shaped. A good design will be *embodied with* our everyday practices, beliefs, attitudes, culture, and bodily ways of being in the world. As phrased by Djajingingrat and colleagues: "Part of the embodiment challenge, then, is to create a physical, contactual and dynamic fit between human and product" (Djajadiningrat, Matthews, and Stienstra 2007, 661).

Although this approach was inspirational to our work at the time, Dourish's concept of embodiment never really concretely addressed the actual, physical body as such. Embodied interaction did not speak of our muscles, our nervous system, the ways we can and cannot move, our skeletons, how emotions are processed throughout our brain, releasing hormones, activating muscles, attention and perception, and how those elements would change and be shaped by new interactions. Nor did it speak of the designs and interactions that would create interesting, meaningful, and aesthetic relationships among movements, actions, and interactions—making them fit with one another. Furthermore, embodied interaction did not provide any ideals about what kind of aesthetic experiences we could and should engage users in. To designers, embodied interaction did not offer an *ideal* for what to design, but instead an analytical framework—a very important contribution that shaped much of our analysis at the time, but lacking in some respects.

The second important trend at the time was a resurrection of the role of emotion in human life. As discussed by Picard (1997), emotion had been seen for a long time as the irrational side of human behavior, the factor that messed up our decision making and rational reasoning. But a new wave of research pointed to the importance of emotion to regulate behavior—for survival, for making decisions, for sociality, empathy, and human experience. This in turn spurred interest from the artificial intelligence field, as well as from interaction design. If emotion was this important to human behavior, then as designers we could not continue designing as if people could be modeled only as rational machines. Picard's seminal work on affective computing (ibid.) significantly influenced my thinking. Here I found inspirational knowledge on how our bodies function and respond to external stimuli. Emotion, she argued, makes up an important part of our corporeality, guiding our actions in a millisecond, long before our rational brain has figured out what is going on. These very basic emotional processes are intimately connected to and changed by our experiences, reasoning, and culture. Our experiences flow back and forth among perceiving, paying attention, attributing appraisal to situations, acting, learning, and *feeling*.

Unfortunately, the theories presented in the growing field of affective computing were not primarily focused on feeling or aesthetic experience. They did not emphasize emotion, perception, and corporality as something shaped by the world we live in—including by the systems and technologies we are surrounded by. Instead, emotion and body were seen as "objects" that could be studied, understood, and modeled by a computer system (Boehner et al. 2007). Human emotions were seen as units that could be isolated, classified, and predicted in interaction with technology, rather than embodied phenomena ranging over the whole technosocial system, changing with our experiences and interacting with others, with technology, and with ourselves. Most importantly to my colleagues and me, this approach lacked an account of the aesthetics and felt experience of those interactions.

Standing at the crossroads of embodiment and theories of affective computing, I was utterly confused. I had no clear guidance for how to approach design in a way that was intimately connected to our physical, corporeal realities, that interacted with, and at the same time altered, the conditions we experience.

Most of all, I did not have a grip on the *felt* experiences and aesthetics.

It was obvious that whatever technology we might create to be worn on our bodies or to respond to our movements would also change our capacity for certain experiences, as well as our practices and our understanding of our own bodies. For example, a simple tool like a pulse meter can change our sports practice; today, runners all over the world attempt to optimize their running so that their heart rates stay at the "right" level (whatever that might be). The pulse meter allows runners to isolate one factor relevant to running, allowing runners to scrutinize that factor and measure its change over time, to compare their performance with others, and to control their heart rates when running by adjusting speed and movement patterns. Although it is by no means simple to assess what that "optimal" heart rate might be, because many factors are involved, over time such monitors have led to a consensus that an ideal heart rate will not exhaust your resources and will optimize your performance; in fact, a practice has developed. Heart-rate tracking and sharing has become a cultural phenomenon. Runners exchange experiences and knowledge about how to engage with this technology; they discuss when to use it and how to make it an embodied part of what they refer to as "being in the zone" or getting to the right "feeling" (Tholander and Nylander 2015).

We might at first react quite negatively to this use of technology, perhaps arguing that runners should be able to feel their heart rates just by listening inwardly. However, this requires us to consider carefully what it means to know yourself. Is there really a conflict between inward listening and using a tool to help you listen? Isolating a single body signal—in this case, heart rate—and mirroring that single measurement back to the user comes with a risk. If runners forget about the complexities of the running experience, focusing solely on keeping the heart rate at the right level, they might exhaust themselves, forget to drink properly, hurt some muscle or ligament, or forget to listen to any of the other signs and signals their bodies are emitting. However, if properly used, for many it becomes a learning tool, technology that provides one piece in the puzzle, turning attention in one direction that, step by step, can be embodied with the complex understandings of the whole sporting experience. If used properly, heart-rate technology embodies a form of bodily learning, supported by a "prosthesis," that runners are invited to share. Tacit knowledge that advanced runners develop by listening to their heart rates is thus made accessible to novices. When taking part in the vast culture around pulse meters, a whole practice exists that guides this process of embodiment. It supports the practice; then, later, runners can get rid of the crutch and instead rely entirely on the *feeling* of a good running experience, integrating the many signs and signals their bodies emit into a whole (Tholander and Nylander 2015).

But how do you design in the vacuum that exists before such a whole practice has developed? And beyond designing to optimize some sports practices, what would render *aesthetically* interesting interactions? If aesthetics is concerned with training your ability to attend to sensations, to appreciate them, to engage fully with them, then you have to work quite hard to make a pulse meter part of your aesthetic experience of running. At least initially, a pulse meter will force you to understand your body as an object—not as an embodied subjectivity. Only later can you come back to the feeling of running, attending to all the parts that come together into the whole experience.

This brings us to the third concept that was shaping interaction design as we started our work: user experience. In the so-called third wave of human-computer interaction (HCI) (Bødker 2006), researchers asked not only how interactions could be made more efficient and usable (first wave) or how to make teams work together efficiently (second wave). Instead, they started to ask what conditions afforded good, interesting, scary, boring, important, addictive, shallow, profound, ludic, or any other of all the possible experiences we might design for. Digital technologies were entering all walks of life: games, home life, social interactions, sports, health. What would make people intrinsically motivated to engage with these technologies? It was no longer enough to make systems usable and efficient; they also had to create the basis for experiences that users would be interested in. I became particularly inspired by McCarthy and Wright's pragmatist account of experience and what it could do for interaction design (McCarthy and Wright 2004a).

McCarthy and Wright argued that experiences are always unique. Every time we play a computer game, for example, the experience will be slightly different. We will be in a slightly different mood, we will vary our behavior a bit, our experiences from the previous session will influence the new experience, and so on. Only sometimes will this lead to a strong aesthetic experience that we can clearly delimit afterward, with a clear beginning and end and with some emotion as a congruent force tying all the different aspects together. They based their reasoning on, among other sources, the work by the pragmatist Dewey, who wrote *Art as Experience* (Dewey [1934] 2005). Dewey attempted to shift attention from trying to tie aesthetics to the art objects themselves, instead framing experiences as arising in dialogue between some art piece or situation and the person engaging with it. Similarly, McCarthy and Wright argued that user experiences of technologies could not be seen solely as properties of the design, but instead should be viewed as unique experiences arising between the end user and the user's interactions with a system.

McCarthy and Wright's framing of unique aesthetic experiences was very inspirational to me—and influenced the whole field of interaction design. But I had to turn to other pragmatists to find a stronger engagement with the bodily, subjective side of these experiences. Through important and early work by Schiphorst (2009a, 2009b) and Petersen (Petersen et al. 2004), I found the somaesthetic theories by Richard Shusterman (2000a), a continuation of the work by Dewey and other pragmatists. Shusterman (2008) created the concept of somaesthetics from a combination of *soma*—our subjective self, body, emotion, and thinking—and *aesthetics*—our perceptual appreciation of the world.

Although Shusterman's ideas immediately appealed to me, some of his conceptualizations at first did not make any sense to me. Only when I engaged in some of the body practices that he spoke of did they started to make sense. In fact, I was totally amazed by how body practices such as kung fu or the Feldenkrais method (Feldenkrais [1972] 1977) spurred aesthetic experiences I did not know I was capable of and that I had never felt before. The engagement with Shusterman's somaesthetic theories lead to a whole new wave of creative work in my research group—and to the ideas, designs, and methods that I will introduce in this book.

I want to make one important point clear at this stage: there is a huge difference between engaging in an existing body practice, such as Feldenkrais, and creatively designing entirely novel interactions, shaping new practices and new experiences. We might be inspired by some existing body practice or aesthetic expression, but designing with somatic engagement is something else. Instead of experiencing what is already orchestrated for us, we need to design such orchestrations, scaffolded by digital technologies. Adapting Shusterman's approach into a design process took quite a lot of translation work, as well as a long period of massaging ideas through practical design work. Shusterman accommodated for some aspects of this translation; his theories gave me and my research group some conceptualizations, as well as a practice that allowed us to start exploring. But only after engaging with our design process for a long time, repeatedly designing, feeling, redesigning, were we able to translate and make use of our gained somatic understanding, fashioning it into a novel design with the qualities we sought. Our design process was long and winding, challenging in a way I had not experienced before. But the reward was worth it. At the other end of the long design journey, I finally had the conceptualizations and tacit knowledge I first sought back in the year 2000. The process gave me a renewed interest in interaction design research and practice and a passion for somaesthetic design work that I feel the urge to share.

Mixing Personal Life with Research

After immersing myself in somaesthetic theories, I was lucky to meet with Professor Shusterman in several different contexts. Finally, in 2016, I spent part of my sabbatical at Florida Atlantic University (FAU), where he currently works—a rewarding time during which I could engage directly with his ideas and ask all the questions I had.

What surprised me at first was how personal he was in explaining where his experiences and theories came from. In his writings and in our discussions, he gave accounts of his years in Paris, dancing in clubs with female professional dancers, later going to Japan to learn Zen Buddhism practices, training to become a Feldenkrais practitioner, and so on. Not only did he speak about his own experiences and the journey from those transformational experiences in his own life, he often interpreted others' theories and philosophical inquiries about similar accounts of the philosopher's personal life. For example, when we discussed William James and his detailed and insightful accounts of mental illnesses, he repeatedly spoke of James's own life; his hypochondria made him extremely attentive to psychological signs and signals, which in turn shaped his understanding of psychology. Step by step, I started to see the point of interpreting theories against the personal backdrops of their creators.

My own academic journey started in natural science, and my undergraduate training was in computer science. For a long time, I held my work to extremely strong objectivist (and reductionist) ideals. The idea of connecting my own personal experiences to my research was quite foreign to me. It took me years to untangle my knowledge views, uniting my understanding of what research can produce with my everyday experiences of living my own personal life: of being a mother, a grandmother, a horseback rider, a woman. I have slowly arrived at a point at which I recognize the need to provide, or even the necessity of providing, some account of my own personal journey as a backdrop to understanding my scholarship. Without that, you, the reader, cannot probe and evaluate my insights, and you might not even understand where they come from or what they really entail. Parts of this book therefore will be written from a first-person perspective. I will try to describe my own somatic engagement, my values, and my creative practice. Rather than seeing those subjective descriptions as less valuable, less objective, less generalizable, I believe they have the opposite effect. If you come to this text with the same background as I had, however, you will occasionally struggle with my writings, distrusting them, looking for generalizations and solid, objective proof, and perhaps not (always) finding them. Hopefully, if you get through the whole book, you will be curious enough to try out some of the tactics I describe in your own design practice. Only then will the realities behind my personal accounts and experiences be available to you and make sense.

Intended Audience

I foresee three groups of readers who might be interested in soma design. First, design researchers aiming to increase design knowledge relating to aesthetics, values, and engagements of the self and compassion in design work. Second, students at the PhD or MSc level with either engineering or industrial design backgrounds interested in extending their repertory of design skills. Third, the book is relevant to design practitioners. In particular, it will appeal to practitioners who have run into design problems related to wearables, full-body interaction, health applications, dance, games, or other aesthetic practices.

In my experience, design practitioners are already engaging with processes similar to those discussed in this book. The Internet of Things and new materials entering the market have demanded a shift from designing web or mobile apps mainly accessible through a screen to designing interactions taking place everywhere. Many design practitioners are already engaging with these Internet of Things materials and their imagined use contexts through aesthetic and first-person perspectives, touching, feeling, and shaping the materials into meaningful designs. I believe that the time is ripe to introduce a coherent somaesthetic design theory to support design researchers and students in academia.

Lately, more interpretative, subjective accounts of aesthetics, design processes and experiences of technology have been introduced to the academic field of HCI. There are, for example, more autoethnographic accounts of using technologies (Höök 2010; Williams 2015). Our design processes, we now recognize, problematize and increasingly work with autobiographical design processes. In an autobiographical design process, the researcher acts as researcher, designer, and end user to gain deep, subjective knowledge of what works and what does not work in a design (Neustaedter and Sengers 2012). Jeffrey and Shaowen Bardzell have done a better job than I can do here of connecting these trends with century-old traditions in the humanities (Bardzell and Bardzell 2015). For a proper grounding in those traditions, I recommend turning to their work.

What I will try to add to this growing body of design knowledge is the beginnings of a *soma design theory*. Similar to how Shusterman frames somaesthetics (Shusterman 2008), this will not be a theory that can be understood solely through an analytical engagement and by reading this book. Instead, soma design must also, by necessity, be a *pragmatic* study of methodologies to improve our functioning and a *practical* study in which we test those pragmatic methods on ourselves to render experience and design concrete. To really grasp the somaesthetic design experiences introduced here, an *active* stance is required. The somaesthetic interaction design project demands improving our designerly skills through engaging the whole self in creative activities.

To a design practitioner, the idea of autobiographical design is not novel: there is no way of designing without "living" your own design—in your imagination, as well as repeatedly once it exists. But some specific tactics that somaesthetic interaction designers have found inspirational will probably be new to you.

If, on the other hand, you have never worked as a designer, you might struggle with some of the accounts provided in this book. If so, I propose engaging in some of the practical exercises that I describe here and there in the text. After experiencing somaesthetic design, the conceptualizations will be filled with meaning that are difficult obtain in any other manner.

Writing This Book: On Honesty and Personal Experience

I wrote the bulk of this book during my sabbatical year, in 2016, away from my everyday work at KTH Royal Institute of Technology in Stockholm. I first spent some months with Richard Shusterman at Florida Atlantic University, often sitting under a big tree on campus, discussing philosophy, values, ideas. I also spent many hours on the Boca Raton beach doing yoga—both on my own and with a class. I was not used to being away from my family, living alone. This meant I was, in a sense, forced to meet myself, to face my beliefs, attitudes, behaviors, and anxieties. It became at times what Thoreau speaks of in *Walden*: an awakening of the senses (Thoreau [1854] 2016). I could not distract myself with the business of everyday office work or my busy family life. Instead, I indulged in turning my eye inward. I made myself experience the somaesthetics concepts analytically, pragmatically, and practically.

The second half of my sabbatical I spent with my colleague Katherine Isbister and her research group at UC Santa Cruz. Here, I continued to engage in bodily practices, but I also got the chance to discuss concepts with my colleagues in interaction design. For years, Isbister has been involved in designing movement-based games and various wearables. Her research interests overlap with mine, and we have done a lot of work together.

What I have struggled with in writing this book has been to provide honest accounts of my own somatic and aesthetic experiences. It is easy to overstate or put in too strong language the simplicity of somaesthetic experiences. It is, after all, simply an engagement with your own body, emotion, thinking, and sociality: nothing magical or spiritual. At the same time, we do not attend to all these signs and signals on an everyday basis because they require attention and focus. I also encountered entirely novel experiences, discoveries of new possible ways I could move, feel, and act in the world, new experiences I did not even know I was capable of. I was, for example, surprised by the joy in the very simple movements in the Feldenkrais lessons. The playful, basic, joyful experience of rolling on the floor, imitating the rolling of a baby, was totally unexpected to me.

In summary, the best way to read this book would be to simultaneously engage in some body practice that you have never tried before—perhaps some sport or meditation practice. Whenever you come across some claim or conceptualization in the book, return to that body practice and what you have experienced. This will provide you with the groundings and realities behind these words on paper. Even better would be to engage in a design activity in which you can draw upon your own soma, your own somaesthetic engagement. Only then will your understanding be filled with the kind of experiential creative groundings that can be turned into design insight and knowledge.

Acknowledgments

The ideas presented here are grounded in the design work performed in my research group. The group has had many members throughout the years, but one person is special: Anna Ståhl. Nothing much would have happened without her. With Anna, I can effortlessly share ideas, aims, and design engagements. We have worked together for more than fifteen years. Anna is not only my colleague, but also a dear friend with whom I've shared many struggles—not only work-related, but also in life in general. In many ways, this book is also hers.

Anna and I have worked on the soma design ideas with some very talented friends in academia and industry. In particular, I am grateful to Jordi Solsona Belenguer, Ilias Bergström, Eva-Carin Banka Johnson, Martin Jonsson, Anna Karlsson, Jarmo Laaksolahti, Johanna Mercurio, and Kristina Strohmayer.

Our joint work was performed in the Mobile Life research center, cohosted by KTH Royal Institute of Technology, Stockholm University, and RI.SE SICS. The center was funded by Vinnova together with industry partners for ten years, from 2007 to 2017. The center's credo—"Always Explore! Always Create! Always Enjoy!"—captures why it was the perfect setting for our soma design work. To my colleagues and partners in the center: I miss you!

This book itself would not have existed without the generous sabbatical grant provided by KTH Royal Institute of Technology, alongside funding from the Mobile Life center, Strategic Research Foundation (SSF) and VR (Swedish Research Council). I would like to thank the head of the MID-unit at KTH, Ann Lantz, who supported my decision to go on a sabbatical, and Maria Holm, Professor Barry Brown, and Mikael Ydholm, who took care of the Mobile Life center while I was away.

I am deeply indebted to Richard Shusterman, professor of philosophy and English at Florida Atlantic University, and Katherine Isbister, professor in computational media at UC Santa Cruz, who not only hosted me during my sabbatical, but also shared their knowledge and passion for the topic. They are both amazing scholars. Not only did I learn a lot from them, I also regard them as my close friends.

I also owe big favors to my friends who took the time to read and comment on my manuscript: Jeffrey Bardzell, Katherine Isbister, Airi Lampinen, Pedro Sanches, Richard Shusterman, and Anna Ståhl.

The work presented is inspired by workshop discussions, design encounters, and discussions with many talented soma designers around the globe—in particular: Kristina Andersen, Marianne Graves Petersen, Mads Høbye, Caroline Hummels, Katherine Isbister, George Khut, Lian Loke, Elena Márquez Segura, Stina Nylander, Thecla Schiphorst, Dag Svanaes, Vygandas Šimbelis, Jakob Tholander, Elsa Kosmack Vaara, and Danielle Wilde. Throughout the years I have had inspiring conversations with Paul Dourish and William Gaver on the ideas behind this work.

I want to thank Doug Sery at the MIT Press and the anonymous reviewers he recruited. Their input was crucial to my process. A special, heartfelt thanks goes to Christine Larson, who never, ever complained about all the work she had to do with my Swenglish and messy book structure (remaining mistakes are all my own!), and to Vicky Lo at Boris Design, who created the amazing artworks and book cover.

A special thanks goes to all my horseback-riding friends from all over the world: Jarmo Laaksolahti, Josie Taylor Law, Lotta Jörsäter, Katarina Monfils Gustavsson, Stina Nylander, Heidi Benson, Johanna Enström, Sandie Stegenberg, Tina Wagnås, and many others. I know we share a special bond in our love of this noble animal and the riding experiences they so willingly provide us with. You are the ones who truly understand my somaesthetic experience of the rare moments when I become my centaur-self.

Finally, I am privileged to be part of a big, bustling, loving family, who kept my spirits high and encouraged me throughout the writing process: my children, Adam and Axel; my daughter-in-law, Jenny; my beautiful, amazing granddaughters, Alma and Tilda; my parents, Gunnar and Evy; my siblings, Åsa and Johan with their families; and my lovely aunts and uncles and cousins. Special love goes to the anchor in my life, my dear husband Sverker, always encouraging me to "finish the bloody book" and patiently listening to endless worries and anxiety attacks about content, structure, and time plans.

As I was finishing my book project, my father passed away. My father was always my biggest supporter. At crucial moments in my life, he provided me with direction. I remember, for example, when I was trying to figure out what to study at university, he said, "Kia, you can be whatever you want." As a young woman in a small village in the countryside, I found his support was crucial to me. Without his ability to show me that there was a whole world out there that I could and should contribute to, I would not have had the courage to make the choices I did. My father's first question when I phoned him, even toward the end when he was very ill, was always "And how is work?" He took great pride in all my achievements, and I wish he could be around to see this book now that it is done. Most importantly, he loved me unconditionally, and I miss his love and support immensely. I dedicate this book to him.

1 Why We Need Soma Design

We are shaped by our designs. The technologies and interactions we develop encourage certain movements, certain aesthetic experiences, certain practices and responses, while discouraging others. They shape our interactions with information and with other humans—socially, intellectually, collaboratively—while also influencing our understandings of our bodies.

Our designs, of course, are also shaped by available technologies. Right now, we are in the middle of a new wave of digital transformation. Smart materials,[1] autonomous technologies, and ubiquitous systems, connected through the Internet of Things, are already altering the way we relate to our devices, infrastructure, and each other. These new technologies offer the potential to automate and hide much of the tedium of our everyday lives: logistics, transportation, electricity consumption in our homes, connectivity, or the management of autonomous systems such as robotic vacuum cleaners.

These changes offer an enormous opportunity—indeed, a necessity—to reinvent the way we interact with the inanimate world. Once-familiar, everyday objects, from our phones to our vacuums, require novel interaction models—not just typing text on screens, but also, increasingly, movement-based bodily communication.

Sometimes we get these new interactions just right. For example, Apple managed to design interactive gestures for touchscreens that we thoroughly enjoy; it's fun to swipe and swish. Apple's gesture design is mentioned often as one driver behind the huge commercial success of the iPhone and other devices. These friendly little movements popularized and Apple's devices and made them accessible to many, including previously hard-to-reach populations such as children and seniors. What is it that they got right? The gestures are smooth, supple, pliable, and elegant. Strikingly, the design does not build on ideas of what might be "natural" to people, but instead makes use of unique affordances of touchscreen technology, creating a harmony between device and gesture that makes immediate sense to us.

But designing such engaging interactions, which harmonize our movements, our biodata, and our nonverbal social behaviors, turns out to be difficult. In our design processes, we often get it wrong. The interactions we create are not smooth or inviting; there are cracks and breaks that interfere with the feeling of being one with the system, often leading users to abandon them after a few tries. The movements or engagements we are invited to experience feel rigid, repetitive, boring (Isbister and DiMauro 2011). We see it in movement-based games, sports technologies, and attempts to create gesture-based interactions in the home and other everyday settings. If you've ever tried to search for a movie on your TV using your remote control for text entry, you've experienced the frustration of failed interaction design.

It is interesting that it is so difficult to get movement-based design right, given how many very simple tools we have in our everyday lives that we enjoy using over and over: everyday tools for cooking, crafting, sports, and so on. Why is it so pleasurable to perform a repetitive movement over and over when knitting, but not as pleasurable to move your computer mouse repeatedly to click on web pages when searching?

Getting the design right is important for many reasons—and not only to sell more products or enable interactions that are functional and smooth. The importance goes far beyond usability and utility. With the proliferation of interactive technologies, they begin to shape our cultural expressions and, as I mentioned earlier, they start to shape *us*. We see it already with technologies such as the smartphone altering everything from how we meet, socialize, or play to our bodily movements themselves (Ferreira and Höök 2011). The smartphone is already shaping our everyday practices; we struggle to set screen-time limits for our kids, we worry about a decline in social skills, but we also enjoy the experience and the benefits of being in touch with others all the time, everywhere (Weilenmann 2003).

There are mistakes we can make. The biggest mistake, perhaps, is reinforcing the separation of mind from body. Although we may think of bodies as passive machinery consisting of nervous system reactions, bones, and muscles, all research shows that movements, emotions, experiences, and thinking are inseparable. This in turn means that we cannot design as though the body is a mere machine, an object that can be perfected by the technologies we strap onto it or surround it with. What we hear from the interdisciplinary worlds of health, neuroscience, emotion, physiology, and cognitive psychology all speaks of strong links among all aspects of movement and thinking, and particularly psychological well-being (Davidson, Sherer, and Goldsmith 2009). This merging of mind and body proves true for even the most abstract subjects, such as mathematics, which turns out to be firmly grounded in our spatial, bodily ways of being in the world (Papert 1980).

Most design practices to date have reinforced the separation of mind and body—and favored the mind. Most human-technology interfaces are language- and symbol-based. We will see throughout this book how neglecting to account for the merging of mind and body, for the self that is in fact both, will not suffice in the coming era.

This leaves interaction designers, at this moment of technology change, in a position of enormous responsibility. If indeed, as I have argued, our technologies are part of our lifeworlds, shaping us as much as we shape them, then interaction designers are positioned to change and even improve human experience. They are called on, then, to pay attention to what we shall call the *soma*—the self that is a united whole of mind and body, in which our physical being produces and affects our thinking, and our mental and emotional experiences influence physical outcomes (Shusterman 2008). Designers must attend with care to the movements, rhythms, postures, or kinaesthetic-tactile experiences we build into our systems. Our movements will spur and shape other movements—sometimes (often by mistake or ignorance) causing pain (as in repetitive stress syndrome), sometimes causing pleasure.

This book argues that for designers to fulfill this responsibility, for them to create designs and systems that create harmony between the soma and the object, a new design program is needed. This program would help designers cultivate somaesthetic sensibilities, so they can better and more deliberately shape the space of movements invited by technologies, increasing the possibilities of pleasure, somaesthetic experiences, and more meaningful interactions with our lifeworld. This new design program would link movement and bodies to rational thinking and language, but also to aesthetic appreciation of the world we live in. Aesthetic appreciation is cultivated through our senses. If we design only for instrumental goals, engaging users in gestures designed to achieve tasks, their aesthetic potential might be overlooked. A key topic of this book is how to approach and craft aesthetics of bodily movement.

I believe that, done properly, this new approach opens a vast and exciting possibility, a novel space of movement-based interactions. With all the new interactive technologies—sensing, new actuating, new wireless connectivity—a huge space of design possibilities lies before us. In fact, I would like to claim that the domain of body-, movement-, and biosensor-based interactions is *as big as or even bigger* than all the desktop and mobile applications we have seen so far. In this book, I will substantiate that claim by presenting soma design examples relating to work tasks; crafts; exertion games; slow, inward-looking interactions; arts; health applications; and many other domains.

Why We Fail

Why is it that Apple got its swipe gestures right while so many others failed? We might argue that failures are not surprising; digital technologies have not been around for long, and we still have taken only baby steps toward knowing how to design for sustained aesthetic bodily engagements. But what I argue here is that the problem lies not so much in how immature the field is or in how our technologies lack expressive power. Instead, I argue that designers today make two major mistakes.

First, many designers are on a misguided quest to identify "natural movements" or emotions. This type of design encourages a research and design cycle that starts with studying human movement, figuring out a formal way of describing those movements in some computational model (which is always, by necessity, a limited mirror of rich movements and context), and then attempting to figure out how to respond to these movements.

But this approach raises a question: What is natural? After all, there is nothing *natural* about the gestures we use with a smartphone. Those smartphone gestures are designed. They must be learned. They are, of course, constrained by the limits of what the human body can do—our morphology—but they do not arise from any natural bodily state. We would not be able to perform a video study of people in their natural habitat (wherever that would be) that would discover the swipe gesture for opening the iPhone. The whole idea of what is "natural" is a misunderstanding of the basic condition of human movement and survival: we creatively, dynamically, adjust our movements to the situations, tools, and practices of our culture. Of course, there are certain movement patterns, facial expressions, movements, or reactions shared across cultures, because our bodies are constituted in a certain manner, yet there are always variations, changes due to culture, context, or individual experiences. When we engage with one another, we derive meaning from the entire situation—not from one isolated factor, such as the movements of the muscles around the eye. And we often fail to connect despite the richness of communication between us. We misunderstand each other. We sometimes even fail to understand our own reactions. As we all know, we can obsess about events in our lives that changed us and still not understand our own reactions: we can spend hours and hours figuring out what we really feel. Most importantly here, the tools and practices of our culture—for farming, clothing, hunting, eating, moving, playing, socializing—shape our movements.

Beyond questioning the groundings of "natural" movements and emotions, figuring out how to model them computationally is also problematic. Even if we could develop an omnipotent technology capable of recognizing every possible human movement, facial expression, or fine-grained detail of our biodata, it would not necessarily be useful in designing for new movements, new interactions. We learn "commands," whether lexical or movement-based, via the tight coupling between what we do and how the system or tool responds to those commands (Norman 2010). We *change* in response to how the world responds to our activities.

Even if these contradictions did not thwart our omniscient computer model, creating it might not be worth the effort, because our bodily signs and signals often contradict each other. A heartbeat might lead us to one interpretation, a facial expression to another, and bodily movements to a third. This is not just a reflection of the limitations of our models; this cacophony of data is inherent in the nature of the human body, which rarely feels or portrays one single, solitary mood/emotion/intention/health state at a time. Many different processes happen all at once, feeding into one another, reinforcing or increasing our propensity to move, feel, or behave in a certain manner at any given point in time.

A design tension exists between movements that can be recognized by a given technology and the movements or inputs required for the application to achieve its goals. Sometimes, it is better to start from the requirements of the system—what is it supposed to do for us?—and create recognition algorithms and computer models based on those requirements. In techspeak, we need to start with the actuation rather than the sensing and computation. Once we know what the system is going to do, we can reverse engineer it to recognize our users' movements, facial expressions, or other signs and signals. Or, as discussed by Benford and colleagues, we should aim to recognize the movements that are desirable from an application-driven point of view (Benford et al. 2005). Too often, design fails because the sensing function drives the actuation.

This does not mean that biosensor or movement data and its semantics are irrelevant to our design process. We need to design with a keen eye to the affordances of technology and data-driven models. Otherwise, we might end up fighting with the technology to make it fit with the application actuation (Fernaeus and Sundström 2012; Sundström and Höök 2010)—or we might miss out on design opportunities that such modeling offers.

Apart from the complicated issue of identifying so called natural movements, or creating a mesh of affordances and desired function, there is a second, more fundamental reason interaction design struggles to come to terms with aesthetics and somatics. Based on a strong and growing body of evidence, I posit that to create designs involving our bodies, movements, and biodata, we need entirely new design processes, fundamentally different from those now prevalent in the HCI and interaction design fields. Existing design methods for web and mobile app design now are successfully addressing symbolic, language-oriented, and predominantly visual interactions. This stands in stark contrast to the methods employed by those who successfully address and design for movement-based interactions. The difference lies not only in which questions are asked about the computer models of our movements, but in the *qualitative shift required, from a predominantly symbolic, language-oriented stance, to an experiential, felt, aesthetic stance permeating the whole design and use cycle.* This claim is at the core of this book and we will return to it frequently, disentangling what we mean step-by-step. Throughout, I will argue that designers interested in aesthetically oriented, movement-based applications need to cultivate this alternative experiential, felt, aesthetic design stance. In other words, new materials and new technologies demand new processes of design.

From Language to Movement

I have already suggested that it is critically important in this moment to develop these new processes and approaches, to shift from a symbolic, language-oriented interaction style to an experiential, felt, aesthetic, movement-based interaction style. Why is that urgent right now?

In a sense, major HCI paradigms have always followed technology and infrastructure innovations (Grudin 1990): Desktop interaction followed the advent of personal computers. Collaborative applications were only possible after computers had become networked. Now-ubiquitous computing interactions required the miniaturization of computing, memory, and batteries, as well as access to wireless connectivity. And so on.

In this new wave of digitization, many possibilities arise to improve human existence—but few succeed. We need new processes to unlock the potential of smart materials, autonomous systems, and the Internet of Things and to find ways to significantly improve how technology benefits everyday life. Yet existing systems are beset with manifest human-interaction problems (Harper 2006; Taylor et al. 2007)—notably, (1) limited attention span, (2) lack of human (and sometimes machine) predictability, and (3) our reliance on inherited design paradigms and metaphors that no longer apply.

Things That Go "Beep" in the Night
Our houses, cars, and offices are now filled with interactive "things" attempting to grab our attention. The fridge warns you with a beep if you leave the door open, the washing machine signals when it is finished, and even the chainsaw now warns you when you have been using it for too long. We are overloaded with interactions calling for our attention. Most of those interactions are designed with the traditional, symbolic, dialogue-driven model in mind. They require active engagements in a turn-taking dialogue style. Processes that have been more or less silent in our homes, such as the thermostat regulating the temperature or the fire detector, now call for our attention, asking us to change their batteries or manipulate their state, or simply telling us that they are still "alive," doing their jobs. There are researchers who think we should move even further down this lane, "making unloved objects loved" (Rose 2014), in effect turning all machines we surround ourselves with into attention-seeking, demanding, dialogue-driven interactive objects. Although making interaction with thermostats or fire detectors delightful may be a worthy subject, we must ask ourselves what the totality of all these interactions will be. What will it be to live in the smart home, smart garden, smart transportation system, or smart city, where everything calls for your attention, asking you to engage in dialogues?

Life Is Improv
The problem lies not only in how much time and attention we have to devote to all these interactive designs (not to speak of the time spent recharging their batteries or making them talk to the network or each other). There is also a mismatch between devices that need limited, specific, predictable input and the richness and variation of our everyday practices. Frequently, the design of interactive digital objects assumes that everyday practices are regular and even predictable. The smart thermostat assumes that you will come home from work every day at a particular point in time and that the temperature should be raised right before that so that the house saves energy when you are not around and provides comforting warmth when you are. But, as Lucy Suchman points out, human action is

"essentially situated and ad hoc improvisation," responding to situations as they arise (1987, 51). There are always exceptions, changes, and shifts in how we engage with the practices of our everyday life. For example, the smart lighting system that is turned on automatically when the homeowner approaches his or her apartment may not have been designed for the sharing economy in which someone else rents the apartment while the homeowner is on vacation (as happened to a colleague of mine). In that case, it will not be enough to hand over the keys to the tenant who comes to stay temporarily. The tenant also must install the lighting app on his or her mobile device. Even more importantly, when the tenant moves out, the homeowner must make sure that he or she uninstalls the lighting app; otherwise, the tenant can still control the lighting from afar.

There is an even easier way to think about how your everyday behaviors are not algorithmic and regular: Just think back over the last few days in your life. How many times did you get up at exactly the same time every morning or get back from work as regularly as these systems assume you do? Studies of smart homes both in the past and today confirm that, despite decades of research and design work, these rationalizations are still infesting the idea of what is considered "smart" (Harper 2006; Jenson 2014).

Furthermore, machines sometimes interact with each other in unexpected ways when connected to the Internet. There are stories of lawnmower robots running off, leaving their gardens when mistakenly connected to someone else's network. Different parts of your entertainment system may turn the volume up and down outside your control or fail to connect smoothly. Each smart object comes with its own form of interaction, its own mobile app, its own upgrade requirements, and its own manner of calling for users' attention. Interaction models have been inherited from the desktop metaphor, and some mobile interactions have their own apps that use nonstandardized icons, sounds, or notification frameworks. When put together, the current forms of smart technology do not blend. They cannot interface with one another. Most importantly, as end users, we end up with a cacophony of interactions calling for attention.

Contrary to the functional and aesthetic ideals that may govern a different interior design style, there is no strong aesthetics governing smart home products to make them all come together like puzzle pieces. There is a lack of unifying interaction paradigm and overall aesthetics.

Interfaces Aren't What We Thought They Were

The HCI field makes certain assumptions about what an interface is and how it works—assumptions that may no longer hold true today, and certainly will not tomorrow. Perhaps most importantly, HCI researchers almost always assume that users will work with devices in "an interactive loop" in which the user's attention is focused on a single system in a rich, immediate form of interaction and feedback—often through a screen interface, fundamentally based on a language-based dialogue. This idea was questioned by Marc Weiser, who coined the idea of *ubiquitous computing* (Weiser 1991). He and his colleagues envisioned an area of calm computing that would be like walking through a forest, beautiful, calm, and not calling for attention unless we decide to attend to it (Weiser and Brown 1997). As Verbeek (2015) points out, nontechnological systems interact with us in a much wider range of ways than existing technology, ways such as overhearing a conversation, walking on a path, or feeling our own internal body. Yet to make use of these interface modes will require a risky and radical break with existing ways of thinking about how people should interact with computers. To make this radical break, we cannot glue on yet another direct manipulation metaphor in which dialogue is the fundamental organizing principle. Instead, we may have to go back to the fundamentals of what it means to be a moving subject reacting and interacting in some specific context.

As we will argue here, though explicit, symbolic, dialogue-driven interaction is perhaps one of the most advanced ways we interact with our fellow human beings, meaning-making processes do not *start* in symbols and language. If we want to fundamentally alter the way we design interactions with machines and seek alternatives to the human-computer dialogue model, we need to turn to some of the fundamentals of what it means to be an organism able to move, interact, and create meaning from a complex context of nature, other people, culture, tools, and sensory engagements with the world. As I will argue here, meaning-making processes arise when we are babies, long before we can speak. Meaning is grounded in our own movement and in watching others move. The rich soil of movement is the basis for how we create meaning. In fact, purposeful actions and complex behaviors allow all sorts of animals to survive in the world—even those without language and the ability to engage in proper, turn-taking dialogue behaviors. If meaning originates in movement, then our interfaces could be far more dynamic and diverse than we currently imagine. But to get to as-yet unimagined interfaces, we must first imagine—and implement—a new approach to design. This is not a dismissal of dialogue-oriented interfaces or the use of symbols and language. I expect that the most powerful interactions will move between implicit and explicit interactions seamlessly.

An Aesthetics of Experience

When questioning the dialogue model in HCI and looking for alternative ways of designing for interaction, it is, in my view, not enough to look for utilitarian purposes, such as fulfilling work tasks. Because these systems are everywhere, moving into every aspect of our lives, aims beyond fulfilling work tasks as efficiently as possible must govern our work. We need to bring novel *ideals* to our design practice.

The work presented here belongs to what has been named the *third wave* of HCI (Bødker 2006). As discussed in the preface, the first wave dealt with designs for one user and one computer, using rigid guidelines, formal methods, and a cognitivist grounding. In the second wave, computers became connected and we had to consider groups of users working together. This lead to an interest in sociology, ethnography, and activity theory, as we needed to design for assemblages of technologies, practices, and the requirements shaped by work.

These two waves left an important aspect of design untouched: *first-person felt experiences*. In fact, most early usability work did not speak of experiences at all, but of values such as efficiency, usability, and learnability. The overarching aim during the first two waves was to support work practices—and, indeed, they delivered many useful insights for those settings. Early work on user experience was often motivated in relation to utilitarian aims, such as efficiency in task completion. A good user experience was valued because it could generate a positive mood and engagement and thus lead to better work productivity.

But an aspect of work that we often fail to see or that comes as an afterthought is the enjoyment and experience of work. It is therefore not so strange that much of the development in the first and second waves ignored aesthetics and experience. Although productivity and utility obviously are important aims, there is a point to turning the question upside down: What if user experience was the main design challenge, with usability and efficiency in use as secondary, supportive endeavors? The relationship is clear when we move outside the work domain and speak of, for example, computer games. A game obviously should be usable, but that is not enough. Usability aims must help create the intended gaming experience.

In a sense, each of these three waves was prompted by specific technological advances. The first wave dealt with the advent of the personal computer. The second dealt with networked computers. Now, in third-wave HCI, we find ourselves surrounded by a plethora of new, digitally enabled technologies that move digital interactions into the world. The most notable are smartphones, but other examples include home gaming consoles, biosensors worn on the body, interactive clothes, tangibles, virtual reality, and wearable computers.

These technologies promise to unleash wonderful new possibilities. They can extend our senses, making us superhuman, altering how we experience the world and ourselves. As such, these new materials have released a wave of creativity. But the third wave also puts new demands on academics who study HCI. How can we explain why some designs spur evocative, aesthetic, fun, playful interactions, while others do not? Even more importantly, what are the methods and ideals that can inform our design practice? To address these questions, the third wave of HCI design, starting about mid-2000, introduced theories of play, movement, emotion, felt life, empathy, and aesthetic experiences. Many academics turned to the arts, humanities, or other practices to inform this shift. In industry, the illusive concept of *user experience* became both the Holy Grail that would help sell products and a difficult, unmeasurable, hard-to-grasp entity. In academia, design and HCI researchers turned their interest to games, social media, interactive arts, and other aesthetic practices to understand how better to design for the richness of all sorts of user experiences.

To deal with this user experience turn, new theories and ideas were introduced and translated into interaction-design practice. Unfortunately, few of them explicitly addressed how we engage with the world somatically. For the most part, they focused on our subjective ways of being in the world, without grounding their analysis in our bodies and senses and how those in turn connect to our subjective selves—moving, perceiving, engaging, feeling, and reasoning.

There has been a growing dissatisfaction in the field with this lack of engagement with the realities of our physical, experiential subjectivities—our bodies. Bodies are mentioned in the abstract, but we rarely get to hear about their corporeal realities—for example, the position and feel of our bodies, of our sitting bones against a chair, the touch of a feather on your skin, or how a strong rhythm in an interaction can speak to us. Rhythm perhaps most strongly comes through in game designs where it is used to increase, decrease, or sustain rapid keystroke or joystick movements. But as argued by Löwgren (2009), rhythm is probably present in most applications whether it is intentionally designed for or just by mistake. Design researchers and practitioners have been asking for concrete knowledge and design methods involving muscles, the nervous system, emotional expressions, proprioception, tactile sensibilities, and kinaesthetics. Despite all the work we have seen in HCI in designing for embodiment, the actual corporeal, pulsating, live, felt body has been notably absent from both theory and practical design work. Most design work relating to our bodies and movements has taken quite an instrumental view of interaction: our bodies are there to be trimmed, perfected, and kept free from illnesses and bad influences. Placing some sensors on our body and collecting data on ourselves is supposed to change our bad habits and make us healthy, beautiful, and able to live long lives (Purpura et al. 2011). Or, in another strand of design work, the body is seen as an "input device" that can be used in game design. Bodily engagement has not been seen as the primary path to aesthetics, but simply as an instrument through which we make mind rule over matter. The aesthetic pleasures have been confined to those that arise from social engagements or intellectual games. Although it has been clear that our human constitution is an integrated whole in which movement, emotion, and thinking are tightly interlinked, it has been difficult to achieve a holistic grip on the design process, addressing aesthetics from this perspective. These instrumental approaches leave out important aspects of human experience, and thus impoverish the kinds of designs we might be able to imagine for new materials and conditions.

My claim here is that there is no shortcut to design for and with our "whole" selves. Although we can pick apart experiences and provide various piecemeal facts—such as how certain facial expressions correlate with certain emotional experiences or how touch differs when an object is felt by the hand versus higher up on the arm—such facts will never be enough to create meaningful interactions. To properly address our somas, the whole subjective self has to be present in both the design and use processes, which both define and alter the experience.

But how do you, as designer or user, engage somatically in a design process? What are the alternative design stances that will not distract from our somas, our aesthetic experiences, or our ability to compassionately engage with others and their somatics? What will help deepen understanding and engagement with our selves, as well as help us become more empathic with others?

This book is my attempt to answer these urgent questions. I argue that we need a theory and practice of design that accounts for the unity, rather than the separation, of mind and body—an approach I call *soma design*. Soma design allows us to "examine" and improve on connections among sensation, feeling, emotion, and subjective understanding and values (Khut 2006). It engages with bodily rhythms, touch, proprioception, and bodily playfulness, but also with our values, meaning-making processes, emotions, and ways of engaging with the world. It is individual, as well as social. It deals with self-care, as well as empathy with others. It has to do with movements and bodies, but addresses the whole self, body and mind as one. It concerns the orchestration of the "whole," emptying materials of all their potential and thereby providing fertile grounds for meaning-making.

In that sense, to me, soma design will be relevant to all forms of design. My goal for this book is to lay out a program that includes a set of ideas and practices and a vocabulary that will allow us to identify, discuss, and evaluate soma design in action.

Why: Theoretical Groundings in Movement and Somaesthetics

If we are serious about designing for everyday life, for social communication, for people moving, feeling, interacting in every walk of life, we need groundings in aesthetics and theories that incorporate the full range of what it means to be human. I will focus on two strands of work that have been inspirational for my research group. These two theories together can offer a new perspective on design, providing a coherent, holistic perspective, as well as aesthetic ideals and guidance, for our design work.

The first of these theories can be called *primacy of movement*. I will focus mainly on the work by philosopher, dancer, and choreographer Maxine Sheets-Johnstone (2011). She bases her work on evolutionary biology, phenomenology, and analysis of aesthetic practices such as dance. This has led her to question the idea that human perception and reasoning is first and foremost a language-oriented, symbolic, representational process. Movement is in one sense obviously the basis of life: Without movement, there is no life, no perception, no experience. Without the movements of the heart, muscles, and nervous system, we are dead. Beyond forming the basis of all organic life, however, Sheets-Johnstone shows us how movement is always varied, always adapting, and always in dialogue with the changing world around us. From an evolutionary, biological perspective, movement in organisms attempting to survive must always respond to the local, lived environment. When it comes to the human condition, our bodies, their morphology, and their potential movements are the foundation of all human meaning-making processes. It is in this movement that language is grounded. Movement comes first, language second. Sheets-Johnstone's theory posits a somatic-first perspective, instead of a language-first position. Through an account of her theories, offered in chapter 2, I aim to reorient our understanding of interaction design, from the *predominantly symbolic, language-oriented stance* mentioned previously, to one in which movement and sensory appreciation comes first.

The second theoretical grounding, *somaesthetics*, from philosopher and Feldenkrais practitioner Richard Shusterman, combines the concept of *soma* with *aesthetics* (Shusterman 2008). It blends a phenomenological, pragmatic perspective with practical bodily practices and aesthetic sensitivities.

By *soma*, Shusterman (2008) refers to a bodily subjectivity, a living, purposive, sentient, perceptive body, in which movement, body, emotion, cognition, perception, and sociality are tightly interlinked. That contrasts with a perspective in which we separate intellectual reasoning from our bodily realities, or an ethnographic perspective in which we do not speculate on the inner, subjective experiences of people. It is instead a full recognition of our subjective selves.

Aesthetics is a notably complex concept, taking on many different meanings depending on the purpose and context. Shusterman approaches aesthetics as an active skill, an ability to appreciate our experiences, one that can be trained and sharpened. He argues that if we develop our perception and senses through close attention to our experiences, we can reap from them more richness, depth, and interest. If, for example, we attend to how we eat food, we can more richly experience its texture, taste, fragrance, its movement from the plate to our mouth, the way we swallow, and the overall sensation of letting food enter into our body. Training your aesthetic ability is, in essence, no different from educating your intellect and reason: it requires study, time, and engagement. If we train our sensory abilities, we will be able to better appreciate our experiences.

Shusterman differs from Dewey ([1934] 2005) and, later, McCarthy and Wright (2004a) in that he does not restrict aesthetic experience only to those unique, heightened experiences that stand out from everyday life. Instead, his perspective embraces aesthetic experience in everyday, mundane, engagements. He emphasizes that, through dedication and training, we can become more aware, more present in our everyday practices. Ultimately, this may lead to what Thoreau ([1854] 2016) speaks of as an awakening from the mindless, joyless engagement that results from a lack of attention to the senses.

What: Introducing a Somaesthetic Design Program

Earlier, I mentioned that I seek to lay out a design program, defined as a set of ideas and practices and a vocabulary that will allow us to know soma design when we see it, and to give us a set of guidelines and terms to discuss and evaluate it. I want to touch here on what I mean by design *program*, which I'll elaborate in chapter 5.

As Redström (2017) writes, the way we frame design knowledge can range from pointing to a single, *specific design*, to describing a larger and more encompassing *program*, which forms a consistent universe of design knowledge or explorations, incorporating certain aesthetics and interaction patterns, and perhaps spurring certain behaviors. Within such a program, specific designs may serve as prototypical examples, similar to how a particular building may serve to describe a whole architectural style in architectural studies. The specific design in this sense becomes a definition or a fact that we can use in our reasoning to denote a whole class of systems or interactive experiences. This book seeks to set forth such a program—by offering aesthetic examples and suggesting certain practices.

It is important to recognize that this soma design program cannot be reduced to some objective rules or design patterns that can be replicated over and over and that will always generate the same aesthetic experience. Each engagement will be a unique aesthetic experience. But if every design process and every meeting between an end user and an aesthetic design is unique, then what do we mean by a *soma design theory*? What is the design knowledge and internally consistent theory we can bring forth, and what potency will it have in generating viable designs?

In many ways, soma design resembles another aesthetic practice: music (Kosmack Vaara 2017). A musician will train his or her tacit knowledge for years, engaging with his or her instrument until it becomes "ready-to-hand" (Merleau-Ponty 1996), an embodied part of the musician, allowing him or her not only to produce sounds in the most rudimentary manner, but also to dynamically shape the aesthetic expression of the score. Musicians spend hours physically exercising with their instruments to train their bodies to handle it. But they also learn a repertory of music pieces; a terminology to describe them; a set of genre-specific concepts; music scores, in some cases; and terminology for speaking of the temporal and emotional gestalt the composer aimed for. They need to make all of this knowledge readily available the moment they draw upon it to play music live.

Soma design will require a similar process of training and theoretical understanding. If, as a designer or user, you have shaped an aesthetic interaction, then various articulations and conceptualizations will start to make sense to you. You will be able to connect your tacit understanding to accounts that other designers provide, and you can engage in a more informed practice. The combination of your tacit understanding and the conceptualizations you use to describe interactions form your *design knowledge*.

Similar to how music knowledge cannot guarantee that the composer creates beautiful music or that the musicians in an orchestra create a perfect experience, there are no somaesthetic design rules or patterns that will guarantee perfect designs. Similar to how active music training will improve the musicians' skills and appreciation of music, however, so too will somaesthetic practice improve your designerly skills. As we shall see later in this book, it is notable that the outcomes of soma design processes share certain design sensitivities, certain family resemblances, and certain forms of engagements. As a designer, you can learn to appreciate and shape those qualities in your own practice.

Here, is it important to note that the design process does not end when the product leaves the designer's hands. As discussed by Redström (2017), "design*ing*" is an ongoing activity that starts when the designer shapes materials into orchestrated experiences, but those experiences continue to "be designed" as end users partake of and engage in the interactions. We are always actively involved in shaping and being shaped by technology. An ongoing somaesthetic design*ing* process, as opposed to a static design process, is what we are aiming to achieve.

Soma design knowledge must be firmly grounded in the affordances of the *sociodigital material*: that is, both in the human side of the interaction—the involvement of our somas—and in the role and form of the digital/physical materials used to build applications. These two aspects come together to form the interactive aesthetic experience. Because we are designing with a sociodigital material, our own somas (both designers' and imagined users' somas) are also a design material of sorts. In a soma design process, our bodies and our subjective experiences, feelings, values, meaning-making, and movement-based engagements are altered by the design process. The designer's (and end user's) *lived body* becomes a resource in the design process.

How: Four Elements of Soma Design

To help the reader see where we are heading, let me start by providing a very short introduction to what a soma design process may entail. Some of the ideas here might not make sense to you yet—unless you have been involved in a similar design process of your own. To help you start imagining what might be involved, try the following exercise to create a shape-changing chair (see figure 1.1):

Figure 1.1
Imagining an interactive chair

Sit back in your chair with both feet firmly placed on the floor. Close your eyes. Try to imagine how to design an interactive chair. Start by locating your sitting bones, and explore how they meet the firmness of your chair. Are you sitting equally on both your sitting bones? Is one placed more forward on the chair than the other? Is your weight supported equally from the chair up through your sitting bones, all the way up through your spine, reaching your shoulders, allowing your head to balance comfortably on the top of your spine? Now continue to let your focus move from one part of your body to another; from feeling your sitting bones, move your awareness down, feeling first your thighs, then knees, calves, feet, soles of your feet, and your toes. Then turn to your breathing, and feel how each breath alters your weight on the chair. Also direct your attention to the different parts of the chair you are sitting on: How is your whole body supported through the chair and the floor?

Now imagine that the chair can alter its firmness, altering your sitting experience. In your imagination, give your chair different properties—more or less firm, more or less bouncy, and so on. Also try to imagine an interactive chair, dynamically, subtly changing its form, behavior, or expression in response to you. Perhaps the chair has a beat, like a heartbeat, perhaps mirroring your own heart. What would that feel like? Make very, very small, subtle, controlled movements, millimeters back and forth, rocking from one sitting bone to the other, putting more weight on your left or right foot while engaging in these imaginings.

As you work through this imaginary design exercise, I would like to draw your attention to four elements that will be characteristic of soma design: (1) *lived experience*, (2) the *slowing down* of design, (3) testing and *retesting* against the desired aesthetic, and (4) *sociodigital materials*.

Lived Experience

First, soma designing emphasizes a first-person, hands-on, active engagement and experience. The designer's *lived experience* must be in place to feel the fine nuances of different movements, tactile experiences, or mirrorings of our bodily processes in interactive design. To arrive at a position from which we as designers can engage in such lived experiences and shape novel design, we first have to train our *aesthetic sensitivities*. By repeatedly engaging with different body practices or touching, feeling, and probing the qualities of different movement-based digital materials or applications, we can develop the ability to differentiate between small nuances in the bodily responses to different interactions. This resembles other artistic practices in which artists always start by learning about their materials before they can mold them into artistic expressions.

I emphasize the training of designers' aesthetic sensitivity for movement-based interaction for two reasons. First, in the academic research fields of HCI and interaction-design research and practice, we often have underestimated the need to engage deeply with and get to know our materials before shaping designs (Isbister and Höök 2009). We have been obsessed with the idea that an HCI design method should be easy to grasp for anyone and cheap to perform. Given the history of HCI, this focus is not so strange: The discipline was trying to establish itself as an important field of knowledge alongside traditional computer science. Designers and researchers had to show that our methods were not too expensive and could be taught quickly within the realms of a traditional engineering course.

Training aesthetic sensibility to prepare for soma design entails a deep engagement with your own self, your own soma, during the design process. It involves cultivating a somatic sensitivity, making movements very, very slowly to properly feel them or repeatedly touching and feeling interactive materials to make full use of their experiential potential.

Slowing Down

The second reason aesthetic sensitivity is important relates to the difference between designing a symbolic-oriented interaction and a soma-based one. The latter, as we shall discuss in depth later, requires a slower, more thoughtful design process. For instance, in the exercise outlined earlier, as you sat in the chair, you had to turn your attention very slowly from one aspect of your bodily experience to the next to really discern the feeling of each.

One approach to becoming more sensitive to these nuances lies in learning how to *articulate* bodily experiences. In the shape-changing chair design challenge above, I provided some orienting questions to help distinguish different visceral, bodily experiences—imagined as well as real—in the interaction: questions related to firmness, bounciness, changing form, and heartbeat. This (hopefully) directed your attention to different aspects of your bodily experience. But maybe you also felt other aspects of your sitting experience that you struggled to articulate and that did not fit with these particular concepts. Maybe you discovered symmetries or asymmetries of your body, pain in different limbs, or the connection between the sitting bones and the muscles going all the way out into your heels. These aspects need to be articulated in your mind for you to be able to distinguish between them and address them in your design. Whether you articulate them in the sense of giving them lexical representation, a name, or an articulation in the form of a distinguishable bodily experience is perhaps not as important as learning to be sensitive to and appreciative of their existence. This is a slow learning process; it requires giving attention to internal experiences that are not always readily available to us.

In fact, the soma design process is much slower than what we are used to in symbolic visual design—both because it takes more time to engage your whole soma, shaping and being shaped by the design process, and because the designer must be more thoughtful and reflective. Language provides a shortcut in argumentation, as in our design processes. We can quickly sketch and articulate ideas so long as the symbols and language are known to us. Movement-based ideas require a different engagement. To share them, we have to experience them. We have to engage in a fine-grained understanding of what they are. I will repeatedly come back to this thoughtfulness, or slowness, in the design process as I seek to provide some of the theoretical underpinnings of this distinct difference from other design methods.

Iterative Testing

Say that, after imagining your interactive chair, you start building it. How will you know if you're getting closer to the aesthetic experience you are hoping to achieve? You will have to return to it again and again, on your own and with your team. This is why, for example, the company Harmonix, creators of both *Rock Band* and *Guitar Hero*, made everyone in the company play in a rock band. According to a *Wired* article about the design process for *Rock Band*, these employee rock bands "get together every week to rock out to the latest build, then pass their thoughts on to the designers. ... This organic, iterative design process gets everyone in the company involved in tweaking all the different minutiae that go into accurately replicating the rock star experience on plastic faux instruments" (Kohler 2007). Repeated engagement, immersion, and *feeling the interaction* as it is created are key insights from their design process.

Sociodigital Materials

A soma design process relies strongly on a first-person, bodily, felt experience of *digital materials* and their affordances—or how properties can be shaped in materials to fit with our corporeal selves. Although traditional interaction design also relies heavily on thorough knowledge of algorithms, visualization genres, screen properties, and so on, the need for touching, feeling, and physically, slowly engaging with them has not been at the core of our practice.

Digital materials have a unique quality regarding how they can change in and through the interaction with the user; they are digital but have a social aspect. This means that designers have to shape the *dynamic gestalt* of the system (Löwgren and Stolterman 2004). The dynamic gestalt (sometimes named the *interaction gestalt*) is not a property of the design itself, but the experiential identity of the interaction as it unfolds between user and design. Over the course of an interaction, the design will reveal how it responds to users' activities with its tempo, rhythm, and aesthetics. To shape this dynamic gestalt, designers need to engage with and experience what the system "feels like" when interacting with it over time. When the required input or engagement from the user consists of movements, gestures, heart rate, or some aspect of their emotional expressions, designers must put themselves in the users' position, feeling the possible or desirable movements. They need to shape an aesthetic experience that unfolds over time, in dialogue with bodily processes. As bodily processes cannot be changed as rapidly as those involving mainly our symbolic processing abilities, the engagement with the sociodigital material must, by necessity, be a slow process. Our sensual, bodily abilities develop slowly; they rely on altering muscle strengths, nervous system reactions, and perception over time.

Why We Care

By now, you might be wondering whether all this work—all this thoughtfulness, slowness, and engagement—is worth the effort. Will it necessarily render better design?

There are many different ways of answering that question. One is to ask whether this slow process has opened new design spaces, populated with potential designs that we would not have brought forth otherwise. In this book, I will describe a wide range of design exemplars from both academia and industry, where new ideas are being explored. We will see examples in which the interaction subtly encourages users to attend to their own bodies, enriching their sensitivity to, enjoyment of, and appreciation of their own somatics. Sometimes those systems lead to enjoyment in the moment, sometimes to well-being in a longer-term sense, and sometimes even serve instrumental productivity purposes. Body-, movement- and soma-based interactions are also starting to play a role in the new wave of digitalization moving from the "screen" into the world. In various forms, such as the *Internet of Things, ubiquitous computing, tangible interaction, wearables,* or *ambient intelligence*, this new wave of digitalization means that-HCI design now needs to engage with "faceless" systems. We must interact with devices or systems lacking a screen, or ones for which the traditional idea of a dialogue between user and system is no longer present (Hallnäs and Redström 2001; Janlert and Stolterman 2015; Ju 2015). In settings including our homes, our gardens, and our city lives, we need to shift away from communication based on a traditional desktop metaphor, with explicit dialogue through a glass screen as its main way of communicating. Instead, our movements, body postures, gestures, breathing, biodata, or facial expressions will trigger responses from the systems in our environments, mixing with the traditional desktop dialogues, or even sometimes entirely replacing them. Soma design offers one piece of the puzzle in creating such faceless interactions.

But the question of whether soma design is worthwhile should perhaps also be asked in a different manner: Can we really continue to design interactions as if we do not have bodies, or, as I will phrase it here, no soma? I argue that a somaesthetic design perspective provides a better chance to craft user experiences that harmonize with the pleasures and displeasures, beats, rhythms, and richness of the living, felt, bodily subjectivity—our human condition. Note that I am not speaking only of "nice," beautiful, or fine arts cultural experiences. I am speaking of all sorts of experiences: beautiful, ugly, painful, shallow, exhilarating, utilitarian/work-oriented, habitual, and nonhabitual behaviors.

Complementing or Replacing Current Design Practice?

I will not argue that a soma design stance should replace other methods we already know and successfully apply. As always, theoretical concepts and methods need to be used with discrimination and be applied with expertise. A good designer knows when to use one or the other.

Rather, my aim is to propose that soma design be added to the repertory of the interaction designer (Schon 1984). With this book, I want to propose a path to design, a set of tactics or strategies, to help interaction designers make the necessary shift from designing mainly in symbolic dialogue forms and toward instead designing aesthetically evocative body-based interactions. My ultimate hope is that this approach will be taught at engineering schools, as well as industrial design schools, alongside methods such as user-centered design, personas, or task analysis—for example, in basic HCI books such as that by Rogers, Sharp, and Preece (2011). It should be one tool in the designerly toolbox—but as such, it is quite foreign to our mainstream practices today (especially in the design educations residing in our engineering schools), and much more research is needed to determine how we can best introduce this form of engagement (Hummels, Overbeeke, and Klooster 2006).

While soma design becomes another tool for designers, it is not simply an add-on to the repertory of design tactics we already know. It is not a matter of adding a layer of user experience on top of products. It speaks of changing ourselves, our appreciation capability, our creative practice. It speaks to the fundamentals of what we are, what it means to be human.

How to Read This Book

This book is structured to show three things, step-by-step: Why, What, and How.

Why Soma Design

In part I, I will more fully develop the arguments I laid out earlier, showing why we need a new design approach and the theoretical motivations for this program. I will discuss how movement is basic to the human condition and how emotion, movement, and thinking are tightly interlinked (chapter 2). As mentioned, I will organize this discussion around two main theoretical strands: the primacy of movement by Sheets-Johnstone and the theory of somaesthetics by Shusterman. I will also address questions of what it means to design for one's individual soma, when bodies and their political and cultural conditions vary so dramatically across culture, class, gender, economic conditions, and other considerations. My belief is that attending truly and deeply to one's own soma ultimately cultivates a deep empathy and respect for other somas, which will benefit more liberating, less oppressive forms of design.

What Is Soma Design

Part II of the book is comprised of chapters 3–5, describing various soma designs and then defining what they are. There is a whole growing field of somaesthetic design works, both in academia and in industry. To explain their appeal and what is somaesthetic in their design, I will provide a personal account of six encounters with self-identified somaesthetic designs (chapter 3). These six are chosen because they show the wide range of somaesthetic interactive experiences we may design for: social interaction, meditation, health applications, interactive arts, theatre props and functional applications to be used as part of your everyday life.

Next, to answer the question of how to design a somaesthetically inspired system, I will describe in depth three somaesthetic designs created by my research group together with the IKEA and Boris Design companies: Soma Mat, Breathing Light, and Sarka (chapter 4). The aim is to describe how we trained our own somaesthetic appreciation skills as designers, our engagements with various digital materials, our engagements with an imagined future user and use practice, and how we brought in other users to experience our designs. I will draw upon my own experience to describe the somaesthetical "realities" behind our design decisions.

Finally, I formally define the criteria we might use to recognize what constitutes a soma design in chapter 5. Based on work by many different researchers in this field, these ideas will be introduced in the form of a *program* (Redström 2017) for which certain aesthetic criteria hold. Those criteria separate the more generic somaesthetic theories from those specifically addressing an active, creative somaesthetic design stance.

How to Design with Your Soma

In part III, I will explore how one might go about recognizing and practicing soma design.

Apart from the methods we used when creating our own designs, discussed in chapter 4, many other tactics may be applied in a soma-conscious way (chapter 6). Existing literature offers a wide range of methods—some borrowed from dance and other body-based practices, others developed specifically for interaction design. In chapter 6, we focus on methods to improve your own aesthetic sensibilities, while in chapter 7, we focus on methods directly engaging with design and soma imaginations. At the end of chapter 7, I will make a brief comparison with standard HCI methods. That, together with an elaboration of the qualities of design theory, will pinpoint the qualitative difference between language-based, symbolic, visual interaction and soma design.

In chapter 8 I will acknowledge a range of issues that must be resolved to validate this approach to design. I readily admit that this book tackles only some of the potential, some of the thorny political issues, some of what can and should be done to continue to develop our interaction design practice. Finally, in the last chapter (chapter 9), I outline a soma design research agenda, indicating areas that must be developed and studied as soma design practices mature. In a manifesto, I express the values and aims of soma design. It is my hope that you, as readers, designers, researchers, and students, will take the next steps and fill this manifesto with content.

Engaging with somaesthetic design is not just an add-on to the repertory of design tactics we already know. It is not a matter of adding a layer of user experience on top of products. It speaks of changing ourselves, our appreciation capability, our creative practice. It speaks to the fundamentals of what we are, what it means to be human.

I   Why

2 Theoretical Backdrop: The Primacy of Movement and Somaesthetics

In the preface and in chapter 1, I argued that we need a new design process urgently for several compelling reasons: because design shapes us; because current designs often fail to shape us in the direction we wish to grow as individuals or communities; and because we stand at a unique moment, when new technologies are opening new possibilities for better, more holistic interactive design. I also argued for an approach I call *soma design*, based on theories of movement and on the concept of somaesthetics, which erases the problematic mind/body dichotomy in Western discourse. In this chapter, I explore these theoretical groundings in more depth. Scholarly readers will see how the roots of soma design invoke cognitive science and pragmatist philosophers; practitioners may recognize concepts familiar from yoga, meditation, or other so-called mind-body practices (though I emphasize throughout that this dichotomy is a fallacy).

I also will show in more depth how dualism underlies much interaction design today, focusing almost entirely on the mind, and ignoring almost entirely the body. I will show how Dourish (2001) and others began questioning this dualism through concepts like *embodiment*, which, though problematic, began to move toward a more holistic view of interaction. With this backdrop in mind, I will then explore two main philosophical theories I introduced earlier: Maxine Sheets-Johnstone's (2011) emphasis on the primacy of movement and Richard Shusterman's (2008) concept of somaesthetics. These theories offer terms and ideas that can help shift our worldview and thus have concrete effects on our design work.

But first, a note on terminology.

Some Terminology

Speaking of the Body
It is surprisingly difficult to talk about *the body* as a clearly identifiable unit. In my introduction, I used several different concepts to try to capture our

focus on movement and body: corporeality, kinaesthetic, somatics, embodiment, ergonomics, and so on. At the basis of this difficulty lies a century-old controversy separating body from mind, separating mind from the world we live in, searching for pure ideals, pure thoughts, pure reasoning, not tied to the physical realities of our bodies and our material reality—a problem known as *dualism*. But—as research in many different disciplines has shown, ranging from neuroscience to sociology and anthropology—the body is not separate from the mind, nor can we separate it from consciousness or from our physical, social, and cultural surroundings. As we shall discuss here, the ways we move, feel, think, and interact with our surroundings are inseparable processes that together determine how we create meaning in our everyday lives. The ways we understand others and the ways we react to events in our surroundings are inseparable from the physical reality of our moving bodies, our experiences, practices, learnings, habits, and culture.

If this is true, how can we then separate out the body or our bodily movements from everything else that is going on? Is it only the skin covering our flesh that determines what is *in* the body and what is outside? If so, where can we locate the mind, the consciousness, or our culture and practices? Reducing the "human condition" to our biology as constituted by our brains or vice versa, to our culture and social practice solely, risks overlooking the different, interlinked processes that create our ways of being in the world. If we are going to design for and with the body, we need more clarity.

One issue that we need to address in our design processes is how to be explicit about our bodily ways of behaving, our morphology—the way in which our bodies are constituted. Although we cannot talk about the body as separate from the world, nor from our thinking and the mind, we still need to be able to talk about specific body parts, about specific muscles, reactions, and perceptions, as this will help us create designs in sync with our movements and experiences. Please note that a precise and qualified way of talking about the realities of our movement, body, and experiences is not the same as assuming that the body will always respond in the same way, like some reductionist machinery with a simple stimulus-response coupling that we can build into our machine models. Instead, we need ways to build systems that start from an understanding of how our bodies and movements change through experience, through the use of our muscles, through training our nervous system reactions, our habits, and our social and cultural contexts. Our designs need to count on *change* as we alter our movements and behavior dynamically, moment by moment, in response to events unfolding dynamically around us. This ability to always change is in a sense obvious: How else could we survive in a world that, itself, is always changing?

Informatics professor Paul Dourish (2001) proposed that seeing systems and the interactions they enable as part of our lived worlds, as *embodied*, would help us think about design in better ways. He took inspiration from phenomenologists such as Merleau-Ponty (1996). Through the lens of phenomenology, he introduced embodiment as a key concept to describe this intertwined relationship between us as living organisms, acting, changing, creating tools and systems in the world, and us at the same time making those tools part of ourselves—of our understanding of the world. With this perspective, any design process needs to consider how the system we design will be integrated—becoming embodied—with our ways of being in the world. The design work must care about the specific life world the tool enters.

Dourish's argument spurred a wave of creativity and a new approach that has been very useful to the academic field of interaction design. Despite all the work we have seen on designing for embodiment, however, the actual, corporeal, pulsating, live, felt body has been notably absent from both theory and descriptions of practical design work.

Put more bluntly, embodied design took us some steps toward a nondualistic stance in our approach to design, but it did not take us all the way. By failing to account for the primacy of movement and the lived body, embodied design failed to promote a nondualistic design stance. In fact, Sheets-Johnstone argues that the concept of embodiment "is a lexical band-aid covering a 350-year-old wound generated and kept suppurating by a schizoid metaphysics" (1999, 260). She proposed that the word *embodied* tries to fix dualism—but at the same time, when we use that term, we suggest that there is an alternative—a way to be disembodied. That is, embodied interaction implies that there are users and designs that are sometimes disembodied—which is never the case. As humans, we are always embodied, always in the world, always part of a social context, always moving our bodies, always in contact with a range of designed tools that our culture offers—some badly designed, some fitting perfectly with the task and context. By placing the word *embodied* in front of other words, such as *design*, *robot*, or *application*, are we really on the road to better design? Or are we reemphasizing a dualistic stance?

To investigate this further, we will turn to the theories and concepts introduced by Sheets-Johnstone (2011) in her work on the *primacy of movement*. Through her work, we will put our moving bodies first and use human movement as the lens through which we can understand the human condition—including our thinking, our language, and how we reason. With that foundation in place, we then move on to better terminology for the living, subjective self, introducing the concept of *soma*, denoting both body and mind, and, most importantly, the first-person perspective.

Defining Aesthetics

The second, even more difficult terminology problem we need to sort out is how to talk about *aesthetics*—our sensory appreciation—and connect it to the human realities of emotion and bodily movements. I mean this not in some abstract sense, but, again, in a very concrete manner. What are the different parts that make an upbeat, vigorous, happy, interaction with a system—or, alternatively, that characterize a slow, inward-listening, mindful interaction? What interactions should the system encourage to spur movements that lead to an aesthetic experience that, in a sense, harmonizes or "is in rhythm" with our bodies, our joy and presence? Unless we can describe and discuss the specifics of that interaction, the aesthetic feel of the different movements, and know what we mean, we cannot come together and design with movement.[1]

Again, like how our bodies cannot be separated from our minds or the world, aesthetics comes not from the individual parts of the system we are designing, but from the *whole*. Dewey puts this elegantly when he talks about how all the different parts need to come together and form a whole: "Emotion is the moving and cementing force. It selects what is congruous and dyes what is selected with its color, thereby giving qualitative unity to materials externally disparate and dissimilar. It thus provides unity in and through the varied parts of an experience" ([1934] 2005, 44).

Shusterman's concept of *somaesthetics* builds on the insights from Dewey, but like Sheets-Johnstone, Shusterman wants to ground our understanding of aesthetics even more firmly in the rich soil our bodies offer. Instead of engaging with beauty, he turned back to the original meaning of *aesthetic*: sensory perception. By adding *soma* to *aesthetics*, he is emphasizing how sensory perception requires as subject. His aim is the study and improvement of appreciative perception, including perceiving that which is not pretty or special, but ordinary or even disturbing and unpleasant.

What makes somaesthetics especially useful for our design purposes is that it communicates a strong ideal, a norm for what we should be doing in our lives. Shusterman claims that there are *better* ways of being in the world, better ways of moving, better ways of learning, better ways of improving our sensory appreciation. A drastic way of framing his claim is to return to the old debate on whether it is more important to live this life as it is, or to live as if it is the next life that matters. That is, should we attempt to free ourselves—our virtues and minds—from our bodies, to die liberated from our mortal forms, or should we aim to live with our bodies, our human conditions, in better ways *before* dying? Shusterman refers to the latter as "the highest art of all—that of perfecting humanity and living better lives" (2012, 26). He is clear that living better lives does not come without effort, but through engagement. It is an art.

Although the idea of *embodied design* did not communicate a strong ideal beyond making sure that we designed systems that would harmonize with and be integrated with our lifeworlds, somaesthetic design does build on aesthetic ideals. It aims to deepen our connection with ourselves and to encourage designs that promote empathy with others. Somaesthetics has an overt goal: improving ourselves and practicing the highest art of all—living better lives.

Let us now turn to the two theories I have selected to introduce those conceptual underpinnings that will help us shift our perspectives of the human condition. These are by no means the only theories that speak to themes of movement, unity over dualism, or connection, but they concisely, eloquently articulate key concepts in soma design while offering vocabulary and ideas to assist those who pursue it. Hopefully, these two theories will bring us a few steps closer to seeing design in a new light.

How to Use This Chapter   I will outline these two theories and share experiences on my own. However, to fill the ideas and concepts presented here with meaning, you must turn to your own experience and "act them out." I will only be able to give you examples from the literature and my own life. You need to work to make these concepts an actionable reality, rhyming with your experiences and thereby useful to your design work. I suggest that, from time to time, you stop reading, close your eyes, turn inward, and try to imagine and feel the experiences the text speaks about, linking them to your own experiences and favorite bodily practices.

Primacy of Movement

As a starting point, I have chosen philosopher Maxine Sheets-Johnstone's work and her emphasis on the *primacy of movement*. Sheets-Johnstone started out as a dancer and choreographer; later, she decided to study evolutionary biology to get a better grip on the human condition.

Her writings helped shift my worldview from one in which design was primarily a language- and symbol-oriented activity to one with a more integrative stance. I came to see how language is rooted in movement and that movement is the earliest form of communication, the one that comes first to any living organism—including people.

Movement First, Language Second

Depending on your inclination and your beliefs, you might find Sheets-Johnstone's claim here difficult to accept: she insists that movement, not language, is our primary way of understanding and being in the world. However, she builds her argument carefully and persuasively, reviewing evolution and providing many different examples.

To illustrate evolution on a smaller scale, she turns to how babies develop language skills. It is only when the newborn baby moves or when there is movement in the environment that the world becomes accessible and perceivable. Our perception is geared toward movement, to the extent that we cannot even see that which is not moving. A baby learns the meaning of actions in the world through actively perceiving and moving, as well as seeing others move, gesture, talk, and act in the world. Children first learn the verbs, the acts that are perceivable, through acting and watching others act. Their exploration of the world is tactile and grounded in perception. It is not the case that the way a small child acts is "prelinguistic." Instead, language is rooted in our movements, and Sheets-Johnstone claims we should see language as *postkinetic*—that is, without movement, there is no language.

In development theory, it is a well-known fact that children need to move to make sense of the world. This is why, for example, children with disabilities that inhibit their movement need to be helped to move to experience the meaning of concepts such as "being underneath" something.

Evolutionarily, it also would be strange if meaning and learning could only be tied to language. There must first be meaningful, shared understandings of activities before we can name them. Otherwise, our primate ancestors would not have survived: "Indeed corporeal concepts are the essential without which language cannot arise and could not ever have arisen. There would be nothing to hold language together, no body of thought which would anchor it. Language is not experiences; it is the means by which we describe experience—or try to describe experience, for the gap between experiential and the language is not easily bridged" (Sheets-Johnstone 2011, 148).

Given Sheets-Johnstone's studies of evolutionary biology, this is perhaps not such a strange position. When we look around us, it is obvious that animals move, that the basis for their survival is movement. Without movement, there is no life. Furthermore, with the insights gained in academic disciplines ranging from neuroscience to artificial intelligence, it becomes harder and harder to talk about human traits such as language, consciousness, or tool-making as unique to being human, setting us apart from other species. We are obviously a successful species, able to inhabit different habitats by producing tools of various kinds that let us survive almost everywhere. But through the studies of other intelligent species, it is noticeable how all traits that we once claimed to be uniquely human exist in one form or another in other species as well (even if they are not always as complex and intricate). Tool-making, for example, is not a unique human trait: it is exhibited by birds, primates other than humans, and other mammals. The coordination of action in animals that hunt in packs is intricate and requires situated intelligence and reactive responses in the moment, sometimes above and beyond what humans can achieve. Culture and behaviors that are learned from one generation to the next exist in other primates; for example, one group of chimpanzees will behave differently from another group, learning and developing within the group. Complex emotions and behaviors drawing upon long-lasting friendships, memories, and empathy, such as grief, can be seen in mammals as diverse as horses,[2] elephants, and dogs.

In short, language arises in response to evolution—as a means to better survival—rooted in movement-based activities. Perhaps these activities first arose in response to grooming practices, or maybe to help coordinate hunting practices, but they clearly grew as a means to describe the world around us through our movement and actions.[3] As we move, meaning arises and is communicated; for example, you can see where I am heading by watching my gait and by knowing your own gait and movement. On that basis, it is easy to see how gestures, eye directions, or facial expressions can develop to become meaningful communication. It is with a basis in these prelinguistic, meaning-making practices that language can be invented and be filled with meaning. In that sense, language is postkinetic. It is through movement that we understand and act in the world. Our bodies move. Our thinking is movement. Or, as Sheets-Johnstone put it: "What is distinctive about thinking in movement is not that the flow of thought is kinetic, but that the thought itself is. It is motional through and through; at once spatial, temporal, dynamic" (2011, 421).

Intelligence, Movement, and Kinetic Bodily Logos

Sheets-Johnstone emphasizes *intelligence in action* as the basis for our behaviors. Although we approach situations with previously learned behavior patterns or instinctive behaviors, we always adjust them dynamically to fit the situation at hand. Without dynamic adjustments, we would not be able to deal with changes in the environment. To scholars in HCI, this resonates with, for example, Lucy Suchman's (1987) work on plans and situated action. Through studying how people approach copying machines at Xerox, she showed that we use plans as resources to inform our behavior, but that these plans are always dynamically adapted based on how the system responds to our activities. Any interaction design that assumes that people follow a given plan, step-by-step, without altering their behavior dynamically in response to a specific situation, will fail to capture how people will behave. Suchman's work on situated action has had a substantial impact on design—both in the artificial intelligence domain in which robots are given behaviors through situated-planning or reactive-planning algorithms, but also in the design of any interactive design. In the latter case, we have learned that machines must convey their inner state, making them "readable" to us, providing "inscribable surfaces," to allow us to dynamically change our plans and behaviors to attain our goals depending on what the machine does (Suchman 1997).

Sheets-Johnstone makes a similar argument, but she ties it even more strongly to the movements of our bodies, showing how this dynamic behavior starts there—not only in humans, but in any moving animal. One of the concepts Sheets-Johnstone uses to describe these movement patterns is *kinetic bodily logos*. She argues that we are born with certain patterns of behavior and movement, which are determined by the genetics of our species and our specific morphology—that is, the constitution of our bodies. But these kinetic bodily logos are not static patterns forever set to produce only one behavior in a simple stimulus-response relationship. Instead, these logos can adapt endlessly to any dynamically unfolding situation. In our kinetic bodily logos, thinking (or meaning-making) and movement are not separated. Although other philosophers have given these behaviors other names—such as Merleau-Ponty's (1996) *motor intentionality*, part of the *schèma corporel* (body schema)—Sheets-Johnstone's definition is, to my understanding, more far reaching. By naming them *logos*,[4] she invokes the meaning-making processes these intricate patterns of thinking and movement entail.

One of the many beautiful examples of complex animal behavior that Sheets-Johnstone draws upon to explain this concept of kinetic bodily logos concerns female wasps (Tinbergen 1968, quoted in Sheets-Johnstone 2015, 55–57). This example demonstrates how these patterns operate in dialogue with the surrounding world, adapting to dynamically changing situations and offering endless *kinetically dynamic possibilities*. Her example shows how we cannot reduce movement and animal behaviors to static, instinctive, stimulus-behavior responses. It also shows how movement is not separate from the world in which it takes place (including, for humans, the tools we surround ourselves with as part of our culture).

The female sand wasp (*Ammophila*) lays several eggs in different locations, in nests that she hides in the sand. She brings caterpillars to each larva as food, but only after checking its state and how much food it needs. This means that the wasp can remember where her three different nests are placed, how hungry each larva is, and how to get back to them—knowledge she has derived from her movement in the landscape. Bringing a caterpillar to one of the nests is hard work, as the caterpillar is big and heavy to the wasp. She cannot grab it and fly with it (see figure 2.1). Instead,

> [she] climbs a bush of heather or a young pine tree and then, arrived at the top after a laborious climb, she turns in various directions, as if having a good look round. Then she takes a long jump, which is in the direction of her nest. … The wasp then begins to walk, stumbling and plodding along over the rough ground. Although starting out in the right direction, she might make a wrong turn or even go in loops. She will then again climb a heather bush or young pine, look around again, make another jump—in the correct direction of the nest. Various studies

Figure 2.1
A wasp carrying a larva

clearly show that the wasp's movement is tethered to landmarks, landmarks such as tufts of grass or a clump of pebbles or pine cones—the position of which she has to learn. (Tinbergen 1968, 120, quoted in Maxine Sheets-Johnstone 2011, 444)

The kinetic bodily logos here allows the wasp adjust her movements to the environment dynamically. She learns about landmarks and in which direction to move. But during her hunt for food, the world might be changing; stones may move, grass might wither, new paths may have to be found.

As the world dynamically changes, animals must engage and create meaning through their movements with the world. This is what Sheets-Johnstone means when she says that thinking and movement are not separated. It also shows how these logos can be endlessly adapted to the dynamically unfolding situation. These logos form the basis for how we think. As such, "[they] are the generative source of concepts of agentivity, of if/then relationships, of spatio-temporal invariants. They generate expectations; they are replete with kinetic concepts having to do with energy, distance, speed, range of movement, direction—in short with a complex of dynamic qualities inherent in the experience of movement itself" (Maxine Sheets-Johnstone 2011, 444). These kinetic bodily logos consist of bodily processes such as surface recognition sensitivity, proprioception, kinaesthesia, and the capacity to think in movement.

Given these kinetic bodily logos and encounters with the world, animals can modify their behavior, learn about the world, and learn about themselves. If they do not learn, they do not survive. What the world *offers* to the animals is what they must adjust to—the dynamically changing possibilities of the world (bushes, pine trees, sand, other animals). There is an ongoing dialogue with what evolution will craft.

By choosing examples from what we might consider lower lifeforms such as the wasp, showing how even such a simple animal can act with a great deal of intention, memory, and adjustment to the situation at hand, Sheets-Johnstone helps us see that human activity is not so different from these lower lifeforms. We too act, react, get it wrong, rework our learnings, and, based on input, continuously adapt what we do. This is not only a frontal-lobe, rational, language-driven reasoning process, but in many ways very similar to how the wasp acts in the moment: moving, evaluating, changing our course of action.

Relating this back to design work, note how one of the basic activities in interaction design, designing for *affordances* (Gibson 2014a, 2014b; Norman 1999), involves creating possibilities that engage our kinetic bodily logos. It is not the case that we can design, for example, a doorknob to be intuitively natural to us. Turning the knob will always be a learned activity.

Norman's emphasis on affordances (drawing from Gibson) offers the idea that we should design for meaning-making in our everyday lives, inspired by and making use of our movements and our morphology, the constitution of our bodies, and how we think in action. As we touch the knob, attempt to turn it, that interaction feeds into activities of the hand and arm that are immediately meaningful to us. In fact, every time a person interacts with a system, turning a doorknob or pushing a button, it can be described as a dynamic, movement-based meeting, unique to the situation at hand and reflecting *thinking in movement*. As we act, we also observe, perceive, and react.

Dynamic Congruency between Movement and Emotion
Given the focus on aesthetics and movement in this book, there is one more important concept we can learn from Sheets-Johnstone's philosophical inquiry. It concerns the linking of movement to emotion, a link noted by both Darwin in *On Emotion in Man and Animal* (Darwin 1965) and by William James, the founding father of psychology (James 1905).

The word *emotion* originates from the French *esmotion*, in turn derived from *movoir*: to set in motion, to move feelings. This gives us a first hint of what emotion is: an experience that is both constituted as movement and that at the same time sets us in motion and makes us act.

In the different disciplines studying emotion—neuroscience, life sciences, anthropology, social psychology, and others—there is agreement on how emotion can act as an *appraisal* function that gives different values to different optional ways of acting (Davidson, Sherer, and Hill Goldsmith 2009). In any situation, there are endless variations on what we can do next. Without emotion, it is not clear why one path is preferable to another. When it is a matter of life and death, emotion is what saves us, by spurring immediate action. Emotion is therefore a quick response without much cognitive reasoning before its onset. Emotion is not a state but a process that starts, increases, and, once the act is over, decreases in intensity. This does not mean that emotional processes can be separated from our reasoning and conscious thought. Instead, the more complex reasoning will be woven into the process, but is always secondary to a first, fast reaction in our nervous systems—more specifically, in our limbic systems. (The limbic system consists of evolutionarily "older" parts of the brain, such as the amygdala and hippocampus, in which the emotional processing takes place.) But the limbic system is not separate from the rest of the brain, or the nervous system from the whole body.

For example, in neuroscience, Ledoux (2015) has shown how visual stimuli go both directly to the emotional brain (amygdala and hippocampus) and at the same time to the frontal lobe that controls our reasoning. Based on the very fast appraisal process in the emotional brain, signs will go directly to the body, emitting hormones, tensing or relaxing muscles, controlling our facial expressions, and so on. This means that the body will respond very quickly to threats, surprises, or changes in the environment. But once the reasoning in the frontal lobe happens (which is a slightly slower process), those processes in turn also communicate with the emotional brain, modifying our responses. Maybe what we saw was not a dangerous snake, but a stick? If it was a stick, this insight will calm the appraisal process in the emotional brain, sending signals to the body to calm down and to the perceptual system to further investigate that it is indeed a stick and not a snake. A cascade of interactions takes place back and forth between the visual stimuli, perception, the emotional brain, the body, and the frontal lobe. This process does not occur only in extreme fear situations; it is always ongoing, with varying intensities for our emotional responses.

Research shows that some people suffering damage to emotional centers in the brain will not act rationally (Damasio 1994). They will not know how to respond in a situation because they have no *feeling* for the better course of action. Emotion, as a key to appraisal of activity, clearly plays a key role in our rationality and responses to the world. These findings have made an important contribution to, for example, the design of robots, as they also need to have some form of appraisal function in place to make choices among different actions. Otherwise, they might be stuck in eternal loops reasoning about the benefits or disadvantages of action A or action B. While the robot is stuck in reasoning, the world may change, requiring the robot to start all over. This is not to say that robots need emotions in the sense of replicating the mammalian, emotional brain to make decisions. Rather, they need some form of appraisal function to set values for different actions, allowing the robots to make quick choices in every instant.

What Sheets-Johnstone so elegantly tells us through her writings, however, is that we cannot reduce emotion to an appraisal function located in the emotional brain (the limbic system). Nor can we reduce emotion to what Ekman (1992) refers to as the *six basic emotions*, based on his studies of facial expressions. Such reductionist accounts are a kind of *microscopic phrenology*. Instead, Sheets-Johnstone points out: "Bodily movement coincident with emotion are different from both facial expression and autonomic nervous system activity, these phenomenon being the prime focus of empirical studies of emotion. Studies of the former present emotion in the form of visual stills and deducted facial muscle involvements; studies of the latter measure physiological responses. Neither focus on the whole-body experience of emotion, which means neither focus on the felt experience of being moved and moving" (1999, 272). By this, she does not mean that facial muscle movements or autonomic nervous system responses are unimportant; they just fail to account for the whole experience of our own kinetic/tactical-kinaesthetic bodies as we move and are moved by emotion.

Let us consider an example of a strong, extreme emotion, like fear, to make this clearer. Sheets-Johnstone gives the example of being pursued by an unknown assailant at the night in a deserted area of a city:

> An intense and unceasing whole-body tension drives the body forward. It is quite unlike the tension one feels in a jogging run, for instance, or in a run to greet someone. There is a hardness to the whole body that congeals it into a singularity tight mass; the driving speed of the movement condenses airborne and impact moments into a singular continuum of motion. The head-on movement is at times erratic; there are sudden changes of direction. With these changes the legs bending at the knee, so that the whole body is lowered. The movement is each time abrupt. It breaks the otherwise unrelenting and propulsive speed of movement. The body may suddenly swerve, dodge, twist, duck or crouch, and the head may swivel about before the forward plunging run with its acutely concentrated and unbroken energies continues. (1999, 269)

Even if we have never been pursued by an unknown assailant, we recognize how it would feel from reading this phenomenological account. The felt experience of the dynamics of fear, the tension in the muscles, the abrupt changes of direction, the ducking: We can imagine the experience, even if we are not moving while reading the account. The movement and how fear moves us are analytically one and the same. The dynamics of the movement *are* the dynamics of the felt experience. They are inseparable.

Thus, though it is clear that emotional processes play an important role in our survival by activating bodily processes, these emotional experiences (in the emotional brain) do not always come before movement and muscular behaviors. Bodily movements and emotional processes are tightly coupled, and not only in one direction, from appraisal to bodily action. The activation is a two-way channel. As Sheets-Johnstone puts it, there is "a generative as well as expressive relationship between movement and emotion" (1999, 262). In fact, emotional processes can start in any part of those tightly interconnected systems—in external events perceived, in thinking about past events, in moving in certain ways, or in having certain hormone levels. That is, certain movements, memories, hormone levels, tensions in our muscles, or even digestive processes can also *generate* emotional processes.

Aristotle pointed out that the soul cannot be divorced from the body: "It seems that all the affections of soul involve a body—passion, gentleness, fear, pity, courage, joy, loving, and hating; in all these there is a concurrent affection of the body" (quoted in Barnes 1984, 642). Note how the experience is framed as a *concurrent* affection of the body.

William James (1884), who is often referred to as the founder of psychology, saw emotion without an embodied experience as an impossibility: "A purely disembodied human emotion is a nonentity." James cites an example from Henle to describe the close connection between feeling and bodily movement or experiences: "So small a thing as a bubble of air rising from the stomach through the oesophagus, and loitering on its way a few minutes and exerting pressure on the heart, is able during sleep to occasion a nightmare, and during waking to produce a vague anxiety. On the other hand, we see that joyous thoughts dilate our blood-vessels, and that a suitable quantity of wine, because it dilates the vessels, also disposes us to joyous thoughts" (James [1890] 1981, 462).

This does not mean that we can create a feeling solely through making one of the movements involved. Mimicry alone, as in mirroring facial expressions, will not necessarily be enough to create an emotional experience. All the different parts need to be there for emotion to arise, and we cannot deterministically spur changes to our internal organs or hormone levels through portraying certain movements or facial expressions. But with mimicry, the chance that all the other parts of the emotional experience will follow increases. For example, James ([1890] 1981) described that actors portraying strong emotions reported profuse sweating, even when their characters do not require physical exertion. This phenomenon underlies the technique of *method acting*, in which actors seek the inner motives for why their characters speak or act in certain ways, allowing the actors to not only represent but also activate emotional and subconscious behaviors (Stanislavski [1938] 2017). It is a physically grounded technique in which improvisation is key to "feeling" what the character in the play would have felt.

Returning to Sheets-Johnstone's characterization of emotion as movement, to her the most important insight is the *dynamic congruency* between movement and emotion. By studying emotion as if it was a still picture, we miss its temporal aspects and, more importantly, its outcome: to motivate action. Such action may be needed to survive, but also to communicate and establish relations with peers. Emotional behaviors are, in her view, fundamentally kinetic bodily happenings—being moved in order to move.

The kinetic bodily logos that shape and are shaped by our behaviors and environments also include emotional process shaping and are shaped by our surroundings. This in turn means that there will be endless variations on exactly what is experienced moment by moment. This was true also for William James, who saw endless variations in how emotion was experienced and expressed—due both to individual differences and to every new situation and encounter.

Emotional processes are shaped not in the least by our cultural surroundings. An emotional experience resides not only "inside" our bodies as processes going back and forth between different parts of our body; they are also, in a sense, spread throughout the social setting we are in (Katz 2001; Lutz 1988; Lutz and White 2003; Parkinson 1996). Emotions are not only hardwired processes in our brains; they are interesting, changeable processes that regulate our social selves. As such, they are constructed in dialogue between ourselves and the culture and social settings we live in. Emotion is not only movement to survive in a world full of danger, it is also a social and dynamic communication mechanism. We learn how and when certain emotions are appropriate, and we learn the appropriate expressions of emotions for different cultures, contexts, and situations. Our cultural practices are a form of sedimented, agreed-upon movements, enabling endless variation, enforcing prescribed ways to act. The way we make sense of emotions combines the experiential and emotional processes in our bodies with interaction with others, colored by our learned cultural practices.

The anthropologist Catherine Lutz, for example, shows how a form of anger named *song* by the people of the South Pacific atoll Ifaluk serves an important socializing role in their society (Lutz 1988; Lutz and White 2003). Song is, according to Lutz, "justifiable anger" and is used with children and with subordinates to teach them fitting behavior, such as making their fair share of the communal meal, paying respect to elders, or acting socially appropriately. In my own culture, song is not a clearly identifiable emotion. Although I might also act angrily with my children to teach them politeness, the enactment and experience of that anger is not linked to how I behave with my coworkers.

We often think of emotional experiences and feelings as processes that suddenly overwhelm us, taking away our initiative, making us act without proper deliberation—but this is only the case in extreme situations. For the most part, we actively regulate our experiences; even for extreme experiences, we can train our responses. Ethnographic work by Jack Katz (2001) provides a rich account of how people individually and in groups actively *produce* emotion as part of their social practices. He discusses, for example, how joy and laughter among visitors to a funhouse equipped with distorting mirrors is produced and regulated among the friends visiting together. Moving to a new mirror, tentatively chuckling at the reflection, glancing at your friend—who in turn might move closer—might in the end result in "real" laughter when standing together in front of the mirror. Katz also places this production of emotion into a larger, complex social and societal setting when he discusses anger among car drivers in Los Angeles. He shows that anger when being cut off by another car is produced as a consequence of a loss of embodiment with the car, the road, and the general experience of traveling. The car cuts us off, disturbs our flow of experience, our sense of being one with the movements we are experiencing—and this spurs anger. Beyond the infringement upon the driver's extended body, Katz connects this anger with the social situation on the road; the lack of communicative possibilities between cars and their drivers; our prejudice of other people's driving skills, relating to their cultural background or ethnicity; and so on; he then shows how all of it comes together, explaining why anger is produced. He even sees anger as a *graceful* way to regain a sense of embodiment.

In summary, emotion is not reducible: it cannot be reduced to the object of the emotion; to the feeling of the emotion, in terms of bodily processes in our inner organs, hormones, muscles, or blood vessels; to the appraisal value helping us determine how to act; to the language or conscious reasoning about the experience; or to the practices of our culture, teaching us how to respond and react. It is all these together that constitute the emotional process. At every instance, the emotional experience will be unique, depending on the constitution of our bodies, prior experiences, cultures, and context.

First-Person Perspective on Movement Experience

Sheets-Johnstone's position on movement, being moved, and feeling has consequences for one of the key insights we will use in this book: the importance of our first-person perspectives. As we discussed, our bodies cannot be reduced to predictable stimulus-response machines. Our behaviors are dynamically changing, responding in the moment to changes, and meaning resides inside those movements. Studying the body solely from a third-person perspective, from the outside, therefore will not tell us what is going on.

Instead, Sheets-Johnstone emphasizes a first-person perspective—a perspective we will draw upon in our practical design exercises later in this book (chapters 4, 6, and 7). If we reduce our bodies to machines of some kind, then we are placing ourselves outside of those bodies—looking at them in the third person. But if we instead engage with our living bodies, feeling, acting, and engaging with our aliveness, then we attain a first-person perspective: "Thinking in movement involved no symbolic counters but is tied to an on-going qualitatively experience dynamics in which movement possibilities arise and dissolve" (Sheets-Johnstone 2011, xxxi).

To illustrate what it means to shift from a third-person perspective to a first-person presence with "no symbolic counters," let me provide a first-person account from one of my own studies—an autoethnography (Höök 2010) of myself horseback riding. At the particular moment described ahead from one of my horseback-riding lessons, I had been struggling with my rhythm and posture, working hard at seeing my body from the "outside" with a third-person perspective, trying to actively correct the position of my heels, my knees, my thighs, the direction of my gaze, and so on. My riding teacher, Christian, saw my struggles and started talking about something entirely different: going to the hairdresser, and this and that—chitchatting with me. This distracted my third-person-perspective focus and allowed me to relax into the dynamically unfolding situation at hand—becoming a centaur, uniting my movements with the horse's movements:

> Towards the end of the third lesson, after having been embarrassed, out of rhythm and very confused, I had, in a way, given up all my good intentions of putting my body in the right place and working hard to make it work. Instead, I allowed myself to be distracted by Christian who was talking about something irrelevant, I relaxed and then I finally got the rhythm of the horse. Suddenly, without consciously trying to, I shifted my weight further back in the saddle and suddenly it worked. I rose at the right moment, I was relaxed in the way I was sitting and the whole thing felt fleeting and nice.
>
> At this point, as I was relaxing, just feeling the rhythm of the trot, I was not really thinking of where my different body parts are placed, nor was I thinking about the rhythm as such. I cannot say that any clearly formulated thoughts flew through my mind. Indeed, one could say that I am not thinking at all. Thinking is precisely not what is required, I was simply entirely absorbed by the situation. My muscles were doing what they should be doing, my eyes were directed towards where we should be going, my hearing followed the rhythm of the horse's hooves on the ground, and I felt as one with the horse. We were no longer separated but moved together with one intention, one will. My whole self was simple there, in synch with the movement. (ibid., 233)

The reference to "not thinking at all" should not be taken to mean that movement control occurs without thinking. What I am referring to is that there are no symbolic counters that can account for the stream of consciousness flowing through my centaur-self. My language-oriented, conscious self was focused on chitchatting with my teacher, Christian. One process did not disturb the other but freed up resources to go with the flow of movements.

There is a longer discussion to be held here about whether I can really be perceiving and acting in the horse's world, or if I am always restrained by my morphology, stuck in what is "available" to humans[5]—or, vice versa, if the horse can be in my world. What best characterizes my experience is a mutual sympathy (Ingold 2017), meaning-making grounded in our joint movements.

The process of acting in movement was picked up on by Alan Kay (1987) when he, together with the team at Xerox, invented the desktop metaphor. In a video from 1987, Kay recalls watching a TV show in which an instructor taught a woman who had never played tennis before to perform a forehand stroke, background stroke, and serve in twenty minutes. By distracting her rational reasoning by making her sing and chatting to her, the instructor allowed other parts of herself to relax into simple imitation behaviors—key to all social animals, especially primates. Kay's idea was that it should be possible to replace the command-based interfaces of computers at the time. A command-based interface requires remembering the names of commands, learning a whole vocabulary, almost learning a new language. After seeing the tennis player learn so quickly, Kay thought it would be better to make commands by gestures, physical, movement-based acts paired with clear feedback—as in, for example, point-and-click or drag-and-drop. This in turn frees up our more linguistically oriented, conscious thinking to perform other tasks.

Lexical Band-Aids: Mind as Consequence, Not as Embodiment
This brings us back to the question I asked at the start of this chapter: How can we talk about the body? What terminology should we be using? We should now understand that the question itself presumes that the body is a simple machine of flesh, blood, and bones that carries around our brains—a machinery essentially meaningless in understanding our minds. Instead, what has fascinated us—often due to religious beliefs—has been to pin down what is uniquely human, qualities that set us apart from other animals. This has put emphasis on our language and consciousness, our ability to stand outside of ourselves and make rational arguments, the

third-person perspective. But through reading Sheets-Johnstone, the question is turned upside down. We are first and foremost organisms that move. The difference between us and other organisms is not a qualitative one. We actively seek movement, and it is only when we move that we can feel, think, and create meaning. We watch others and learn from their behavior and recognize their intentions through our own. Even our language arises in and through that movement.

But to say that everything is movement and that this term is all we need would also be a reductionist statement. There are reasons we might want to talk about different parts of our bodies, different parts of our internal processes and our cultural practices. Once we have language, we can also jointly reason and work on much more far-reaching and complex topics together. By naming and differentiating among the different human traits, we can engage in a more qualified discussion, recognizing and honoring the different qualities of different parts of our reasoning and ways of being in the world.

The answer to the question of how to talk about "the body," therefore, is yes, let us use the term *body*, and let us name and discriminate among limbs, muscles, inner organs, and nervous systems. Let us talk about the different parts of the brain and how signals travel through them back and forth. Let us talk about perception, cognition, consciousness, movement, and emotion. This is not the problem. The real conceptual problem is when we speak about our thinking, mind, and consciousness as if those can be separated from movement. Instead of talking first about our mind and thinking and then second about our bodies, we need to start in movement, learned in interaction and then internalized as individual capacity, as this is where the thinking happens. Even as I sit calmly writing this sentence, my body is moving.

This does not mean that language is not an absolutely unique and wonderful invention, forming an intrinsic part of our morphology, the movements of our living human bodies—and human consciousness is intrinsically linked to language. But as Sheets-Johnstone says: "Consciousness is thus not in matter; it is a dimension of living forms, in particular, a dimension of living forms that move" (1998, 276). Language and the ways it shapes our consciousness allow us to view ourselves from the outside, with the third-person perspective. Language helps us discriminate among different experiences, to the extent that it is harder for us to discern those experiences for which our culture does not have a name. Speaking therefore is acting, moving, and influencing ourselves and the world around us. We live in and thrive on this world of language—but it is always grounded in our bodies, movements, and context.

As I described earlier, the term *embodiment* attempted to bridge the gap that was created between mind and body. But Sheets-Johnstone argues that the term is a mere "lexical band-aid" to remedy a problem that is, in fact, nothing less than a fundamental misunderstanding of the human condition. As there is *never* any chance for us to be disembodied, it does not make sense to speak about embodiment. We are always embodied. Adding the concept of *embodiment* to any human activity or computer agents, such as in the *embodied mind* (Varela, Thompson, and Rosch 2017) or *embodied agents* (Cassell 2000), does not make sense. It is in our animate forms that life begins and where emotions are rooted, where concepts and language start—not in something that Sheets-Johnstone might term *mental life*.

But what term should we use instead of *embodiment*? How can we talk about the unity among thinking, moving, and feeling—our first-person perspective? What term might we find that does not create and reinforce an artificial separation between body and mind?

To answer this question, I turn to the somaesthetics theory proposed by Richard Shusterman and draw upon his use of the term *soma*, which is "the lived, sentient, purposive body that implies the essential union of body-mind" (2012, 188). This is the term we will use whenever we need to remind ourselves of the first-person perspective, the unity of mind and body, and the interlinking of our experiences, thinking, and feeling.

Somaesthetics

As we saw, Sheets-Johnstone's philosophical inquiry builds on theories of evolution and survival, as well as scientific studies in biology and psychology. She draws upon a line of reasoning from Aristotle via Merleau-Ponty, starting from the biological configurations of our bodies and emphasizing how we are shaped by evolution. This is why I picked her as a starting point for introducing the primacy of movement and the role of emotion in our lives. I wanted to remove any remaining worries you, my reader, might have that there is some mysterious, spiritual side to what I want to convey in this book. I also wanted to show that what we are discussing here is not out of reach of rigorous study and inquiry, irrespective of your stance toward what constitutes rigor.

Sheets-Johnstone's account of the human condition also concerns aesthetics. She is an artist, a dancer and a choreographer, interested in emotional qualia,[6] art forms, and cultural expression. In her description of the primacy of movement, she provides beautiful accounts of dance improvisation, emphasizing the wonderful rhythms that Jane Goodall refers to as our "bipedal swagger" (Goodall 1972, quoted in Sheets-Johnstone 2015, 313) and upright bodies bring. However, her work offers little practical guidance for how to go about creating aesthetic designs based on movement and holistic understandings of the self. Therefore, we will not go deeper into her accounts of art, aesthetics, and movement, but will instead move to Shusterman's theories on *somaesthetics*, which speak more directly to the relationship between aesthetics and somatics that we seek to uncover and work with in our somaesthetic design processes.

In the following section, I will first explain Shusterman's concept of somaesthetics and its relation to the pragmatic tradition and understanding of aesthetics. I will then show how Shusterman builds upon Dewey's ([1934] 2005) argument that aesthetic quality is not an inherent property of an object, but rather the result of active engagement and experience. But where Dewey emphasizes the unique, romantic, and beautiful, Shusterman understands somaesthetics as the critical and meliorative study of appreciative perception—not only of the pretty, but also the ordinary or even the disturbing. Finally, I will outline his argument that we can train our somatic sensibilities, much as wine connoisseurs train their palates, to distinguish a wide and subtle variation of distinct somatic experiences. This argument undergirds the rest on this book, for it suggests that by training ourselves somaesthetically, we can develop designs that help us live better lives, by creating experiences and systems that shape us in the ways we want to be shaped.

Soma + Aesthetics = Somaesthetics

Somaesthetics is an interdisciplinary field, grounded in pragmatist philosophy and phenomenology. Shusterman defines it as the "critical study and meliorative cultivation of the soma as a site both of sensory appreciation (aesthesis) and creative self-fashioning" (2012, 111). By combining the word *soma* with *aesthetics*, our sensory appreciations, he draws our attention to the importance of our bodily movements, our ways of being and thinking—but more importantly, the aesthetics of those experiences.

To understand the implications of this term, we first need to discuss what we mean by aesthetics. For much of history, aesthetic qualities like beauty were seen as a property of objects themselves. Scholars looked for measurements that determined those properties. The golden ratio, for example, was a way of describing what a balanced painting should look like to be beautiful.[7] By making beauty a property of the object we perceive and interact with, the active, interpretative, moving perceiver—the human counterpart—was left out. The idea was that art objects, literature, paintings, or music could be and were set apart from everyday life, confined to a separate arena of art. Their properties had to be scrutinized free of context; it was not the music performance that the aesthetic critique should care for, but the notes on the sheet of paper, which represented the pure art object: these were platonic ideals.

Dewey, however—one of the pragmatists that Shusterman builds on—stressed the aesthetic *experience* rather than aesthetics of the object as such. Two insights from Dewey are particularly relevant to our creative design practice.

Aesthetic Experience Set Apart From the Everyday   First, Dewey sees an aesthetic experience as set apart from the general flow of experiences in our everyday life. It typically has a clear beginning and end. It is something that we can refer to afterwards in definite terms: "An experience has a unity that gives it its name, that meal, that storm, that rupture of a friendship. The existence of this unity is constituted by a single quality that pervades the entire experience in spite of the variation of its constituent parts" (Dewey [1934] 2005, 38). Dewey refers to this unity as *emotion*. Note how the experiences he refers to include the context (the storm), matter (the meal), and other people (the friendship), as well as the subjective experience of that totality.

Because any experience, even the most mundane, is always unique, Dewey set aesthetic experience apart by the emphasis on "that" meal, storm, or rupture of a friendship. This emphasis on aesthetic experience as something outside the ordinary is problematic to some of our somaesthetic design aims, as we may also want to talk about the aesthetic experiences of the everyday, of the repeated engagement, or experiences that are perhaps not so memorable that we can talk about them as "that" experience. But for now, let us think about aesthetic experience as an unfolding of events, with a clear beginning, a clear end, and a unity that is unique. Note also how the beauty of an aesthetic experience is not equal to only the positive emotions or safe experiences. It may well include scary, unsettling, or disturbing experiences as well.

When McCarthy and Wright (2004a) brought pragmatism into the field of interaction design, this articulation became problematic to some. After all, if every aesthetic experience is unique, then how can designers make it more likely that a future user will feel the "aesthetics of the temporal gestalt" they have crafted? Surely, we must be able to talk about aesthetics of our interactive designs without necessarily speaking of the uniqueness of an experience when everything comes together into a once-in-a-lifetime memorable moment. Perhaps some of the explanation lies in the difference between the aims of the arts versus the aims of industrial design. In art, a unique expression is crafted, whereas in industrial design, we seek to provide useful tools for mass production endowed with certain experiences.

McCarthy and Wright's introduction of Dewey's account of aesthetic experience to HCI also introduced a second difficulty: aesthetic experiences remain removed from lowbrow experiences. If we are attempting seriously to bring aesthetics into our everyday lives, then the pleasures of some silly television program, or enjoying the touch of the ladle you use every day, over and over, to stir food, must also be seen as "aesthetic experiences." The everyday, much-repeated gesture to open your smartphone, for example, must be meaningful and pleasurable; this is what designers think of when discussing the aesthetics of interactive designs.

That said, McCarthy and Wright's points resonate with Sheets-Johnstone's observations about the uniqueness and flexibility of our kinetic bodily logos. In both cases, each interaction with our smartphones, devices, or other technologies occurs in a slightly new setting, with a slightly new goal, with infinitely small variations of movement and needs. For example, Ingold (2006) provides a beautiful account of sawing a plank, discussing the uniqueness of each plank that he saws through. The meeting of the blade of the saw and the wood must be adjusted for the unique properties of the specific plank, his strength at each moment, the lighting conditions, and so on.

By shifting emphasis away from heightened, sublime aesthetic experiences and toward everyday aesthetics, we can overcome the problem some have had with this account of aesthetic experience. In particular, if our aim is to build better interactive tools that people can use in their everyday practices, such as smartphones or emerging Internet of Things applications, then (as we aim to show here) somaesthetics could help us see aesthetics as far more than "mere surface decoration" and instead as part of the foundation for a purposeful system (Petersen et al. 2004; also discussed in Bardzell and Bardzell 2015) without turning to highbrow, unique, beautiful experiences.

Aesthetic Engagement and Improvement A second insight we should glean from Dewey's account of aesthetic experiences is how we can achieve them—both as artists/designers and as viewers/users. Dewey sees aesthetic experience not as something that happens to us, but as something we engage in, actively and subjectively.

When we craft an aesthetic experience, we should, according to Dewey, attempt to "empty" the material of all its potential. We should try to use every aspect, every material we bring, to create the art. Ideally, all different parts will be explored and exploited to their fullest, while avoiding clichés and shortcuts. In a video game, for example, materials include the narrative, the roles players take on, the graphics, the music, the visualizations, and so on. Each of these parts—each trajectory through the experience (Benford et al. 2009)—must be crafted so that they all come together as one whole. Or, if we want the different materials to speak against one another, creating ambiguous or disharmonious combinations, then we need to design this intentionally to create that kind of experience on purpose, not by mistake.

By bringing the living, sentient body into the equation, Shusterman takes Dewey's pragmatic stance toward aesthetic experience another step closer to the realm of life and practice. Although Dewey mentioned the body and "the lower cognitive skills" that let us experience beauty, his interpretation of aesthetics was not fundamentally grounded in the movements of our bodies as Shusterman's is. Shusterman writes: "My concept of soma as a living, purposive, sentient, perceptive body or bodily subjectivity provides an altogether different direction. We can, as I have tried to demonstrate, improve our perceptual faculties through better use of the soma" (2012, 141). Here, he brings our soma, our bodily movements, into the equation as a "living, purposeful, sentient body." But in the second sentence, he also adds the possibility to improve through "better use of the soma." Training their aesthetic sensibilities has been a long-standing aim for those interested in the arts, but Shusterman emphasizes that the route to doing so goes through the soma.

Training the Soma

Shusterman's aims are grounded in the original purpose of all philosophy: to improve oneself. He does not take aesthetic experience as a given, an experience to be studied as an object out there; instead, he wants to engage us all in actively, creatively changing and improving our experiences. By educating ourselves, he argues we are engaging in "the highest art of all— that of living better lives." In his book *Body Consciousness*, he goes back over centuries of philosophy, all the way back to the Greek philosophers, noting that in the work of Socrates and many of his followers, educating the body was as important as improving the thinking. Socrates himself danced every day. He worked in the "gymnasion, the place where physical exercises were practiced ... the same place where philosophy lessons were given" (Hadot 1995, quoted in Shusterman 2008, 16). But Plato, who came to dominate much of Western philosophy, instead saw the goal of life to be training for death, to divide "the soul as much as possible from the body ... until it is completely independent" (quoted in Shusterman 2008, 16). To Shusterman, this dichotomy has hurt Western philosophy for centuries; only recently have we started to see some reconciliation. A wave of research has swept through philosophy and many other academic disciplines, resurrecting and reevaluating the roles of emotion and body in thinking and living.

But what does Shusterman mean by the art of living a better life? First, like Sheets-Johnstone, he emphasizes the importance of the body: "For the body is our indispensable tool of tools, the necessary medium of our being, perception, action and self-presentation in the world" (Shusterman 2013). With somaesthetics, Shusterman takes this understanding one step further. Not only are movements and the living body the lens through which we can understand the world, this "tool of tools" itself is also moldable. By learning, improving, and playfully engaging with movements involving our muscles, nervous system, and senses, we may extend our experiences and create richer and potentially better ways of being in the world. To Shusterman, learning body awareness and better use of our bodies is as important as educating our minds. This applies both to the motor system, such as when learning to ride a bike, and to the sensory system, learning to interpret and make sense of our bodily experiences. Thus, by increasing our body awareness through engaging in various forms of training, we can become more perceptive and aware in the physical world in which we live and act. Through such training, we may enjoy novel playful, engaging, pleasurable experiences, as well as painful ones.

In his definition of somaesthetics, Shusterman also speaks about *creative self-stylization*—by which he refers to all the ways we decorate our bodies. Tattoos, piercings, clothes, and hairstyles are all part of putting our bodies out there, to be identified with certain styles, movements, and ways of living our lives. We will not go deeply into this side of somaesthetics here but will instead focus on somatic care, the training of our aesthetic sensibilities through body practices.

What Is Aesthetic in Somaesthetic?

What sets apart *aesthetic* movements of the soma from just any movement or any experience? If everything is movement and our experiences basically consist of movements—movements of our muscles, organs, nervous systems, hormones, cultural practices (sedimented movements making up our cultural habits)—then what sets apart an aesthetic movement experience from any other experience?

In his writings, Shusterman repeatedly comes back to the need to disrupt habits and become more aware, discerning the different parts of a movement or emotion, feeling every little change in your body. For example, training your breathing to achieve better focus, or correcting your eating habits from what is "habitual" to shape new, more reflective, thoughtful movements. Returning to Dewey, Shusterman (2008) discusses the difference between "routine, unintelligent habit" and "intelligent or artistic habit" that is fused with thought and feeling. To Shusterman, the art of somatic reflection and conscious control is thus itself a "refined intelligent habit emerging from and coordinating a background of countless other habits that constitute the developing bundle of complex, unstable, opposing attitudes, habits, impulses we call the self."

But what is it that we achieve if we disrupt the habitual, if we listen more attentively to our own movements, discerning all the small changes and processes that are involved in moving? What is it that we will perceive that appeals to us, to our sense of beauty? Shusterman talks about what we will "discover" via two different possibilities. First, we may experience *rediscovery* of what we already know—the ways we moved as babies or children, a reminder of the joys of those movements we have already experienced but that we do not engage in anymore—for example, skipping rather than walking, rolling on our backs from one side to the other, or grabbing our toes. These are simple, pleasurable, innocent joys, which can, in turn, lead to disrupting habits in more complex behaviors, such as eating or having sex, to deepen our joys and potential for novel experiences. Second, we may *expand our repertory of possible movements* through learning from different body arts. In yoga, Feldenkrais, meditation practices, and so on, we can learn, for example, how to control our breathing, which is interesting itself, but also can lead to better focus and ways of handling our everyday stress.

These discoveries or learnings *may* lead to better appreciation, richer bodily ways of being in the world, and more beauty. But somaesthetic experience cannot be defined in the abstract; it is not a process of trying to find some generic qualities that can be can be put into, say, any meal to serve as a guarantee that the experience will always be somaesthetic. The experience is always specific and unique. The somaesthetic experience of eating is always tied to a particular dinner, with particular people eating, all with their unique taste, prior experience of food and dinners, hunger, eating pace, level of care, and knowledge of how to move, chew, and swallow, as well as the unique care taken by the cook when combining textures, tastes, how the table is laid, the culture in which the meal takes place, and so on. The somaesthetic experience lies in how all these different parts come together into a whole for some individual, in some instance. With somaesthetic training, that experience can be richer and even more meaningful. Shusterman talks about an "awakening" from mindless, joyless behaviors through attending and appreciating (referring to Thoreau [1854] 2016). Most of all, somaesthetic engagement is a project of learning to *appreciate*.

Accounts of somaesthetics will therefore always be tied to accounts of specific events. But this is not the same as seeing them as Dewey referred to them, as "that" experience, the unique, special instances almost of enlightenment in which everything comes together into "that meal, that storm." Shusterman has a more down-to-earth way of seeing aesthetic experience, even if he recognizes that art is often discussed in that those terms and that those experiences are possible: "Heightened qualities of affect or emotion are often an important and valued feature of aesthetic experience (both of art and nature), but such a heightened feeling or emotion essentially involved bodily reactions along with cognitive content" (2012, 147). These "heightened qualities" are not necessary to define an experience as a somaesthetic experience. This is important to our work as designers. We want to bring beauty to the everyday interactive designs people use. They might not have a heightened affective response every time they use an interactive design, but if the designs are crafted well, people will enjoy these interactions, and the aesthetics of the interaction design will be discernable in the interaction. It will be constituted as a message from the designer to the user in the form of a communication of movement from one to the other through the temporal gestalt of the interaction.

In a sense, all art/design is movement in this manner. A painting will be made of the movements originally made to create it and my movements as a viewer when I actively perceive it. As Game noted, "The movement of music, riding, writing, lives in us as we live in it" (2001, 8).

Crafting Somaesthetic Experiences

That brings us back to the problem of whether somaesthetics is a property of the interactive system itself. We dismissed that idea earlier. But as designers, of course, we love to hear about good examples, ways in which we can work with our design to open possibilities, the properties of the design that users are compelled by. Surely, there are properties of the interactive design that will increase the likelihood of a rewarding somaesthetic experience. That is, though the properties of the object itself cannot be used to define aesthetics, the properties of the object (or rather the consummation of the experience created for us to engage in with all its different parts) can be more or less well-crafted, more or less good at achieving the experience the designer intended to communicate.

This should not be confused with an idea that it would be possible to isolate somaesthetic properties from the overall aim of the system. As Gaver (2009) says when he writes about putting some particular "emotion" into a design: "From this point of view, designing for emotion is like designing for blue: it makes a modifier a noun. Imagine being told to design something blue. Blue what? Whale? Sky? Suede shoes? The request seems nonsensical. Similarly, focusing design on emotion without a grounded sense of the situation in which emotions are meant to gain meaning appears to be a category error. Instead, we need to understand how to design for engaging experiences more generally." Isolating a factor like emotion from the overall totality of what we are designing is *nonsensical*. Likewise, it is nonsensical to design for somaesthetics as a generic ingredient that can be dropped into any design, the way tomatoes are an ingredient in canned Campbell's soup.[8]

As with any design process, the overall design purpose must be made clear—as we will discuss in detail later (chapters 3–7)—but within this purpose, certain qualities can help us open the design space and approach the somaesthetic qualities that speak to our human ways of moving and experiencing. For instance, to generate a somaesthetic experience, we know that we need to stimulate the *kinaesthetic-tactile* experience; we need to regulate the *pace* of the consummation of the experience; we know that *rhythm*, *touch*, and certain stimulations of our nervous systems, following our morphology (the specific constitutions of our limbs, our skin, our nervous system reactions), will make certain experiences more likely and others less likely.

Shusterman himself also speaks explicitly about some specific somatic experiences that people enjoy: rhythm; balance (as in, balancing your posture); returning to movements you performed as a baby or young child; sexual pleasures; slow, thoughtful movement when eating; dancing; and so on. He is specifically interested in those enjoyments that come not so much from overwhelming our sensory system with stimuli, but instead through careful, slow, deliberate attention, allowing us to notice the small movements and enjoy them. In fact, Shusterman does not shy from claiming that certain somatic experiences will be better for us than others. Removing pain, engaging in deliberate inward attention, shifting from the habitual to a flexibility of mind and movement, and so on, are all specific practices and experiences Shusterman promotes; he is less keen on experiences involving self-inflicted pain, as in Foucault's experiments with sadomasochism (Shusterman 2000b). Or rather, Shusterman critiques Foucault's focus on drugs and S/M as unnecessarily narrow and unhelpful to form the basis of somaesthetic pragmatism. Shusterman instead wants to upgrade the status and value of careful, slow, deliberate experience. He wants to make such experiences as valued as the exhilarating, unique, fast, strong experiences of S/M, extreme sports, or merry-go-rounds.

Drawing on Burke, Shusterman writes: "Aesthetic taste is based on natural 'sensibility' to 'the primary pleasures of sense' as further developed by the powers of imagination and honed by judgement and understanding. As our mental life is nourished by the bodily senses, so Burke argues, our mental activities rely on corporeal forces" (Burke 1998, 74–75, quoted in Shusterman 2005, 326). To any designer, this resonates with the idea of *design judgement*: the value we put on different design options to make informed choices (Nelson and Stolterman 2003).

Coming back to the somatic pleasures of rhythm, balance, rolling, and so on, it is notable that any human culture on earth has its forms of dancing; singing; music; art; tools; self-fashioning of the body through clothes, tattoos, and piercings; and so on. This is part of our human condition; "man has always danced," as Sheets-Johnstone (2015, 313) wrote. But it is also notable that these practices, these habitual cultural movements, are always unique experiences, with their specific variations, whenever practiced. Like Sheets-Johnstone's kinaesthetic logos, prescribed patterns and rules govern these experiences, and yet they form unique instances with each repetition. And as cultural expressions, these rules and patterns evolve constantly, sometimes disrupted by new ideas, new forms of art, yet the underlying themes—rhythm, moving together with others, identity display through clothes and body postures, and so on—recur and seem available in many cultural forms.

My interpretation is that, as designers, we need to cultivate our aesthetic sensibilities, starting with knowledge of bodily movement. We need to understand what attracts us, what qualities, like rhythm or touch, bring us pleasure (or displeasure). By building on this knowledge, we can shape novel interactions with our designs that spur somaesthetic experiences. We communicate our somaesthetic movements through the shape of the system, the way the user is invited to partake in the interactions. The interactive design becomes an expression of movement and a dialogue between designer and user.

The Art of Living: An Example

Shusterman repeatedly refers to his endeavor as "the art of living," instead of the "art of dying" that Plato advocated. A trained Feldenkrais practitioner, Shusterman has treated people with pain and disabilities to help improve their lives. This practice holds that increasing a person's kinaesthetic and proprioceptive self-awareness leads to increased function, reduced pain, and greater ease and pleasure of movement. In short, Moshe Feldenkrais ([1972] 1977) built his bodyworks on the idea that a deliberate, slowed-down movement sends signals through the nervous system, activating patterns in the brain, making that movement more readily available. As we grow older, we start relying on habitual ways of moving, and we rarely engage in the nonhabitual variants. This is all fine, but if we have pain somewhere, we might have to remind ourselves of the alternatives.

What perhaps intrigues Shusterman most about this work is less the removal of pain and more the reconnecting with the joy of movement. In both cases, a better life is the aim: more joy, more engaging movement, less pain, and aesthetic experience in and through the movements. Or, as Feldenkrais ([1972] 1977) described it, "A limited repertoire of movement becomes a limited repertory of experiences."

To make this less abstract, let me provide an example from the Feldenkrais practice. Some Feldenkrais lessons reconnect us with how we moved as babies. One of my favorite Feldenkrais movements is lying on my back, with legs and arms lifted, either letting my hands hang in front of my face or holding my knees or feet in my hands, and then rolling slowly, slowly, back and forth, from left to right. The rolling back and forth is fun! The joy is concrete, residing in the movement, the rolling rhythm, and the holding of my feet, that I otherwise rarely touch. Holding my feet also lets me connect with my whole legs, feeling how strong and sturdy they are. I feel my back touching the floor, feeling sensations from all the different parts of my back. I am reminded of pleasurable movements, long forgotten, being a child, discovering and exploring the limits of my body (see figure 2.2).

What Feldenkrais aimed at through such lessons was not stretching or muscle training, but rather a reminder for us, mainly through our nervous systems, about the many different ways we can roll. The aim is not so much flexibility of the body as flexibility of mind. For every habitual way of moving, such as walking, standing, crossing your legs, looking over your shoulder, breathing, or rolling, we should have a couple of alternative ways of performing the movement; this accomplishes many positive results, not

Figure 2.2
Laying on your back, holding your feet: a Feldenkrais experience

the least of which is to better handle pain or avoid straining our bodies. To learn these alternatives, or remember the many different ways we could be standing, walking, or rolling, Feldenkrais asked participants to perform the movements extremely slowly, several times. The idea is to send signals back into the nervous system, activating or creating new patterns for movements. These new patterns allow the patient to move in a different manner, one that might not spur pain in the damaged muscle or body part. This requires making the habitual accessible to us so that we can distinguish between all the small parts that make up the bigger movement schema. Feldenkrais wrote:

> If a man does not feel, he cannot sense differences, and of course he will not be able to distinguish one action and another. Without this ability to differentiate there can be no learning, and certainly no increase in the ability to learn. It is not a simple matter, for the human senses are linked to the stimuli that produce them so that discrimination is finest when the stimulus is smallest.

If I raise an iron bar I shall not feel the difference if a fly either lights on it or leaves it. If, on the other hand, I am holding a feather, I shall feel a distinct difference if the fly were to settle on it. The same applies to all the sense: hearing, sight, smell taste, heat, and cold. (Feldenkrais [1972] 1977, 59)

The philosophy behind these slow movements is key to Shusterman's understanding of *aesthetic appreciation*. Although he does not rule out "limit experiences," in which we expose ourselves to pain or exhilaration as part of the somaesthetic inquiry (as advocated by Foucault), he stresses gentler, subtle means to probe and challenge our habitual (and thus no longer noticed) movements. Instead of flooding our nervous systems with impressions, slower, more reflective introspections can help us discern the small, sometimes barely perceptible changes in muscle tensions or emotional reactions that otherwise flow by in the stream of impulses and impressions. By exploring, for example, our habitual breathing rhythms, trying out alternative ways of breathing or even holding our breath, we can become more sensitive to all the different perceptual differences involved when pulling in air into our lungs. The sensitivity we train through such exercises, be they Feldenkrais lessons or some other body practice, helps us to appreciate the *aesthetics of our own soma* and, ultimately, our experiences of the world.

To me, it is important to point out that this process also leads to empathy with yourself, acceptance of the shortcomings and fragility of your body, the pains and aches you have—but also, within those limits, to enjoying the pleasures of moving.

Insight from Practice

To attain this sensitivity, somaesthetics as a philosophical discipline cannot only be concerned with reading, thinking, and writing—as we are doing here. It must also engage in practical exercise. Our movements carry our insights. To engage in the higher art of living, we must cultivate our somaesthetic sensitivities.

Shusterman therefore divides the somaesthetic project into three related processes: an *analytical* study of the body's role in perception and experience, which in turn means studying its role in moral and social life; a *pragmatic* study of methodologies to improve our functioning; and, finally, a *practical* study in which we test those pragmatic methods on ourselves to render concrete experience. When working from a somaesthetic perspective, Shusterman points out that people learn differently. Some people cannot go directly to the practical study without first grasping the analytical side, whereas others start in the practical and only later seek to understand from an intellectual point of view.

At this point, it might be a good idea for the reader to lie down on the floor and gently, slowly, rock back and forth, as in the Feldenkrais lesson discussed earlier. Even better is to follow a proper Feldenkrais lesson, many of which can be found online.

Articulations of Bodily Experiences

As Shusterman points out, when we use verbal accounts of the body and our aesthetic experiences, we run the risk of lying or distancing ourselves from the reality of movement. To make our accounts real, to fill them with content and meaning, the experiences must be felt, enacted through movement and experience. At the same time, however, language can serve us well in the process of discerning different experiences, helping direct our attention to different parts of our bodies or movements.

There lies an interesting contradiction here, one that we will have to deal with somehow. Bodily, aesthetic ways of knowing can arise from your bodily acts without any language translation. The feel of muscle tensions, the touch of the skin, the tone of the body, balance, posture, rhythm of movement, the symbiotic relationships with objects in our environments: these all come together to form a unique holistic experience. Although our language and words can pull our attention to different parts of this holistic experience, deconstructing it (even reducing it), it is also the movement experience itself that constitutes its understanding, meaning, and knowledge. Naming an experience—say, associating the word *flow* with the experience of being totally absorbed in an activity or *grief* with the unhappiness felt after losing someone—will not necessarily mean that you know what it feels like. Unless you have experienced flow or grief, it becomes an empty concept, without any perceptual reality behind it. You can try to imagine it, but the imaginings will be mere shadows of the experience, not able to fully transport you into the feelings (expressed through the movements) involved in those experiences.

Changing the World, Changing Us

What have we learned from all this philosophy so far? First, what we can bring with us into design work is the understanding that movement is foundational to the human condition, and therefore design of interactive artifacts needs to be in dialogue with movement. But our movements are not limited; there is nothing we can study as "natural" human movement.

Instead, our movements are dynamically changing in response to *kinetically dynamic possibilities* in our environment. Those possibilities, of course, include any tools and designs we create, cultural practices, and so on.

Our *kinetic bodily logos* are by necessity infinitely varied in their details to allow us to respond to changes in the world. We recognize these bodily logos in ourselves and thereby also in others. They provide the roots of meaning, consciousness, and communication.

Second, because we are interested in crafting user experiences, we should note that *emotion and movement* are tightly connected; there is "a generative as well as expressive relationship between movement and emotion" (Sheets-Johnstone 1999, 262–263). This in turn, as we shall see later (chapter 5), provides a fertile ground for opening new design spaces in which our interactive designs enter into such emotional dialogues with users.

Third, somaesthetic experiences arise from the training of our sensory appreciation, rooted in the rich soil of our movements, in turn shaping emotion and experience. They require "a living, purposive, sentient, perceptive body or bodily subjectivity" (Shusterman 2012, 141).

Because our designs (art or everyday tools) are part of our lifeworlds, shaping us as much as we shape them, interaction designers have a responsibility to pay attention to the movements, rhythms, postures, or kinaesthetic-tactile experiences we build into our systems. Our movements will spur and even shape certain other movements, sometimes causing pleasure, sometimes (often by mistake or ignorance) causing pain (as in repetitive stress syndrome). Through cultivating our somaesthetic sensibilities, we can better shape the movements invited by the system, increasing the possibilities of pleasure, somaesthetic experiences, and more meaningful interactions with our lifeworlds.

II What

3 Showing, Not Telling: Six First-Person Design Encounters

In the preface and in chapter 1, we discussed why we need a new approach to design: new materials and new ways of connecting our technology offer designers new opportunities and new responsibilities to shape users and society in ways that we want to be shaped. Then, in chapter 2, I explained why primacy of movement and somaesthetics offer a promising theoretical grounding for a new approach to design: they correct dualism and overemphasis on our thinking brains in the design on interaction.

But these theories do not speak explicitly about how to design. Shusterman, for example, relies on his experiences and the analyses of body practices developed by others; he takes for granted the technologies and bodily practices of the world and focuses on the effect that designed practices may have on our somas. He wants to know how these existing practices or designs change us, how every encounter will be a new experience, letting us reexperience ourselves in a new light, extending our aesthetic sensibility.

In all this, Shusterman does not account for the fact that these technologies and practices are themselves designs that may be changed or even created from scratch. He is not addressing how somaesthetic sensibilities might better equip designers to create novel body practices, novel interactions with technologies, novel ways of "being" in the world.

That said, many artists and some designers have been inspired by Shusterman's theories, creating art and designs based on his ideas. (Shusterman himself has been keen to explore and participate in such design activities.) I want to describe six of those designs here, to create a shared vocabulary and sense of the qualities that might make up a soma design experience or product. This may seem unusual in a book like this, in which theory and description may well precede specific examples. However, because soma design is intimately involved with feeling, intuition, and actual, holistic experience, I believe that imagining the feeling and experience of these designs will help readers absorb the potential outcome of soma design practice. In later chapters, we will return to more abstract considerations of the theory and practice of soma design.

Although I cannot provide descriptions that fully capture what it feels like to interact with these six systems, I hope to at least provide some glimpses into what they are like, through rich, first-person descriptions of my own encounters with these interactions.

The six systems I describe have different aims, contexts of use, and functionalities. In this way, they hint at the breadth and width of the design space. They also illustrate how somaesthetic design can shift us from simply replicating movements and qualities of already existing body practices to creating new experiences, new ways of moving, novel sensations, and unique ways of being in the world—with and through interactive technology. Each of the six examples highlights a specific quality or attribute of soma design; through these, I hope to establish a common vocabulary and sensibility that will help us discuss soma design theory later in the book. For instance, in the first example—centered on the swiping gesture on a smartphone—I highlight the interaction's pliability and sense of pleasure. Other examples highlight their own lessons and qualities. These examples include the Ears and the Tail by Svanæs and Solheim (2016); Embodied Encounters Studio by Hummels (2016); Mediated Body and Touchbox by Hobye (2014); the BrightHearts project by Khut (2016); and *Metaphone* by Šimbelis et al. (2014).

Encounter One: Swiping—Pliability and Enjoyment

Almost everyone who reads this can relate to my first example: the swipe gesture on the mobile phone. When Apple introduced this interface in 2007, we had already seen a range of similar solutions. Bits and pieces of the same idea had appeared both commercially (in particular, seen in future vision videos quite early on) and in academia as early as in the 1960s (see, e.g., Johnson 1967; Myers 1998). Popular media, including movies like *Minority Report*, also anticipated such interactive motions. Despite this, most users were surprised and delighted by how effective and pleasurable the interaction was. Apple managed to design just the right gestures, with the right device, at just the right time to make them accessible and aesthetically appealing to many people, which no doubt helped the product's commercial success.

I remember the first time I saw a colleague interacting with his mobile phone: It looked like he was caressing the device. First, he showed me how he opened the screen with a sustained, but light, swipe gesture. He pinched a map to show me how he could make it smaller with the touch. Although he was learning the gestures and he didn't always get the pinching right to resize images, or the spreading motion to expand them didn't always work as expected—overall, I felt like I was watching a choreographed dance.

As I later tried them myself, these interactions came to set the bar for what I would expect from any gesture-based interface. As a result, other movement-based interfaces often have disappointed me. For instance, I still remember how let down I felt when I first attempted full-body gestures in the air in front of a video game controller. The video-recognition system repeatedly failed miserably to "see" me or respond to my gestures. The embarrassment of moving my arms into positions the system could calibrate—failing repeatedly—destroyed the whole joy of the interaction for me.

Of course, it's much easier for systems to read gestures on a glass screen than through images because the physical object can discriminate touch in much more detail. From a technical perspective, the mobile phone gestures themselves require little precision from the user: they are fairly large gestures that do not demand that the user touch an exact spot on the glass surface. In the words of wearables pioneer Thad Starner (2014) of Georgia Tech, who has been wearing various technologies on his body for most of his life, the iPhone can accept "cruder gestures"—and yet, from interaction and aesthetics points of view, the overall effect feels anything but crude. Instead, it achieves a desirable use quality that interaction design professor Jonas Löwgren (2007) calls *pliability*. In a pliable interaction, the union between the command and the resulting interaction feels "involving, malleable and tightly coupled" (ibid.). As I zoom out on a map via pinching gestures or zoom in with the zoom gestures, I feel as if I am *inside* the map, a very different experience than when using a control panel on the side of the map. In other words, there is a tight coupling between my movement and the map. This renders immediate pleasure and a sense of involvement. The objects inside the system become tangible and real to me.

Not only does pliability make interaction more fun, but it also can offer more equal access. Apple's gestures made its devices seem far more accessible to populations that previously had difficulties using computers and mobile phones, such as the elderly and very small children. We've seen videos of kids as young as two years old fully capable of managing a mobile phone or tablet.

Some writers refer to these gestures as *intuitive* or *natural*, but as Norman (2010) pointed out, these are designed gestures: there is nothing natural about them. He argues that designers must tune and craft these gestures carefully to harmonize with what happens on the screen. Otherwise, they do not make sense, nor will they be easy to remember. For example, when we scroll in a document through a flick of the finger, the scrolling must "continue after the flicking action has ceased," but the momentum must be coupled with viscous friction. That is, the scrolling cannot continue to the end of the file, at the same high speed, without coming to a halt (ibid.). Instead, it needs to slow down and stop at a speed relative to the one used to flick the finger. The gestures need their context and feedback loops to make sense to the user. When designers get that coupling right, they can be easy to learn. When we also get a lightness of touch, a compelling coupling to the visualizations and haptics, we may achieve an aesthetic experience of the interaction.

Coming back to our understanding of somaesthetics, we might ask whether these gestures increase our aesthetic appreciation ability and lead to living better lives. In my view, they do. Computer and mobile interactions take up a large proportion of our lives: if the basic interaction mechanism does not harmonize with our abilities to grasp objects, turn them, touch them, manipulate them, and enjoy those movements, then a basic soma pleasure will be missing.

Encounter Two: The Ears and the Tail—Extended Lived Body

The Ears and the Tail are two projects by Svanæs and Solheim, involving mechanical body extensions designed for theater settings (Svanaes and Solheim 2016). The idea is that the tail and the ears extend the actor's body, creating a richer array of expressions.

They originally designed the Ears for a theatrical performance for children, starring a red elephant. The actor wears large, floppy, mechanical ears, equipped with motors, controlled wirelessly by a glove with sensors on the middle and index fingers.

The Tail was created for a troll in a Peer Gynt performance. It responds to the swaying of the actor's hips, using an inertial measurement unit with an accelerometer and gyro. As you sway your hips, the tail exhibits different behaviors (see figure 3.1).

Svanæs and Solheim (2016) described their motivation: "The lived body is our experienced body, the body through which we live our lives, which is different from seeing the body as an object in the world. Designing for the body with the first-person perspective of Merleau-Ponty makes us aware of how technology is incorporated into the experienced body, and how it thus changes us."

Figure 3.1
Dag Svanæs wearing the Tail

I got to try the Ears and the Tail at a workshop. At first, I felt mildly embarrassed walking around with a tail wiggling evocatively behind my back, arousing smiles and embarrassed laughter from my workshop friends. Once I overcame my discomfort, though, I found the experience strangely expressive. To make the tail wiggle, I had to move my hips in different patterns—for example, a circular motion in the sagittal plane, or a smooth sashay from side to side, or a tilt as if I was putting the tail between my legs. As I performed these movements, I could feel the tail as a clear substance, a counterweight, not too heavy nor too light, changing in response to my movements.

The circular movements of my hips encouraged movements that I associate with a feminine, sexy, flirtatious way of walking. As the flirtation was directed backward—behind my back, so to speak—I repeatedly turned my head, cocking it, nodding, smiling, to check out the effect on others behind me. My entire body posture and movement schema was altered. The feeling I had was that my tail happily wriggled in a sashaying, almost slightly aggressive, "look at me," cat-like manner.

Putting the tail between my legs put bodily reality and substance into the expression of cowardice and shame. I could feel my face crumble into a sad, embarrassed expression—again, looking behind me to see the effect on others, but now looking under my brows, with a facial expression saying "excuse me." The tipping of my hips required a conscious movement that could not be done while walking, or at least not in the few minutes I wore the tail.

The flapping ears affected me less powerfully—and in some ways, this shows how soma engagement is not easy to design for. Rather than an experience in which my movements immediately spurred the ears to move, feeding back into my experience of myself, I felt more removed as my hand made gestures with some effect on the ears, which I could not sense or see myself. Perhaps training in front of a mirror to synchronize these movements with my facial expressions or feeding off the reactions of others watching my ears might have created a more embodied experience; I am guessing that this is what the actors had to do to make their performances expressive and seamless.

In the workshop, one participant figured out that she could wear the glove while another participant wore the ears. This became a playful interaction between them in which she tried to match his facial expression by flapping the ears in the right tempo and direction. As it turned out, we all felt we knew how the ears should be turning to express certain emotions, probably from our experiences of cats, dogs, horses, and other domesticated animals, as well as from various media—theater, movies, and so on.

While the point of the Ears and the Tail is to extend on the repertory of expressions for the actor, they had strong effects on my body posture and associated feelings. Even in my brief encounters with these technologies, they started to become part of me. As Dag Svanæs observed in an interview: "One of the most interesting experiences for me was when I took off the tail after wearing it for an hour, and I had a surprising physical feeling of being tailless" (Brandslet 2015).

Encounter Three: Embodied Encounters Studio—Social Playful Engagements

Caroline Hummels has a long-standing track record in incorporating soma-based design into all her work, as well as making it a strong component in industrial design education at Eindhoven University of Technology. In one of her projects, she set out to engage with one hundred inspirators across the globe, envisioning a sustainable future for the world—in products, business models, or political ideas. The topic of the project is interesting itself, but what I want to discuss here is the tool she created to brainstorm and provoke discussion of a different ilk with the inspirators.

Hummels's (2016) vision is to engage the people she meets in "sense-making based on ongoing sensorimotor couplings in a social situation." She observed in her earlier research that different stakeholders collaborated much better if they could engage physically, building something together, using their hands. It created both engagement with the topic and respect and empathy for one another. Rather than interviewing the inspirators she wanted to meet, she invited them to join her in building ideas, explaining business plans, solutions, and problems, through a new tool she devised: Embodied Encounters Studio. The studio supports nonverbal communication and social coordination in action, instead of a more dialogue-oriented discussion in which messages originating in one "mind" are sent to another. The idea behind the design was to encourage two or more participants to brainstorm and engage in participatory sense-making through playful encounters with objects in the studio. By doing so, she notes "bodily encounters seem to lower the threshold to merge the perspectives from people with different backgrounds" (ibid.).

The studio consists of an intriguing and beautiful kit of objects and technologies, small enough for Hummels to carry conveniently as she visits the inspirators. The centerpiece is the Embodied Ideation Toolkit that she created with Ambra Trotto: a set of small, magnetic objects of various abstract shapes and undefined functions (see figure 3.2). The studio also includes a tool for recording video, a way to scribble notes that are placed into a visual trace of the discussion, RFID tags that are placed on discussion cards used to start conversations, and more.

I had the opportunity to play with the toolkit, in a full interview/ building situation, but as a short encounter in which we discussed the evocative nature of the toolkit objects when opening playful dialogues between people. I was immediately drawn to the magnetic objects. Hummels had included old radio antennas that could be extended, serving as "pointing" devices or as a way to pick up the magnetic objects. I extended an antenna and started picking up objects with it. Some objects were too heavy to stay on the antenna and would fall off. Other participants playfully chipped in with their antennas or other objects to help, or started dragging around objects attached to one another through the magnetic force. The effect on all of us was immediate: We instantly became playful, engaging one another through joining forces or stealing objects from one another. We touched the objects, explored their qualities: the space they occupied, their velocity, their affordance for movement, whether they could be combined into larger forms without breaking apart, and their capacity

Figure 3.2
Parts of the Embodied Ideation Toolkit

to sustain play between us. We touched, fiddled, built, destroyed, explored, and engaged both with ourselves and with one another. It opened a path to social play.

Hummels told me that when she met with inspirators, these objects seemed to spark a loosened attitude and quickly broke down barriers between herself and those she engaged with. It also broke down barriers *within* people—between the different roles they take on in their professional and private lives. The intriguing activities somehow got under their skin and touched their subjective selves. For example, she mentioned a very successful and well-known city planner who opened up and told her about his personal life, passions, and dreams, going well beyond his professional role. Experiences like this have led Hummels (2015) to observe that "exploiting bodily skills in a co-design process stimulates a 1st person perspective."

In her writings, Hummels, drawing upon Suchman (2007), discusses cognition as always an ongoing achievement of social coordination, including "social interrelations, roles, norms, culture and politics" (Hummels 2016). When discussing the future with these inspirators, Hummels needed them to imagine a situation different from the present, closer to their honest desires and dreams. The toolkit allowed her to break the norms for how to engage socially, creating different roles for her and the inspirator. This breaking down of roles is of course not without risk. There are reasons we might want to stay in our professional roles, in our third-person perspectives. But if used consciously, this approach can allow different visualizations of the future that can be examined from new angles.

Encounter Four: Mediated Body and Touchbox—Empathy and Connection through Touch

In 2010, Mads Hobye created an interactive art installation designed to subvert barriers to touching the bare skin of a stranger. He created a suit he named Mediated Body to be used at the Burning Man festival.[1] Mediated Body is akin to a theremin.[2] When the "performer" wearing the suit touches the bare skin of a "participant," it generates musical sounds in the headphones they each wear (see figure 3.3).

At Burning Man, the suit led to a whole range of intense meetings between the performer and participants, from intimate, sometimes flirtatious encounters to social, explorative, playful, or awkward meetings. One performer described his experience:

Figure 3.3
Mediated Body. Photo by Mads Hobye

Sometimes people get aware [of themselves] after a while, pull a little away, smile at me, and then throw themselves into the play again. These moments are really beautiful—I feel I completely emerge myself into that other person, as they are not aware of me, I lose my self awareness also and for a moment I only exist to enhance their experience. I lose myself as they lose themselves. It's fantastic how strong an emotional connection is built in a state of not being aware of each other. Even after trying the suit hundreds of times, I still have really intense experiences of what I could call complete presence. It is beautiful taking the headphones of a person after such an experience, look each other in the eyes as humans (almost like blushing after making love), get a big hug, and separate. Isn't it beautiful: meet a stranger, have 3 minutes of the most intense experience of intimacy and exploration, and then leave as strangers but connected [by virtue of] a common experience. It's like one night stands when it is best—just better. (Hobye and Löwgren 2011, 41)

I had read about Mediated Body before I got to try another version of it, Touchbox, at a demo session during a conference. Touchbox is similar to Mediated Body but does not require a performer. Instead, it is meant to be used by two participants. Both wear headphones connected to Touchbox. When the participants touch, sounds are generated.

I tried Touchbox during what was more or less my first real meeting with Richard Shusterman. Although we had a professional relationship, we did not know each other well and were not yet friends, which made for a multilayered encounter. The intimate experience of touching him, generating sounds together, became a bit too much for me at the time, and I was very embarrassed. I believe he was more open to the experience, more experienced in being exposed to art-based interactions of this kind. But, step-by-step, we worked out how to touch, how to move, and were amused and intrigued by the sounds we were able to create (see figure 3.4). But our movements probably erred on the side of being too strong, too forceful, rather than the small, intimate gestures, almost not touching, that would have generated a less harsh soundscape. Standing in the middle of a busy conference, with many demos surrounding us, I was extremely self-aware and restrained. Given the context and my embarrassment, I was happy to not engage in a too-intimate experience, so the way our interaction developed fitted me well.

Hobye points out that the context of use and the story the performer tells the participant when inviting him or her to share the experience will determine the experience. The performer at Burning Man invented a story of an aura to facilitate the meeting with a new participant:

> Aura is the best description, and one that really facilitates a great interaction. Once people hear it is about aura, they intuitively become really slow and start working in the area of almost touching. Mediated Body has a background noise that is there all the time and changes slightly, so even without doing *anything* people already then have the impression that they hear their aura. Starting from such a sensitive state of mind, even the smallest touch is really a great experience. How can I formulate this—telling the aura-story makes the sound effects last a lot longer and have a much higher impact. It's amazing how important the story or frame of mind is! I cannot stress this enough. (Hobye 2014, 127)

Mediated Body and Touchbox were but two art objects in a range of art experiments Hobye has been working on. In a manifesto describing his aims (ibid.), he explains he wanted participants to engage in a form of social play that would go beyond trying to figure out what this "object of curiosity" could be. A failed engagement, to Hobye, would be one in which the participants figure out how the system works and then move on, like a puzzle that has been solved and set aside.

Hobye instead wants there to be a prolonged meeting between participants, one in which they creatively engage with one another and thereby share an experience, honestly and openly. What he found through his design experiments was that "open-ended, poetic, gentle and subtle interaction spaces tend to create such a space, whereas fixed narratives—strict, brutal or destructive interactions—tend to prevent the participants from finding their own pace and interest in the interaction" (Hobye 2014, 15). I

Figure 3.4
My first meeting with Professor Richard Shusterman, playing with Touchbox

particularly appreciate the idea that by being poetic and gentle, you invite participants to a form of social play.

Many of Hobye's art experiments engage with movements, touch, rhythmic engagement, and breaking taboos. I find it particularly interesting when he engages with touch. It seems as if we all long to touch, yet there are many social rules that stop us from touching each other. Digital interactions enabling or spurring touch and empathy are notoriously hard to create, but perhaps one of the most important design aims to achieve profound somaesthetic experiences.

Encounter Five: BrightHearts—Biofeedback Engagements

George Khut (2006) is an artist and researcher engaged with aesthetics and biofeedback interaction. He has built several art installations in which participants' physiological data is fed into the artwork, generating evoca-tive, colorful animations. He is particularly interested in interaction with our autonomic nervous systems and ways that we can use interactions to stimulate the parasympathetic branch of the autonomic nervous system (PSNS). The PSNS is responsible for diverting energy inward, toward proc-esses of recuperation and self-care, in contrast to the sympathetic nervous system (SNS), which directs energy outward for rapid mobilization (the fight-or-flight response). The PSNS system is activated when we are resting, affecting blood pressure, pulse, hormones, breathing rhythms, and other bodily processes. When we get externally represented data fed back to us—for example, as sounds or images describing changes in our heart rates or breathing patterns—these changes become tangible to us and we can learn how to influence the processes being measured.

At this point, it might help if you engage in an exercise:

Sit back, close your eyes, and allow your breathing to become softer and slower. Aim to take six breaths per minute. Focus on gently extending your outbreath, and purse your lips as you blow out—imagining you are blowing out through a drinking straw and exploring how far you can extend this breath—with as little effort as possible. Notice the sensation of breathing in and out throughout your body—and notice how you can feel some of this movement deep into your belly and pelvis. After a while, turn your attention to all the rhythms of your body. Feel how your mind calms down, the heart beating slower. Enjoy the sensation of breathing. Finish by opening your eyes and returning to this text—slowly.

Although this exercise shows how we can listen to various rhythms in our bodies without any technology in the loop, biofeedback technology allows us to vividly differentiate these autonomic nervous system reflexes and better probe and discern the biorhythms of the body that might be hard to feel and thereby regulate. Heart rate variability and arousal, as expressed by skin conductance, are examples of processes that are harder to get a proper sense of.

What is interesting is how these exercises, once learned, can be used anywhere and anytime. Khut (2016, 3860) notes how such practices can be found in many traditions: "My interest in PSNS activation stems from an interest in the psychologically restorative potential of these processes—the altered subjective perspectives that arise via increased PSNS activity are central to many contemplative, devotional and meditative traditions, achieved through the manipulation of breath via recitation and sing-ing, attention to body-sensations, and other practices such as fasting and immersion."

I got to try out the BrightHearts app, one of the many different biofeed-back art installations that Khut has built. It mirrors heart rate in colorful animations, portrayed in a circular pattern on a screen. As you relax and decrease your heart rate, the interface goes from warmer, reddish colors, toward cooler colors, and the circular layers contract inward to the center of the screen. The calculation compares changes in your heart rate that can be influenced by your breathing and autonomic nervous system reflexes with an average of your heart rate recorded at the beginning of the session. The circles appear in the middle of the screen at the onset of each heartbeat and then move outward. The animation looks a bit like when you throw a stone into a lake, but with a continuously pulsating beat in the middle of the circles (see figure 3.5).

I tried the BrightHearts app at a workshop that I was running. I was quite stressed about the whole situation: I was trying to keep track of the progress of the workshop, orchestrating activities, making sure everyone got to try out all the demos participants had brought, trying to facilitate discussions, pushing us toward the interesting topics we wanted to debate. Once I was hooked up to the system, I was also stressed about the fact that everyone could see how my relaxation was progressing through watching the interface (portrayed on an iPad placed on the floor between us). I am usually able to calm myself down through deep breathing and turning my focus inward, but here it took me a while to calm the animations and change the colors from warmer to colder. As my mind was scurrying in all directions, with the workshop and the situation at hand, the chitchat and discussion from people sitting nearby distracted me. But the animations of my heart

Figure 3.5
BrightHearts visualizations

were also mesmerizing. I remember wishing that I could go and sit in a corner on my own to explore my connection to the system.

Khut has used the BrightHearts app to help children with serious illnesses, requiring them to repeatedly visit the hospital and take various tests to gain control over their fears. They first train with the system, and then use it while, for example, getting a shot.

Encounter Six: *Metaphone*—Uncomfortable Interactions

The encounters so far have reinforced the idea of gentle, fun, playful interactions, but, as mentioned earlier, aesthetics in interaction is not limited to the traditional ideas of beauty. As we discussed, somaesthetics, according to Shusterman, does not shy from negative, self-destructive, painful experiences—or, as he refers to them, *limit-experiences*. In the world of digital interactions, Benford et al. (2012) have explored what they refer to as *uncomfortable interactions*. Here, I would like to introduce my experience of a machine of a machine created in the art project *Metaphone* (Šimbelis, n.d.; Šimbelis et al. 2014). *Metaphone* was created by artist Vygandas Simbelis and colleagues.

I tried an early version of *Metaphone* that contained three main elements. The first element was a bio-ball I held in my hand, picking up some of my biological signals: sweat (picked up by a galvanic skin response [GSR][3] sensor) and pulse, as well as how far away I stood from the rest of the machine. The data was sent wirelessly to the other parts of the machine. The second part of the machine converted my data, in the form of sounds, into drawings on a large piece of aquarelle paper placed underneath it. The machine consisted of a large shaft (around two meters long) on two wheels, rotating on the floor; a cart with color tubes would move back and forth along the shaft, squirting color in patterns feeding off my data. The apparatus took up at least half the small room. The third part of the machine was a sonic core, creating what I perceived as a slightly creepy soundscape also feeding off my data. The GSR data generated screeching, electronic, noise-like sounds; beneath it, I could discern my heartbeat represented as a dark, repetitive sound.

My first private session with *Metaphone* took place in the cellar of a sixteenth-century building in the old city of Stockholm. The cellar was a tiny crypt, a small white room with an arched ceiling. The space was ill lit by a single small window, placed high up. Spotlights in the room illuminated the strange and silent apparatus standing on the floor. The machine dominated the small space.

With the bio-ball in my hand (see figure 3.6), I was left alone in the crypt with the machine. I knew quite a lot about this project, so I had already decided how I wanted to engage, and I had all sorts of ideas on how I would control the output from the machine. I decided to begin my session by lying on the floor with my eyes closed and with the ball in my hands. I aimed to breathe slowly, attempting to calm down the sounds and movements of the machine and thus generate a painting that expressed calm and evenness. I also wanted to calm down myself, as I had had a stressful, quite negative day at work. But as it turned out, I had no control whatsoever, and the whole experience became something entirely different. As I wrote after the session:

> My eyes were closed, but the music and the movements from the machine entered into my experience—strongly! They pulled me into an experience where I was listening to the response from the machine and acting with it, or even becoming strongly influenced by it. Some of the sounds were, to me, dark and a bit depressing. Pulling me into a dark side of my experience. Not necessarily a bad experience—in fact, the contrary. It was interesting as it resonated with my whole

Figure 3.6
Metaphone

day. I listened to the tick-tick-tick from the movement of the color-wagon and by squeezing the ball, I listened to the disturbing GSR-related sounds. It felt as if I was rhythmically pulled into the interaction. I forgot my intention to manipulate the machine and my painting and became entirely absorbed with the interaction. [...] But I felt no need to influence the machine—it was more interesting to simply take the whole experience as an influence on me: the sounds, the movement, the wheel turning, the colors.

Metaphone pulled me into its sphere of behaviors and aesthetics, rather than letting me control it. This made for a strangely relaxing yet still creepy experience.

The *Metaphone* project reminds us that interaction aesthetics can touch our somas in many different ways. It also reminds us that, as designers, we are designing half of the interaction; the other half is added by the user, entering the stage with her own experiences, ideas, attitudes, moods, and ability to engage.

Somaesthetic Familiarity

These six encounters map out a space of quite different interactions. They exemplify different design contexts, different aesthetics and aims. Yet my experiences of them made me feel a sense of familiarity, even though they opened entirely new and quite different spaces for experiences. They all entailed a careful sensitivity to movement, to playfulness, to proprioception, to rhythms rhyming with my own biorhythms or the rhythm of the social encounter they mediated. My experience of these systems is quite different from that of the standard tools on my desktop computer or my mobile apps. They touched my soma through tapping into and engaging bodily processes already known to me, but asked me to access them in novel ways, with new experiences and sometimes even new movement patterns, extending my experience. Between the system and myself, a *dynamic gestalt* (Löwgren and Stolterman 2004) took form—sometimes immediately graspable and present, sometimes accessible after engaging with the interaction for a while.

Although many of the designs described in this chapter concern artistic or expressive needs, there are also examples of redesigning widespread, everyday, interactive objects through a pragmatist, somaesthetic perspective. In 2004, for example, Graves Petersen et al. (2004) designed somaesthetics-inspired remote controls for televisions. One of their remote control designs controlled music through movement: for example, you could raise the volume of the music by raising the remote control (with the motion picked up by an accelerometer).

Another example of an everyday object being entirely redesigned is Haptic Beats, a music controller by Mailvaganam and Bruns Alonso (2015). The handheld device allows users to shuffle, change volume, and express whether they liked a piece of music or not. The feedback is entirely based on tight loops of movement—haptic feedback.

How do you arrive at designs like these? In the next chapter, I will provide an account of a somaesthetic design process that I was involved in myself to show how and why a first-person perspective serves a particular role throughout the whole design process.

4 Soma Mat, Breathing Light, and Sarka: An Autobiographical Design Account

In the last chapter, I outlined examples of soma design and the types of qualities we might expect to see emphasized in such projects. In this chapter, I explain my own attempts, and that of my lab, to develop a process to generate soma designs while also attending to the soma in the very process itself.

To do so, I will describe a somaesthetic project we developed in my research group.[1] At the time, we were working together with IKEA, a large furniture manufacturer. The company was curious about interactive furniture and, in particular, wanted to explore if there could be health benefits from interactive engagements in the home. We, on the other hand, were interested in somaesthetics as a design stance. These questions came together in three designs we designed over the course of about three years.

As I mentioned in the preface, we had been designing a wide variety of movement-based systems before I came across the somaesthetics theories. One of the designs, named Affective Health (Sanches et al. 2010), aimed to help users regulate their emotions and stress levels. In the Affective Health system, sensors in a wristband measured arousal levels and movements, sending them in real time via Bluetooth to a mobile phone. When we tested this system, users repeatedly asked for support both to help make sense of the data and, even more importantly, to figure out what they could and should change in their lives.

We realized that simply mirroring our bodies, creating designs incorporating biofeedback loops and allowing reflection over time, must be complemented by some form of learning: bodily and cognitively. But what are the best practices for learning about and changing yourself?

This might be a good moment to stop and reflect on this design challenge. Imagine being in a design team that aims to work with body awareness and aesthetics, shaping an interaction that does not simply mirror the exercises we already know, but can, through some digital interaction, extend on them, perhaps even shaping or scaffolding an entirely novel practice. The aim is both to support people dealing with stress reactions and to create an interesting, joyful, playful experience overall, one that you might want to engage in even if you are not suffering from stress problems. To make sense as an imagined product, this should be an interactive system that you can return to repeatedly, not a one-off, exciting experience. It needs to be grounded in knowledge of bodily processes, engaging your senses and attention to help you turn inward and learn something about yourself, even changing yourself. Where would you start?

In the introduction to one of our early design workshops, we started with a poetic adaptation of a passage by Feldenkrais, who writes that we must "expand the boundaries of the possible: to turn the impossible into the possible, the difficult into the easy, and the easy into the pleasant. For only those activities that are easy and pleasant will become part of a man's habitual life and will serve him at all times" ([1972] 1977, 74). After reading about somaesthetics and Feldenkrais, as well as trying out a range of bodily practices (e.g., sourdough baking, qigong, and tai chi), we decided to try using Feldenkrais lessons as a source of inspiration and a starting point.

Shortly, I will describe where this led us and how our process evolved. But first, I think it will be useful to describe the three products we ultimately developed. In this way, you can understand the endpoints we reached and better understand the detours we took on the way to get there. Therefore, the next section is an account of my own felt, somaesthetic experience in using two of our final designs—Soma Mat and Breathing Light—designed to support users seeking to manage stress or pain through breathing and relaxation.

Experiencing Soma Mat and Breathing Light

In the notes ahead, I describe the feeling of lying on the Soma Mat placed beneath the Breathing Light (Höök et al. 2015; Höök, Jonsson, Ståhl, and Mercurio 2016), with my eyes closed, in the exhibition hall of a large conference.[2] This phenomenological account is based on my own experiences and my own learning, in particular to accept some hip pain that I have been struggling with for many years. Others may have entirely different experiences of the same setting; these are my own impressions only.

Feeling My Temperature

I came rushing into the room where we had set up the demo. I decided that I would allow myself to enjoy a session before starting the demoing at the big conference we were attending. The room was a bit chilly and the concrete floor ugly and dirty, and as I laid down on the Soma Mat, I felt stressed and distracted. My jittery thoughts were jumping from one urgent work topic to another and to anticipation of what to say to the conference participants who would soon come. I told myself to push my worries aside and to accept my situation today, in this room, on this mat, and that even if I was not entirely convinced this would work, I would still do it. As I lay down, adjusting my body on the soft mat, I noticed how the pain in my left hip was acute, throbbing with painful nerve signals all the way down into my calf and heel. I briefly reflected on how easy it was to forget the pain when my mind was elsewhere. Now I had to face it.

I put on a set of earphones and closed my eyes. The familiar voice of my colleague Johanna started, asking me to accept where I was today—not to evaluate it, but to accept it. I felt a short pang of empathy with myself and my pain. I was asked to take a deep breath. Through my eyelids, I noted how the Breathing Light above me increased and decreased in intensity, following my breathing pattern. I relaxed the tension in my shoulders and adjusted my heels on the mat. I could feel the air flowing through my chest, down into my belly, all the way into my legs. I released the tension in the muscles that had been holding back my breath, feeling a sense of relief but also a mild surprise at how tense various muscles around my chest were: For what? Why was I tensing those muscles?

Johanna's recorded voice continued by asking questions to help guide my attention to different parts and experiences of my body—my different limbs, my skin, my breathing, my head, my back. As I directed my attention to different parts of my body, the mat subtly heated up underneath those body parts. The warmth came on slowly and dissipated slowly. The experience of warmth was immensely soothing. I noticed how cold my feet were and the pleasure of the warmth. The demo room was otherwise cold and unfriendly, blowing cold air down on my body, but the mat and the lamp created a cozy, secluded space.

Gradually, I became aware of my own body temperature—the inner temperature, as well as the skin temperature. After a while, without me really noticing it, Johanna stopped providing guiding instructions, and a rhythmic soundscape, like waves on a beach, took over. The mat now heated up in a circular fashion: first slowly underneath my left leg, then onwards slowly to my left hip, my left shoulder, and then down my right side. I felt taken care of, totally immersed in the inner sensations of my physical body. The pain in my left hip became less prominent, almost dissolving in response to the warm mat underneath.

There was a form of harmony between my slow breathing and the lamp's dimming in synchrony.

Finally, I was asked to open my eyes and slowly sit up. At this point, I became very pleased by my altered state of mind. I felt totally present in my body, empathic with myself and others around me. I felt sensually aware of my skin and its role as both an inward- and outward-facing part of me. I was surprised at how secluded the experience became, despite the fact that, as I opened my eyes, I discovered a bunch of people standing around that I had not noticed. I did not feel at all embarrassed or awkward, even though they could see me lying down on the floor in front of them with an entirely relaxed facial and bodily expression. Instead, I wished for them to have the same sense of being "collected" and whole.

This first-person account of lying on a Soma Mat underneath a Breathing Light captures some aspects of what it means to direct your attention to your own body and learn more about yourself. Unfortunately, it is hard to capture in words all aspects of the surprise and joy of discovering (or perhaps being reminded of) your own body temperature, the interaction between the skin and the surrounding air, and your own breathing patterns. It may sound odd that I would not know my own body temperature or not be aware of how much I tense my muscles around my chest and my breathing, but if you take a moment to reflect on it, can you feel your own body temperature? Is it different in different parts of your body? Is there any part of your skin that is not covered by cloth? What is the difference between those parts covered by cloth and those exposed to the air around you? How far down into your lungs are you breathing right now?

These simple moments of attending to yourself, creating a space for somatic reflection, does not involve any magic or spirituality (beyond that you wish to add yourself). It is simply a process of knowing yourself. As Thecla Schiphorst frequently says: "The body is generous in providing us with knowledge."[3] By slowing down, turning inward, we can attend to the signs and signals of our own somas, feel them, explore them, and even alter them through being guided in a process like the one described. The discovery relies on Johanna's guiding questions on the one hand, but also on the heat pads warming up and cooling down underneath different parts of your body in Soma Mat and on the dimming of Breathing Light.

We often take for granted that we have immediate access to our perception and experiences of and through our bodies. But inward listening is a demanding activity and thereby not necessarily easy to design for. Carefully attending inward requires focus and time. Being aided by Johanna's voice, the warmth of the mat, and the interactive light helps to sustain focus and aids the journey of discovery.

Let us make a comparison to tools supporting sport practices. In the preface, I mentioned simple tools like pulse meters and how they have changed the way we engage in sports, making runners all over the world attempt to optimize their running to keep their heart rates at the "right" level. The pulse measurement allows them to break out one significant part of how their bodies respond to running, making it accessible for scrutiny and comparison over time, actively trying to improve their bodies' heart rate levels when running. Ideals for exactly what heart rate level is optimal to not exhaust your resources and instead optimize your performance have been discussed and slowly agreed upon: a practice has developed. It has become a cultural phenomenon in which runners exchange experiences and knowledge of how to engage with this technology. They discuss when to use it and how to make it an embodied part of the "feeling" runners strive to achieve.

But as we discussed earlier, isolating one body signal—in this case, heart rate—comes with a risk. If used properly, heart-rate technology embodies a form of bodily learning that you are invited to share. Knowledge that advanced runners have s made accessible to others who are less trained in how to listen to their heart rates. But an amateur might also misuse it, running with a sole focus on optimizing heart rate, forgetting about other bodily signs and signals, such as the need to drink water, slow down, or sense worrying pain. But how do you design in the vacuum that exists before a practice has developed that supports the transition from naive, even dangerous, use to use that can be safely scaffolded and made part of a good way of feeling your running? And why would you pick heart rate in particular as the body signal that runners need to connect with? Why not heart rate variability, stride length, sweating, or any other measurement?

Or, in the case examined here, why did we pick breathing rate and guiding attention through heat as the two bodily signs and processes modeled in Soma Mat and Breathing Light? Why these and not, for example, heart rate, sweat level, or some other measurement? Why would heat, dimming lights, and soundscapes be the right modalities to support an inner journey of learning and changing the self? And, perhaps most importantly, how did we engage with *aesthetics* in our design process?

Three Designs: Soma Mat, Breathing Light, and Sarka

Having read my subjective experience of the mat, it might be helpful now to have a brief, more objective description of Soma Mat and Breathing Light. I will also describe Sarka, a third design we developed, which offers audio feedback as a way to increase somatic perception (Bergström and Jonsson 2016).

Soma Mat—Directing Attention with Heat

Soma Mat (see figure 4.1) uses heat feedback to direct your attention to different body parts while you follow the instructions of a prerecorded, Feldenkrais-inspired lesson. When the instructor says, for example, "How does your body contact the floor right now—your heel, your right heel? Left heel? Is there any difference between how they contact the floor?" the mat heats up underneath your right heel and then your left heel. The warmth comes on slowly and leaves slowly.

The voice instructions are prerecorded and provided through a mobile app. They are inspired by Feldenkrais lessons but altered to work on the experience the mat is scaffolding: the experience of heat on your skin. The activation of one of the six heating pads is scripted to follow the lesson. After you lay down on the mat with your earphones on, you pick one of the lessons in the mobile app. This triggers the interaction to start. The communication between the mobile app and Soma Mat is Bluetooth-enabled.

Breathing Light—An Enclosed Space for Reflection

An important part of the somaesthetic philosophy is the notion that to achieve a better understanding of your body, you have to actively interfere with your daily unconscious routines and create room for reflection.

The Breathing Light prototype supports this practice by providing dedicated space for such activities. It consists of an enclosure made of fabric and string curtains (see figure 4.2) that you crawl under, creating a room within a room, effectively shutting out the external world. Inside this enclosure, we have placed a breathing sensor next to the lamp. It measures the movements of your chest by measuring the distance between the sensor and your chest. The sensor controls a lamp inside the module, creating an ambient light that will dim in cadence with your breathing.

When you lie down on Soma Mat with the Breathing Light module above you, you feel enclosed and taken care of. As you close your eyes, what you see through your eyelids is the gentle pulsing of the light.

Sarka—Reinforcing Small Movements

The third prototype, Sarka, focuses on movement. When engaging in Feldenkrais exercises, you perform very small, slow movements, exploring how they connect to different parts of your body. You might be asked, for example, to make a very small circle with your shoulder—so small that someone looking at you would not be able detect it. The underlying theory is that by performing these coordinated movements in a particular order, very slowly, the brain will get stimuli from the movements and learn or

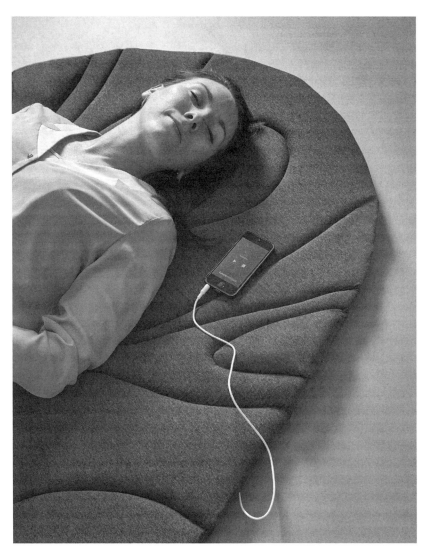

Figure 4.1
Soma Mat

Figure 4.2
Breathing Light

rediscover the combination. This in turn makes the movement pattern more readily available to become a part of your movement repertoire.

Our initial design idea was that we should be able to reinforce and support users in making these movements if we first detected them through, say, pressure sensors in the carpet or camera technology and then provided feedback in some way, such as visualizations projected onto the ceiling. As we shall discuss later, the visualizations proved to be distracting. Instead, sonifications allow users to close their eyes and focus their attention inward. We designed the sonification feedback to raise attention to the relative weight distribution between the upper part of the body (torso) and the lower part (hips), and between the left and right sides of the body. The pressure against the mat either is continuous or consists of momentary movements.

We equipped the mat with three different sound themes to choose from. To give a sense of these soundscapes, I will briefly describe some of the expressions. The first theme related to water. Continuous pressure was translated into a recording of rain. For momentary movements, we used a recording of small, nonregular waves against rocks. The second theme was inspired by nighttime in nature. Continuous pressure was mirrored into a soundscape of crickets and cicadas singing in an open landscape. For the hips, we chose a recording of a moderate wind blowing continuously. For the momentary movement sound, we used a recording of a small campfire. The third sonification was more abstract in nature. For the torso, a continuous sound, a C1 note of a sampled string quartet, is maintained. For the hips, cello and double bass are used. In all three themes, continuous movement was made to sound more distant in the 3-D soundscape, whereas momentary movement sounded as if it was closer to the mat.

When lying down on Sarka, small movements will render interesting, soothing sound experiences, but if you move too vigorously or suddenly, the soundscape becomes big and confusing. The idea is to latch on to Shusterman's proposal that the careful, slow, deliberate experience is as important and interesting as the intense and unique ones.

Process: From Early Slowstorming to Working Designs

From the start, we decided to frame our work as an autobiographical design project (Neustaedter and Sengers 2012). That is, we would be designers, prospective users, and researchers at the same time. We tried many different bodily practices, but as mentioned earlier, we decided to focus on Feldenkrais. The aim of our design work was not to copy Feldenkrais and build tools that supported only that particular practice but to innovate something new, incorporating a practice that emphasized the unity, not separation, of mind and body. Yoga or meditation might have worked just as well, but Feldenkrais intrigued, as it was different from all other body practices we tried and novel to all of us on the design team. Regardless of the practice at core, however, the designs ultimately and by necessity alter those core experiences.

At the beginning of the project, Shusterman came and held a two-day workshop with us. During our mornings, he engaged us in Feldenkrais lessons, interwoven with discussions of somaesthetic theories. In the afternoon, we engaged in brainstorming sessions—perhaps better expressed as *slowstorming*, as the ideas did not come as rapidly as we were used to.

In fact, it took us almost three years from that initial two-day workshop to arrive at the systems I described earlier. The process was highly enjoyable, but very slow—or perhaps better described as thoughtful, reflective, and craft-oriented. This way of addressing bodily engagement required a novel understanding of ourselves, our own somas—individually but also as a joint team experience. It was different from what we were used to when designing mobile apps or web pages.

We quickly discovered that the joint experience and empathic understanding of one another's engagement could not be acquired quickly. We had to attend to our own somas, learn more about ourselves as designers, before turning to and engaging with a whole range of different combinations of digital and other materials. We had to repeatedly touch and feel those materials to shape the temporal gestalt that would unfold once the system was working (see Fernaeus and Sundström 2012; Isbister and Höök 2009; Schiphorst 2007; Sundström and Höök 2010).

In addition, as in any academic design studio, the work was interleaved with working on other projects—students coming and going as participants in our work, as well as adding theoretical and analytical work. This explains in part why the design process took so long. But I would like to argue that this process had to be slower, and not only due to the varying circumstances in academic settings or because this was new territory for us. It was slow because we had to engage with and cultivate our own somatic appreciation of the Feldenkrais method and of the design's gradual unfolding.

Personally, I enjoyed the design process, but as time passed, I also worried about whether we would ever get anywhere and whether I was spending our research funding wisely. On the positive side, I felt as if I was learning a lot about my own body and thereby myself; I learned about the aesthetics of movements, I faced some of my hip pain and started to become more empathic toward my body, and I experienced a new range of somaesthetic experiences that I had never felt before. The design process also brought us together as a team. We had to open up and discuss intimate details about our experiences. I was lucky that we had enough research funding to continue despite the slowness of our progress. I relied in particular on one of my colleagues, Anna Ståhl, whom I had been working with for a long time. I knew that if I could only provide a secure space for our joint explorations, fending off demands from the outside and bringing in the right competences and unique individuals to work with, we would produce interesting results in the end. But I believe that both Anna and I were surprised at how long it took. Luckily, in the end, we were also positively surprised by the quality of the soma experiences enabled by Soma Mat and Breathing Light.

Attaining Somaesthetics Skills

First, we had to explore our own somaesthetic appreciations as designers. For a whole year, we engaged in Feldenkrais lessons without really producing any functioning design. Instead, it was a learning process in which embryonic ideas were tested and often found lacking.

To properly learn a somatic practice like Feldenkrais, you need a knowledgeable instructor. After our two-day workshop with Shusterman, which helped us with both the bodily practice and the philosophical context and framing of somaesthetics, we continued with weekly Feldenkrais exercises led by Kristina Strohmeyer.

A Feldenkrais exercise requires that you turn your attention inward, listening to your bodily signs and signals. In our exercises, we often started by describing our feelings before the exercise and then did so again after the lesson. In the descriptions after an exercise, we would report on, for example, having felt that one leg was longer than the other or that one side of the body felt orange while the other was black and burnt. Stress symptoms, strain, and pain were often reported in a more qualified manner after the exercise. We also found that we spoke more of the functions and experiences of our inner organs—sometimes being surprised that we could learn how our lungs worked or get a feeling for how the hip is connected to the shoulder.

Soma Slowstorming

As we trained own capacity for somaesthetic appreciation, we also had to find ways of translating our insights into design work. One interesting result of the Feldenkrais work was that it seemed to affect our whole beings. After a lesson, we all felt more grounded in ourselves, more honest, more reflective, and a bit slower in movements and reactions. Right after engaging in one of the lessons, we could not immediately shift into doing design work (or any other activity). We needed first to slowly rise from the exercise, talk about it together, and then take a break before coming back to the other work tasks of the day.

But what was even more interesting to us was how these lessons influenced our brainstorming exercises. In a typical brainstorming session, ideas are tossed out aggressively in rapid succession, one person taking up someone else's idea, changing it, turning it around, shifting perspectives. In the brainstorming sessions that followed a Feldenkrais exercise, we found that our ideas were forming more slowly. They felt more honest, closer to our hearts and desires—exposing us. The interactions we came to envision were delicate, sensitive to our bodily processes.

During the project, we slowstormed in many different settings, with different groups of people, for different design purposes; in general, the same experiences and considerations reappeared every time. In particular, we felt that this slower process helped us get a hold on the illusive aesthetics of bodily interactions.

But it was not easy. Let me provide one first-person memory of engaging and struggling with decision making in the design process:

In the morning, Professor Shusterman had explained why the Feldenkrais lessons often probe your bodily experience through questions directed at different body parts or movements. These questions are not meant to be answered and there is no right or wrong answer. Instead, they are carefully constructed so that you divide your body or movements into smaller parts, asking to you focus on one such part. By asking these focusing questions, you can calm the spectacle of your mind that easily rushes from one experience to the other and instead direct your attention to that body part and really sense what is happening there. He then led us through various exercises in which we would feel our own breathing, as well as empathically engage with each other's breathing. In one exercise, we laid down in a spooning position, where the person behind would put a hand on the ribcage of the person in front. Through the arm, the breathing would be communicated.

After the intense and still unexpectedly relaxing morning, we went to have lunch; when we came back, we put pens, papers, sticky notes, and other typical brainstorming materials on the floor. My group consisted of an interesting mix of competences: Feldenkrais practitioner Kristina Strohmayer; Professor Cheryl Akner-Koler from the art school in Stockholm, who specializes in designing tactile, aesthetic, sensual experiences; and me, reasonably knowledgeable in technological possibilities. In my group, we drew ideas and sketches on a big sheet of paper on the floor placed between us. We discussed how we had especially enjoyed feeling our own breathing—the sense of our diaphragms moving up and down. Kristina Strohmayer remarked on how beautiful the diaphragm is: the shape, the strength, and the whole idea of what it does for us. We asked her to draw it, and while she was drawing, I turned my attention inward, reminding myself of the breathing exercise, trying to feel my diaphragm again. It took a while to get hold of the experience, and it was even more difficult to imagine what some interaction with a digital device could add to this experience. We speculated what could be done with sensors or textiles covering the chest, or possibly a camera registering the movements of the rib cage. We struggled even to agree on whether we had all experienced the diaphragm so strongly or if there were other parts of our breathing experience that were more interesting to us. In the end, we abandoned the idea of engaging with our diaphragms.

It took us several more sessions after the two-day workshop before we started to discern some of the core experiences that meant the most to us. We also stopped inviting new people into our design processes, and instead worked hard on forming a smaller, more tightly knit group.

In the end, because our slowstorming always took place after engaging in a Feldenkrais lesson, lying on the floor in our office, the move to designing an interactive mat was not far away. And though the idea of the diaphragm didn't work out, the rhythm of breathing never ceased to fascinate; in the end, our fascination resulted in Breathing Lamp. The slow movements—especially the very, very small circular movements of the shoulder or the diagonal movements connecting hip and shoulder, looking for symmetries and asymmetries in our bodies—had the same mesmerizing effects on us, leading to designing Sarka. That said, there were many other ideas that, given time and money, we would have loved to develop, such as an idea for a soma costume created from interactive fabrics, allowing for interactive feedback close to the skin.

Material Encounters

While creating our three designs, we repeatedly had to experiment with different digital and physical materials, faking interactions and testing them *in situ* to find the ones that would make sense. The interactions had to be simulated and acted out for us to really feel their impact on our bodily experiences. Simply imagining what they would be like was not enough to qualify the experience.

As expressed by Löwgren and Stolterman (2004), we had to test the *dynamic gestalt* of the interaction. In this design, test, fail, redesign loop, we tried a whole range of modalities. We tried vibrations as feedback—but even with very subtle vibrations, they distracted us. We tried 3-D sound with a localized voice as feedback—but again, the movement of the voice did not help us to focus on some specific movement or part of our body and instead drew our attention to the outside world. We tried a moving light with the same negative result. As mentioned earlier, visualizations also proved distracting. And so on. It was not until we engaged with heat, the dimming light, and the interactive soundscape that we found modalities that made sense.

Our search was not entirely uninformed by theory or practice from other fields. For example, we studied compassion therapy (Gilbert 2009) and met with a compassion therapist, Christina Andersson, who told us about heat as an intimate sense that many patients struggled with. The compassion therapist told us how patients with anxiety problems and deliberate self-harm behaviors would typically avoid being touched and would even avoid the heat from their own hands lying on their legs when sitting. Their reaction came from being in perpetual fight-or-flight states in which their whole systems were on aggressive alert. The first step in com-passion therapy would be to approach a state in which the patient could deal with touch, which is intensely intimate. This triggered our interest in this modality.

In our design-test-fail process, we also had to consider the different phys-ical materials that would interact with the heat or dimming light. Soma Mat, for example, had to be equipped with a layer of foam that was neither too thick nor too thin. Here we were informed by the Feldenkrais theories that prescribe having contact with the floor through a thin mattress in order to be grounded and carried by the floor.

On one occasion, we got to test a mattress created for patients with bed-sores. It consisted of many small plastic bubbles that slowly inflated and deflated in a pattern that would subtly shift the weight of your body (see figure 4.3). Here is my personal account of what it felt like:

> The mattress on the floor was quite thick, and the machine filling it with air was a bit noisy. When I laid down on it, I had to close my eyes to not be reminded of my colleagues, standing around watching me. I was lying on my back, eyes closed, the palms of my hands resting on the mattress. I soon started to feel as if I was floating in the air. The feeling was that of being mid-air, rising upwards. There was nothing grounding me, no reference point. It relaxed my neck, my shoulders, and my hips. All the parts of my body that keep my body tonus, my composure, relaxed.

The inflatable mattress led us to many discussions of materials that could subtly change in relation to our movements. As it turned out, it was too

Figure 4.3
Experiencing an inflatable mattress for bedsores

costly to work with this particular mattress, and we found no way to program a controller for each of the tiny bubbles. We also noted that the experience of floating went against the Feldenkrais ideas of being grounded, of having a reference point against which our movements could be felt. We had to abandon this material, but elements of the experience remained in our final Soma Mat.

The Aesthetics of Heat

Soma Mat ended up focusing on heat as a modality for interaction (Jonsson et al. 2016). The mat has six heat pads embedded in the mat. The script triggers each heat pad to warm up at the same moment that Johanna's voice asks you to focus on the corresponding area. The heat comes on slowly, subtly, and subsides slowly, subtly.

To arrive at this design, we explored and attempted to exploit the aesthetics of the material to its fullest. Nobody in our team had worked with heat before. It turned out to be a difficult modality to work with as it depended on a lot of contextual factors, as well as individual differences. If the temperature in the room is too hot, you will not feel the effect, or it might even become unpleasant. Different people are more or less sensitive to heat. Our bodies will always strive for homeostasis, a balanced state in which we are not too cold or not too warm, as the architect Ong described:

Consider an aesthetically pleasing thermal experience like drinking a warm beverage, lying in the sun or taking a warm bath. The aesthetics of such an experience goes beyond the moment itself—beyond just heating up the body. ... If we stop to consider that our daily routine is punctuated by what are essentially acts of homeostasis—adjusting the temperature of our baths or showers, making sure our food and drinks are of the right temperature, putting on or taking off pieces of clothing, and so on—we will begin to realize just how important it is to get the pleasure and satisfaction of these actions right in order for us to function properly. (Ong 2012, 16)

As we experimented with tubes of hot water[4] and heat-transmitting light, we noted how the warmth needs to cover a fairly large area of the body to be at all noticeable. We also learned the precision with which different technologies directed heat to specific parts of the body. Once we picked heat pads as our technology, we had to figure out which cover material would transmit the heat in the best way. The layering of memory foam and cloth on top of the heat pads in the mat created the right level of diffusion and focus—subtle and diffuse, but still recognizable. Furthermore, we learned how to control the timing of the heat pads. They needed to heat slowly and cool slowly.

But most importantly, heat had an important property that other modalities, such as vibration or touch, did not have. It helped us to turn inward and experience our movements and bodily processes from the inside, rather than drawing attention to the surface: "Heat ... has shown the potential to permeate the skin and be perceived inside the body, if all dependent factors are properly tuned" (Jonsson et al. 2016, 115).

Focus Inward or Outward?

One of the Sarka variants we created was an interesting and informative failure that was not able to not able to capture the somaesthetic appreciation we aimed for. Pressure sensors in the mat picked up on the user's movements, in turn feeding into a visualization projected onto the ceiling above the user. It looked very promising because the sensors in the mat could detect very subtle body movements, mirroring them in what we saw as beautiful, evocative visualizations. When people tested this prototype, they usually were mesmerized by the visual interaction. In that sense, it was not at all a failure. Where it failed, however, was in inducing the specific, inward-listening soma experience we were after. The visual focus of this prototype drew too much attention away from the user's inner experience of the movements. The whole idea of learning more about yourself failed. Instead, the focus became a process of controlling the visualization.

Our speculation is that because our visual sense is our dominant sense, there are many habitual processes that immediately come into focus when we engage visually. By instead closing our eyes and lying down on the floor, we immediately leave habitual practices behind. Many of the Feldenkrais lessons are done with closed eyes to help us focus on our inner experience rather than shift our attention to the outside world. Fewer visual stimuli let us focus on movement stimuli that are harder to discern otherwise. Instead of visualizations, we therefore tried out sonifications—which worked really well.

Orchestrating the Whole Experience

As you are designing, you are always shifting back and forth between evaluating and imagining. You try to imagine how the whole interaction will play out if you choose certain materials, certain interactions with those materials, certain ways of making them come together into a string of experiences. We "orchestrate" the imagined experience.

In our project, we came to speak of this orchestration as divided into the *intro*, *mid*, and *outro* experiences. Easing yourself into a space where you attend to your soma always required some kind of ritual. In Feldenkrais, a lesson often started with a body scan[5] to help you land in your body, feeling where you are today, recognizing pains, symmetries, asymmetries, or tensed muscles, or simply the mood you are in. The mid-part of the experience would be some specific exercise, gently leading you through an experience that you might learn something from. Finally, the outro would ease you out of the experience, but also help you to remember it through articulating it—in your mind, in words, or in some form of imagery.

When experimenting with different outro rituals, we discussed the possibility of creating short haiku[6] from the words and phrases that popped into our minds. For a while, we wrote haiku poetry for one another to see what it would be like to generate haiku from our verbal expressions of our experiences. Together with a design company, Daytona, we also experimented with a form of fridge poetry and with putting words on top of a body outline in a mobile app.

Once you start to settle on a particular orchestration of experiences, the devil really is in the details. For Soma Mat, for example, selecting just the right Feldenkrais lesson proved crucial. First, we created a short script of about eight minutes, a good length for demos. This meant working hard on a script that would bring together all the pieces of the experience of heat and one's own body temperature in a relatively short interaction. We had to scrutinize every detail of the script and select just the right voice. Johanna happened to have a soothing voice, a way of speaking that harmonized with what we wanted to convey. But it took quite some tuning before each detail in that script coincided perfectly with the onset of heat in the different heat pads.

Orchestrating the experience entails making every design choice come together into a whole—an interaction gestalt. Johanna's voice, the choice of lesson, the onset of the heat pads, the dimming of the light, the scene where the whole interaction takes place: all these choices need to point in one and the same direction. If the choice of cloth covering Soma Mat had been too interesting itself—for example, if it were a bright color or a velvet—that would have drawn users' attention in the wrong direction vis-à-vis our design intention. Lim et al. (2007) discuss how the interaction gestalt needs to be a unified concept, greater than the sum of its parts. They argue that "only thinking about the user experience cannot fully guide designers to explore a design space of possible aesthetic interactions in a concrete way. This means that designers should have knowledge of how to shape aesthetic interactions in a more visible, explicit, and designerly way" (240). We have to *live* our designs, repeatedly, during the design process.

Interpreting, Borrowing, and Stealing

Design never happens in a void. We are always inspired by what we have seen before, by others' designs, by what the culture might consider novel, interesting, or beautiful. A part of our design process relied on what other designers had done. We read up on the academic literature on somaesthetic design, and we were also inspired by commercial design and arts.

For example, the earlier, failed version of Sarka was inspired by George Khut's *Drawing Breath* (Khut 2006). Based on a person's breathing pattern, Khut created interesting visualizations very similar to our early attempts of creating visualizations in the ceiling above the user. Because Khut was not aiming to scaffold the experience and turn attention inward, but instead aiming to help users learn to control their breathing through biofeedback, the visualizations worked with his design aims but not with ours.

As mentioned earlier, we also found a video of how Lucy McCrae created a tube-based "dress" for the singer Robyn to be used in one of her music videos. The tubes were filled with liquid, air, and vapor in different colors. A pump would move these liquids, creating interesting effects. We borrowed this concept and tried to direct attention inward instead of to the outward expressions with hot and cold water. Unfortunately, this was yet another dead end because it was hard to change the temperature of the water in those tubes quickly enough. But it was the beginnings of our choice to use heat as a modality.

Somaesthetic Appreciation Design

All three of our design exemplars came to encourage a specific orchestrated interaction pattern, a so-called strong concept, a concept we later came to name *somaesthetic appreciation design* (Höök, Jonsson, Ståhl, and Mercurio 2016). When the different parts of such an orchestration come together, users will find it easier to turn inward and experience their own somas.

We found four key qualities central to somaesthetic appreciation design—qualities that set these designs apart from other somaesthetic experiences. The qualities are formed based on experiences from the design inquiry described earlier, as well as from an analysis of the accounts from the participants we invited to interact with the prototypes.

Subtle Guidance—Directing Attention Inward

A first lesson learned when designing for body awareness was that the interactions that guide and direct a person's focus and attention—for example, toward specific bodily or sensory sensations—need to be very *subtle*, sometimes almost barely noticeable. Finding the balance between guiding attention but not grabbing it became a challenge. As noted by Shusterman (2008), building on his work as a Feldenkrais practitioner, as well as the work by William James ([1890] 1981) on introspection, the perception of bodily experiences always happens in relation to the external world, either by moving the body or through sensory interactions with external objects. The sensation of the weight of the foot, for example, can be perceived through the sensory experience of the contact with the floor. When designing interactive modalities that aim to guide focus and attention, the subtleness of the stimuli has a major impact on whether the focus stays on the introspective, somaesthetic appreciation or shifts outward, toward the source of the stimuli and the surrounding environment.

Subtle guidance relies on the interplay between two different concepts that Shusterman has developed further from William James (1905): change and interest. *Change* refers here to the importance of subdividing the bodily experiences into more specific areas or functions and then engaging in activities that shift focus from one area to another and back in order to provide a more nuanced and rich perception of fine-grained movements. The notion of *interest*, on the other hand, deals with finding a way to sustain your focus on one body part or area. As Shusterman

(2008, 162) phrases it: "To reach precise bodily introspection the key is to direct our focused attention first to one part then another, a clearer sense of relations of parts to whole can be obtained. This transition of focus provides sense of change, it also renews our interest in each new body part." Thus, in the framing of somaesthetic appreciation design, the notion of subtle guidance should be understood through mechanisms that provide changing stimuli that help shift attention between areas or functions of the body. At the same time, this subtle guidance also needs to support lingering attention and focus on one movement or area, preventing the mind from wandering.

How does subtle guidance manifest in our designs? In the Breathing Light system, the pulsating light helps to keep the interest and focus on the breath while simultaneously reinforcing and bringing to the fore the experience of change between inhaling and exhaling.

In Soma Mat, the thermal stimuli in the mat systematically guide focus toward different areas of the body and supports a sustained focus on each area.

In Sarka, the soundscape changes subtly in response to users' movements. The soundscape is created solely as a response to those movements. It is not trying to be one step ahead, forcing you to catch up. But the sonifications are more pleasant, soothing, and interesting when you shift your weight slowly and gently between torso and hips, or from one of your body parts to another. In that sense, the soundscape is guiding you.

What is the grounding in design inquiry? Arriving at those particular interactive modalities—heat, pulsating light, and soundscapes—was not trivial. For example, heat was chosen after exploring many ways to enhance and reinforce the Feldenkrais experience: light, visuals, ambient sound, 3-D sound, vibrations, touch, blowing air, and heat. In experiential exploration workshops on sensory feedback, we tested a variety of sensory stimuli, from the inflatable mattresses mentioned earlier to stroking the skin with brushes. Our initial idea was that some form of vibration or touch would help. I remember an exploration workshop that made me giggle so much I could barely stop:

> Anna and I paired up to try a series of three different possible feedback mechanisms. We had set them up in ways that could possibly fake what it would feel like. In one of them, Anna crawled underneath a field bed we had brought to our office, while I got to lay on top. As we listened to a prerecorded Feldenkrais lesson, she then tried to gently push the different body parts I was supposed to focus on. To me, on top, this not only distracted me from focusing on my experience, it was also hilarious. I started giggling and could not hold back. After a while,

we both laughed so hard that it brought tears to our eyes. Not a bad interaction, if our aim had been to spur excitement and laughter rather than slow, inward-facing, bodily attention.

Poking someone from underneath a field bed might sound like a really bad setup to explore haptic feedback. But in an early design phase, before you know whether it will be worthwhile to spend your resources on buying and programing advanced actuators, setting up a design experiment, and spending several weeks before you can even "feel" it, these kinds of fake interactions constitute a useful shortcut for design decisions. But as a designer, you have to really engage as if it is real, trying to imagine whether a "poking" mattress potentially could be designed with such subtle feedback that it would make sense. In my account, it is obvious that Anna and I failed to pretend properly and envision what could be rather than what was. Still, it was clear to us and to the other team members that vibrations or gentle poking did not go well with inward-facing experiences. Anything turning your attention to the surface of your body failed.

As a part of these explorations, we also explored the modality of heat or thermal stimuli as a means of guiding attention, using, for example, sodium acetate instant heat pad hand warmers, wheat-grain-based heat pads, and warm water running in tubes. Here we found that heat captured certain qualities that other sensory modalities we tested did not. All members of the group expressed a positive experience with the heat; it possessed certain subtleness, coming on slowly, lingering in the background, and then slowly fading away. This subtleness played well with the Feldenkrais experience, in which external stimuli easily take focus away from the inward-looking experience. Stroke and touch, for example, became much too direct and took people out of the experience immediately. Their focus shifted toward the sensory experience of the specific stimulus, whereas the heat became a more integral part of a compound experience of a specific body part.

Was there grounding in participant accounts? Although I declared upfront in this chapter that our process was autobiographical, with the design team also playing the role of the user, we sometimes brought in outside participants to experience our prototypes. I would not necessarily regard their experiences as more objective evidence that our systems indeed created or supported the desired experience, especially as outside participants would not necessarily share an understanding of what the desired experience was. Their feedback mainly centers on what is there—not what could or should be. Furthermore, we quickly realized that we would not get relevant feedback unless the people we brought in possessed good body awareness, aesthetic appreciation skills, and a rich language to express themselves.

That said, multiple accounts from participants concurred that heat helped direct attention to and keep the focus on different body parts. Many participants also claimed that the heat stimuli helped bring back focus when the mind wandered (the following accounts are translated from Swedish): "an extra injection to the practice, an awareness of everything arrived with the heat" and "I think in general the heat it is quite helpful also in focusing on the part of the body she [Johanna] is talking about." Several participants also described the heat stimuli as being sensed *inside* the body: "the heat that comes is felt inside the body".

Making Space—Temporally, Interactively, and Physically

A second important quality significant to a somaesthetic appreciation design relies on providing a "space" for reflection. There is an interesting dual meaning to the idea of *making space*; on the one hand, it concerns slowing down the pace of life and actively disrupting everyday habitual routines. On the other hand, it also has a quite literal, physical meaning: in our design work, it became important to build a secluded space, forming a certain atmosphere or a sense of feeling safe, enclosed, taken care of. This also corresponds to Shusterman's (2008, 163) interpretation of Williams James: "Attention to bodily feelings can also be enhanced by the strategy of warding off competing interests, since any form of attention constitutes a focalization of consciousness that implies ignoring other things in order to concentrate on the object attended."

Making space is more than merely creating a physical barrier blocking out light and sound. The environment needs to feel safe, so you feel you are taken care of. For us, it involved creating an aesthetically evocative environment—communicated through the choice of materials together with the interactions created inside this space.

How does making space manifest in our designs? In short, the softness of the mattress in Soma Mat and the heat/soundscape in Sarka help create a cozy and calm experience. The form of the mat also creates a particular space, fitting your body size and your movements, yours to be inhabited. If you look carefully, you may note that the stitching is shaped like a stylized body, indicating where the head and other body parts should be placed on the mat. This helps users to know how to lie down on the mat, but also makes you feel secure and that your body is right where it should be.

Breathing Light has a similar private space mapped out underneath the strings hanging down. It serves both to exclude external stimuli and to make you feel safe and taken care of.

What is the grounding in the design inquiry? Early on, it became clear to us that external stimuli could easily overtake the experience. Whenever we were doing Feldenkrais exercises in our office, we had to make sure the doors were closed, and we always brought blankets to feel warm and covered and yoga mats to lie on to make us feel we had our "own space."

Again, we tested many setups before we arrived at designs capturing what we needed. We tried, for example, to make the whole interaction take place in a tent, but that became too enclosed, almost claustrophobic. We also tried to design a lamp with a shield that covered the upper part of the body, but that also became too enclosed. Finally, we arrived at the fringes hanging down, allowing a slightly more transparent space (see figure 4.2).

Was there grounding in participant accounts? Two experiences related to making space reoccurred in the participants' accounts. The most clearly stated one relates to encapsulation, as the words of four different subjects express: "you enter another room"; "to have your own small space"; "a room in the room"; and "it is slightly open, it does not become so closed in and paranoid in there."

It is interesting to note that one of our participants was troubled by how her legs were sticking out from underneath Breathing Light:

> And then I have the feeling that some part of bottom part of my body, like legs from the knees down, there not so much happened. And I think it's because the shape, like you got this dome thing and my legs were out the entire time and that's why I didn't feel a lot connection with my lower part.

Her experience tells us how important it is to enclose the whole body. Because the Breathing Light shade does not cover the legs, but only the torso, she does not feel that her whole body is inside the space.

The other reported experience relates more to the atmosphere of being in this space, which our participants described using expressions such as "cozy," "calming, soft feeling," and "almost psychedelic."

Intimate Correspondence—Following the Rhythm of the Body

A third important quality of somaesthetic appreciation design relates to the design and characteristics of various feedback loops, such as biofeedback, which can reinforce or mirror felt-body experiences. Here we note, perhaps not so surprisingly, that for such feedback to support somaesthetic appreciation, *immediacy* and *synchronization* is key. If the synchronization between Johanna's voice and the heat feedback is only slightly off, it no longer makes sense. Or if Sarka does not immediately produce sounds in response to your movements, it becomes very hard to figure out how to move. These setups rely on a *correspondence* relationship, and it needs to be constituted as an *implicit* interaction—not explicitly engaging you in an active dialogue in which you must reply to the system, as in most other interfaces.

Ingold introduced the concept of *correspondence* to describe what it means to be human in a world of other people, together with systems and our environment (Ingold 2013, 2017). Correspondence is a type of intimate relationship between a subject and an artifact, such as between a cello player and his cello (ibid.). In the kind of intimate correspondence we are aiming for here, the immediate and synchronized feedback rhymes with the rhythms and flows of the body in such a way that the interactive system is perceived more as an extension of the body than as a separate entity or communication counterpart.

For the feedback to make sense, its expression must also somehow correspond with the bodily experience being addressed. Part of this correspondence has to do with making careful mappings from what the system senses to expressions—be they visualizations, heat, or pulsating light. The feedback must make sense and be meaningful vis-à-vis your own rhythm as you experience it subjectively. The intimate correspondence relationship is similar to the interactions you would have with a mirror, in which you are not really aware of the mirror per se.

Designing for this experience is hard when things don't work perfectly. For example, when biofeedback is out of sync, the user is distracted and focuses on the workings of the system or the outside world rather than on the activity.

How does intimate correspondence manifest in our designs? In Breathing Light, the pulsating light is carefully synchronized with the breathing. In Soma Mat, the wandering thermal stimuli are tightly synchronized with the voice instructions.

Sarka has a more complex relationship, in which different sounds are tied to different parts of your body and to different qualities of your movements. A prolonged, sustained pressure on the mat will render different sounds than quick, shifting movements. Shifting your weight back and forth between hips and shoulders or from left to right will again add to this complex soundscape.

What is the grounding in design inquiry? In the design work, we worked extensively with a problem that might seem very simple to solve—the synchrony between breathing and the dimming light feedback. The problem is that the light cannot lag behind the breathing experience even by a few milliseconds. As soon as it does, users lose their sense of being in sync and their breathing is affected. Because the technologies in the prototypes were not always functioning perfectly, there are numerous examples of accounts from participants of problems with the timing of heat or light creating confusion and breaking the somaesthetic appreciation activity:

> And I don't know if it, it doesn't always sync up, because sometimes when you breathe out in a different way or something then it recognizes it as a breathing in so then the light turns brighter so sometimes it's off. And then it's kind of strange because then you are like "I am breathing out, it should dim but it is breathing in" the light itself breathing in.

Articulating Experience—Providing a Means to Put Words to Bodily Sensations

Finally, the fourth important quality that sets a somaesthetic appreciation design apart from other soma designs concerns the importance of articulating the felt bodily experience. The relationship among language, perception, and how our experiences are affected by our ability to articulate them in words is a well-known and debated linguistic and philosophical topic—as mentioned in chapter 2. Language allows us to shift to a third-person perspective of our experiences. It also allows us to pinpoint and discern different parts of experiences. Wittgenstein goes so far as to claim that we would not experience pain in the absence of understanding the word *pain*. Here, Shusterman proposes the use of linguistic tags as a resource that can be used to improve the nuances of the perception of the body:

> Linguistic tags or descriptions, for example, can make a very vague feeling less difficult to discriminate by tying that feeling to words, which are much more easily differentiated. James argues, for instance, that the different names of wines help us discriminate their subtly different flavours far more clearly and precisely than we could without the use of different names. ... The rich and value-laden associations of words can, moreover, transform our feelings, even our bodily ones. For such reasons, the use of language to guide and sharpen somaesthetic introspection—through preparatory instructions, focusing questions, and imaginative descriptions of what will be (or was) experienced and how it will (or did) feel—is crucial even to those disciplines of somatic awareness that regard the range and meaning of our feelings as going well beyond the limits of language. (Shusterman 2008, 164)

How does articulation manifest in our designs? We engaged with articulation in two ways: the in situ activity of bodily introspection/reflection, and the external expression and description of the experience after the session. In our examples of somaesthetic appreciation design, articulation is encouraged via visualization and verbalization. Johanna's guidance through the Feldenkrais exercise, for example, asks the participants to specifically think about their experiences via certain terms, such as *heavy* or *elongated*.

As part of experiencing Soma Mat and Breathing Light, we also asked participants to articulate their experiences by drawing or writing on a piece of paper after their sessions with the system. We also tested the Sensual Evaluation Instrument (Isbister et al. 2006) and asked participants to mold clay to express their experiences.

What is the grounding in design inquiry? The importance of articulation became very prominent during the early stages of the design inquiry. To figure out at all what we were designing for, we had to find means of sharing the experiences with each other. Because this form of body awareness was novel to several of the participants, we had to articulate the experience first of all to ourselves. But we also had to agree on certain qualities in the activities we were designing for.

As mentioned earlier, we came to speak of the designs as divided into the intro, mid, and outro experiences. In the intro and outro parts, we asked participants to articulate "where they were" before and after engaging with our designs. The aim of the systems we designed was to aid users in actively reflecting on the experiential and emotional aspects of the experience. To externalize these inherently subjective experiences of the felt body, making them available for scrutiny, we had to find some instrument or form of expression. After testing different forms (verbal accounts, the Sensual Evaluation Instrument, free drawings, molding soft clay, haiku, and so on) we decided to use body sheets, inspired by methods used in physiotherapy. *Body sheets* consist of rudimentary drawings of human bodies on top of which participants can draw (or write) with different colored pens what they feel in different parts of their body. Participants were asked to fill in a body sheet before engaging with our system and then another one after the session. They were also given several evocative terms, such as "thorny" and "jittery," that they could place on top of this body sheet to express their experience.

A design firm we were working with, Daytona, later built an app to register the before and after experiences by placing words on top of the outline of a body. The app then formed poetry, a bit like fridge poetry, which could be saved. The idea was to remind users of their earlier experiences and perhaps even look for progression between sessions.

Was there grounding in user accounts? Some user accounts point to the importance of articulation:

if you would have just asked me in passing I wouldn't have noticed any of this. It was just the standing still and focusing and realizing "ah my arms do tingle and my fingers are a bit yeah"

The use of multiple colors allowed users to express nuances in their experiences; for example, some created maps between colors and experiences:

And the warm is orange because it wasn't that warm—it was just about the right warmth

Interestingly, we noted that filled-in colored areas in the drawings typically indicate stronger sensations, such as pain.

Living with Soma Mat and Breathing Light

Although my position is that the design process itself is a form of evidence and validation of the design work and that the autobiographical design process crafts the sought experience, it is of course interesting to document how people engage with what we crafted. Did these four qualities we found interesting "come through" in our designs? Did that in turn help foster a different somatic awareness (or body awareness)?

The final step of our design process, therefore, was to build five copies of Soma Mat and Breathing Light and install them in the homes of five different families. We let the participating families live with them for three months. During that time, we interviewed the families regularly.

As with any research product, our designs were not on par with product quality. Despite this, I've never seen such strong reactions to any other product we've built. One of our participants cried when she had to give back the systems after three months. Another family was visited by a friend—a refugee—who had been denied residency in Sweden. Due to all the stress in his life, he could not sleep. As he lay down on the mat, he was finally able to fall asleep.

In our analysis of the interviews, it seems as if what these designs offered became a dedicated space in the families' homes for self-reflection. You can always meditate or engage in other body practices without any designs, but it is hard to maintain such practices in our busy, everyday lives. Soma Mat and Breathing Light spoke to our participants in an immediate manner. The systems helped users build rituals for self-reflection, spaces where they could engage by following a script that in turn allowed them to take the next step.

The experiences also spilled over into other contexts. One of the participants in the three-month study brought the breathing experience with her into other situations:

> Yes, I notice that I am much more aware of my breathing. And I have tested to do more relaxation exercise at work and so on. I know that this has affected my everyday life too. I think more of my breathing and I try to relax and like that. Take a break. Focus solely on sitting on the chair and breathe. And to do—like maybe—turn my head a little or something like that.

This participant had, to her own surprise, used the systems four times a week. She explained that she had issues with stress and, in particular, headaches after grinding her teeth in her sleep. After using the systems, she had stopped grinding her teeth.

To help someone deal with his or her stress is an important aim, but it might be characterized as an *instrumental* goal. Somaesthetic appreciation goes beyond the instrumental, aiming for "living a better life," appreciating your own somatics, gaining better perceptual abilities. What was interesting to us, therefore, was whether the system increased awareness of participants' breathing; of their skin temperature; of signs and signals from different body parts; and whether it all came together in the unique somaesthetic appreciation experience we were hoping for. The first aims were easy to confirm in the interviews. The participants reported back on learning breathing patterns and on the warmth of the mat and how that helped draw attention to their skin temperature and different body parts. They also frequently spoke of how relaxing the experience was. But what about the unique somaesthetic appreciation experience we sought? Throughout this chapter, I have been trying to capture the experience of turning inward, experiencing your living soma, your inner organs, the way different parts connect to one another. But I fear that I am still struggling to really capture the depth and uniqueness of the experience we were after. But as I know the experience myself, I can see when the participants allude to the elusive and unique experience we were after—even if they struggle to put words to it:

> Yes, but I do not know how to explain it but just as I said earlier, that you think "now I am relaxed." Or right before I am about to fall asleep I am relaxed. But it is not at all the same way of being relaxed. Not at all the same state as when I have laid down on the mat. I do not know how to explain it really. I just feel more relaxed.

Later, the same participant reattempts to explain the experience:

> Because you are entirely relaxed and in contact with your body. You really feel your body. ... I long to feel warm in every body part, feeling the warmth move from one body part to the next, to be entirely relaxed and one with my body.

To "really feel your body" and be "one with your body" is exactly what we aimed to design for.

Other Somaesthetic Appreciation Design Exemplars

As we will explain (in chapter 5, somaesthetic appreciation design is a tentative *strong concept* (Höök and Löwgren 2012); that is, it bears the potential of generating more designs beyond the three introduced thus far. In fact, as we looked at other systems presented in academia, we found several that fit into this category, such as the Sonic Cradle (Vidyarthi, Riecke, and Gromala 2012) and the Slow Floor (Feltham et al. 2013).

The cradle is placed in a dark room from which all external stimuli are removed, except for a soundscape mirroring your breathing. It builds on the idea that losing focus while meditating will alter breathing patterns. By subtly mirroring breathing through a surrounding soundscape, the Sonic Cradle may help nudge you back into focus.

The cradle embraces most of the qualities that we identified as part of the somaesthetic appreciation design concept; making space, both with respect to atmosphere and with blocking out disturbances; subtle feedback bringing attention to breathing patterns; and providing for an intimate correspondence between breathing and immersion with the soundscape. The only quality that is not explicitly mentioned in the description of the Sonic Cradle is the articulation of the experience.

A second exemplar is the Slow Floor (Feltham et al. 2013). The Slow Floor takes the form of six interactive walking pads made from timber and foam, with embedded force sensors measuring changes in weight as someone steps on them. This force and weight data is converted into a tone transmitted by four loudspeakers placed around the floor. The tone creates a "decelerating engine" sonic effect.

Again, note how the feedback is subtle, intimately corresponding to walking on the floor. Slow Floor is located in a confined space that allows for reflection and experience. The articulation lies in the increased awareness of your own footsteps.

From Selfishness to Compassion

Before we move on, let us discuss one of the stumbling blocks involved when we approach body awareness exercises such as those manifest in Soma Mat, Breathing Light, and Sarka.

To somebody who has never tried a body-awareness technique, it may seem a very selfish activity, accessible only to rich, self-obsessed Westerners, turning inward rather than outward toward empathic, social care for others. I admit that I have been a sceptic myself, and I still struggle with some aspects of spending time and energy turning inward rather than turning outward, facing society and others around me. Body-awareness techniques may spur associations with yogis sitting on mountains, attending to themselves and to their god(s), reclusive from the world.

Alternatively, you might take entirely the opposite position, dismissing the experience as a shallow interpretation of ancient Eastern philosophies that trivializes the original practice.

Although both worries are legitimate, there are two sides to the story; otherwise, movement practices would not be such a core part of any rituals keeping a society closely knit together, be they rituals of a religious temple or secular practices. Body practices or rituals do not come with a guarantee of success, however. Attending to your soma might indeed make you selfish, absorbed solely with your own health and well-being. But it may also make you more aware of others, their pains and sufferings, their somas. You cannot attend to anyone else and really understand him or her unless you know yourself. If you do not even know your own breathing patterns, will it not be hard or even impossible for you to register those of your friend? There is an element of compassion in many of these exercises that grounds you firmly in the soil of the human condition—the condition we all share. If we are not aware of our own somas or the signals we transmit to the outside world, then we are, in a sense, shutting ourselves off, not only from ourselves but also from others. You might be sending stressful messages to your coworkers without intending to. You might be sending messages of frustration to your family members. In both cases, the ability to slow down and start communicating benefits everyone involved.

To me, the body practice that most clearly tells me that my body is the locus of communication—inward as well as outward—is horseback riding. Horseback riding is not a language-based practice. It happens through physical signs and signals: the rider uses leg muscles, the placement of sitting bones, bodily balance, head movement, hand and arm connection to the horse's mouth, and sometimes tone of voice. The horse talks back through its movement, direction, pace, activations of muscles that can be felt throughout the horse's body, its head and tail movements, flipping ears, neck bending, and breathing noise. To be a good rider, taking care of yourself as well as the horse, you need to learn this wordless language. As in any language, understanding and communication arises in interaction over time. When you experience a particular bodily schema or kinetic bodily logos together with the horse, this mutual understanding and meaning-making may come to be. If you are not sensitive to what is happening between yourself and the horse, riding becomes a matter of brute control, requiring submission of the horse to your rough handling. To be a sensitive and compassionate rider, you must be present, with your whole soma, in the moment-to-moment unfolding of events.

This said, as with any human activity, some might very well use body practices in a selfish manner, attending solely to their own needs. Sometimes this is part of their whole attitude to life. Sometimes it is simply because they do not have any strength left to attend to anyone else; they might be troubled by pain or problems consuming them.

I also want to reemphasize that soma design is not solely to do with slow movements or turning inward. The design examples in this chapter all centered on such practices, but we could equally well have been designing tools to support horseback riding, running, or playing fast and scary games. No matter the practice, there is always an opportunity to attend to the fine-grained movements and engagements required, achieving better design and aesthetic appreciation.

Impermanence of Self and Intersubjectivity

A second question concerns the effects a somatic practice may have on us. How does it change us? Can it really change us in any profound manner, beyond training some muscles or nervous system reactions?

Nobody will contest that we are capable of learning new movements, but it is perhaps less clear to some how our sense of self changes with those learnings. Most of us feel as if our inner voices, our selves, are always there, providing permanent, ongoing inner dialogues with selves that have not really changed since we were children. Many refer to themselves in terms of given personalities, assuming that they will always respond in certain ways in certain situations. Many also assume that their emotional reactions are given, deterministically arriving in response to some stimuli. They assume that they will always be able to tell (themselves or others) what they are feeling—as if their emotions are always readily available, always accessible for scrutiny. But is this really so?

Turn to your own experience: What are you feeling right now? Can you qualify your emotion and articulate exactly what you are experiencing? Often that question requires quite some time and reflection; it requires turning attention from reading this book toward the self. Otherwise, there is no way of knowing what you are experiencing.

In fact, sometimes our inner feelings confuse us and we seek ways to find out what is going on. We might spend hours discussing some emotional crisis with a friend to put words to a confusing experience—sometimes as a way to deal with it or even change the emotions that come with the memory. Some keep a diary of their experiences to facilitate that process. As Csikszentmihalyi (2009) so elegantly wrote: "To remember the past is not only meaningful in order to create and maintain your personal identity, but it can also in itself be a very pleasurable activity. … To keep the past registered can contribute to quality of life. It frees us from being enslaved by the present and makes it possible for our minds to visit the past. It makes it possible to choose and in our memory keep events that have been particularly pleasant and meaningful and thereby "create" a past that helps us to deal with the future."[7]

In the phenomenologist accounts of the self, our experiences and emotions are not directly accessible to us. We must turn our eyes inward to "know." This process in turn modifies what we feel, altering the experiences through affecting many different processes (emotion, conscious reflection, hormones released into our blood streams, short-term memory, and so on), all feeding into one another. The "self" actively engages with these processes in turn, thereby altering our memory and experience of them. Through these experiences, we alter our reactions. The self changes through these processes, taking on different roles, always rooted in our unique biological constitution but changing with our learnings and experiences. The way we express ourselves is not simply a bridge between our inner mental thoughts and the outside world; in the translation, the manifestations of those experiences will be impregnated with the meaning and experiences of expressing them (Mentis, Laaksolahti, and Höök 2014), thereby changing us.

Mirroring ourselves in others is an important part of learning about the self. The intersubjective process emerges from an intercorporality: "the other's body influences our own bodily movements and sensations, and vice versa" (Fuchs and De Jaegher 2009). In a sense, we construct emotion in dialogue with ourselves, others, the situation, and our cultural notions and interpretations. That is, we continuously engage, interpret, and create meaning. In that process, we change ourselves. Sometimes a dramatic event has more profound effects on us; sometimes it is just the stream of everyday consciousness that alters us slowly. Engaging in a body practice such as Feldenkrais alters our expressions and lets us attend to all the connections between somatic signs and signals—be they movements of body parts, their connections, pain, pleasure, or how emotional processes affect us. In social relations, the other's body influences us in an immediate sense; we mirror and might feel what they feel. Simply hearing the voice of a loved one may reveal a whole fabric of experiences and emotions. Who has not experienced someone close to them immediately asking, "What's happened?" just after they say hello?

What we have learned from designing the systems presented in this chapter, together with our earlier work designing for keeping diaries or communicating with others through gestures, is that our designs empower our users to playfully construct a new sense of self, arising in the moment, transforming through experience. Turning inward to get a hold of your own experiences and expressing those are empowering—both in changing the self and in emphatically engaging with others intersubjectively.

Beyond Individual Design Exemplars

We built the designs presented here as a path to learning a different manner of designing, to find novel qualities in our design work. Our ultimate aim is not to build tools for meditation, even if that is a worthy cause in itself. Instead, as discussed in the beginning of this book, we want to bring these lessons into all of our design work, be it design of Internet of Things products, mobiles, computers, or web applications.

The somaesthetics of the dynamic gestalt and how we shape it in our design processes might, in a sense, be an instance of the somaesthetic philosophy project. Or perhaps more accurately, the somaesthetics philosophy serves as a lens, a particular way of seeing the world, informing the design process. But as such, it has its own specific challenges in how it is projected—created—in a dialogue between the design materials at hand and the somaesthetic sensibilities of the designer. Next, let us discuss what we can ask of a *soma design theory* that may inform that dialogue between designer and materials, orchestrating experiences such as those of Soma Mat, Breathing Light, and Sarka.

5 Soma Design Theory

As you look at the title of this chapter, you might wonder why I waited until now—halfway through the book—to offer a coherent theory of soma design. The answer is quite simple: Because soma design is based so heavily on experiences and somatic feelings, I felt it was necessary to give you, the reader, a sense of what such designs actually feel like—how they work, what makes them unique, and how they came about. Articulating a theory of design in words requires a certain distanced, intellectual approach, and yet I am arguing for designs that recognize the soma as the unity of mind and body, intellect and experience. I hope that by now, you have an intuitive sense of what soma designs might look and feel like, which will make my discussion here of soma design theory more meaningful.

To begin that discussion, I start with the most basic questions: What is a design theory? Why would we want a design theory for soma design? What kind of "potency" can we expect from such a theory? What are the concepts and theories already articulated in academia, through explorative design work? In this chapter, I attempt to address those questions and put soma design theory in conversation with them.

What Is a Design Theory?

Here we will use design scholar Johan Redström's concept of the design research program to frame what we mean by a design theory. According to Redström (2017), a *design research program* starts with a set of axioms or aesthetic values serving as the basis for the work. The program is then filled with content and knowledge produced through design experiments, user studies, and conceptualizations. Together, these experimental activities probe the potency of the program, the generative capacity of the axioms. The experimental design activities also probe what stays "inside" the program and what ends up "outside." This goes on for as long as new ideas arise or until you run out of funding to perform more experiments. Looking at the whole program from the outside lets us ask: "Designing *could be* this; what would be its implications?" (ibid., 97; emphasis in original).

To make it clearer, let us take one of Redström's examples. Consider a research program based on the following axiom: "Design is the use of the basic geometrical shapes of the circle, the square, and the triangle ... to express the functionality of everyday things" (Redström (2017, 96). The first activity would be to redesign some everyday things using only these geometrical shapes. In those design experiments, we look for what is typical—as in the sense of a proto*type* (ibid.). We check whether we can repeat the successes or dissect the failures, articulating design methods and concepts that need to be in place to make relevant combinations of the circle, triangle, and square. After many such design experiments, if successful, the program will be populated with many designs; in other words, a novel design space (Westerlund 2009) has been opened. Each design in the program serves as a fact in the theory being built.

Now we turn toward the edges and extremes of this space to learn new things and avoid mere repetition. As Redström (2017, 96) explains: "For instance, we might set off in the direction designing for the human body, exploring the interactions between strict geometry and ergonomics. Or, we might start asking questions about what kinds of artistic expression are possible within the frames of program, and what 'functionality' really refers to." These probings of the edges and extremes tell us about the limitations of the program, defining where it fails to deliver relevant design for everyday objects.

For this particular program example, Redström points out that it is inherently reductive—visually as well as geometrically—because it only allows for circles, squares, and triangles. It is also reductive in that the purpose of the design is seen primarily as functionality, and the knowledge brought forth applies only to the design of everyday things. These properties follow from the commitment to the axiom. In other words, axioms need to be chosen with care and deliberation.

Besides the design exemplars, a research program will also introduce other forms of articulations of design knowledge, such as *design methods*, as well as various conceptualizations that allow us to speak of familial resemblances between the design exemplars that belong inside the program. The "family resemblances" highlighted by these conceptualizations help us identify unique properties of a program and its aesthetics.

Let us draw a parallel to architecture and different architectural styles. A building can serve as a fact; one might say, for instance, "This is a prototypical Art Deco building." As an architecture student, you will learn about the different elements that help us recognize and distinguish this building as Art Deco and not some other style. For example, you might learn what was going on during that time period that led to the particular aesthetics: Art Deco style arose right after World War I and helped provide a sense of recuperation.[1] To achieve a sense of recuperation, one path was to add glamour; Art Deco buildings often use bold colors, rare and expensive materials, and elaborate decorations—often influenced by ancient Egypt. These facts can help us distinguish between styles. One might say, for instance, "Look at the use of these rare and expensive materials! That makes this Art Deco and not modernist." After a while, we learn that there is a familiar feel to Art Deco buildings: a sense of glamour, of decoration, of being expensive. The architect makes use of stylistic elements, materials, shapes, and forms to achieve these experiences. Certain design patterns are repeated in the Art Deco style, recognizable even if they are endlessly varied. When designing your own Art Deco building, you need to know these stylistic elements, what feel to strive for, and what design patterns to draw on.

In interaction design, our material is interactive. Thus, our conceptualizations need to (1) capture the feel of the system as we interact with it and (2) identify and name successful design patterns to capture the turn-taking between system and user. We sometimes refer to the feel of a system as its *experiential qualities* (Ståhl, Löwgren, and Höök 2014). For example, in a style like Apple's, there is an experiential quality you recognize in all the company's products—not solely to do with the rounded corners, the sleek design, or the use of certain colors, but in the ways it reveals itself when you interact with the system. There is a special feel to how mouse movements are animated on the screen, in the design of gestures used to scroll and move between applications, and so on; put together, this creates a sense of familiarity, a familiar recognition.

The second form of conceptualization, the design patterns, are sometimes referred to as *strong concepts* (Höök and Löwgren 2012) in interaction design. As we are generating ideas for what a system could be, we often talk about them as design concepts. Strong concepts emphasize the idea that some concepts seem to be *strong*, in that they can apply across different design situations and different contexts and can generate many applications. An example is the strong concept of *social navigation*—that is, following the trails of others when navigating a large information space (Svensson, Höök, and Cöster 2005; Svensson et al. 2001). Social navigation takes many forms. We can follow the choices of others when we decide which books to buy, when we choose which movies to watch, or when walking through a city. The trails of others can be collected and made visible in many different forms, but we can recognize that there is a common element in all that we can exploit in our design processes. A strong concept is therefore generative: it can generate more than one design. In my work with Jonas Löwgren, we defined a *strong concept* as follows:

• It concerns the dynamic gestalt of an interaction design, that is, its interactive behavior rather than its static appearance.

• It resides at the interface between technology and people. It is a design element, a potential part of an artifact, and at the same time, it speaks of a use practice and behavior unfolding over time.

• It carries a core design idea which has the potential to cut across particular use situations and perhaps even application domains.

• It resides on an abstraction level above particular instances, which means that it can be realized in many different ways when it comes to interface detailing (cf. concept design vs. detailed design). (Höök and Löwgren 2012, 23:5–23:6)

Coming back to the main question—What is a design theory?—we now have some building blocks. A design theory will start from a set of axioms and then, through design experiments, hopefully open a novel design space, answering the question, "What if design is this?" The design space will be filled with design exemplars serving as facts. Some of those design exemplars we will consider to be prototypical, whereas others will represent the edge of the program. Some will successfully achieve the desired aesthetics and functionality, whereas others will be less successful. Based on these design exemplars, which serve as our "facts," we articulate our insights as design methods (embodying procedural knowledge) as well as conceptualizations, such as experiential qualities and strong concepts.

In summary, apart from articulating the axioms of soma design, we also need to "fill" the soma design research program with design knowledge through providing the following (see figure 5.1):

1. Many design exemplars—or, as Stolterman calls them, *ultimate particulars* (Stolterman 2008)—serving as facts in our theory. Some will be prototypical examples; others will push the borders of the program.

2. Conceptualizations of those design exemplars, to point out any resemblances between them that can help guide new design work: *strong concepts* and *experiential qualities*.

3. Design *methods* capturing soma-based ideals when designing, to help guide the design process (capturing procedural knowledge).

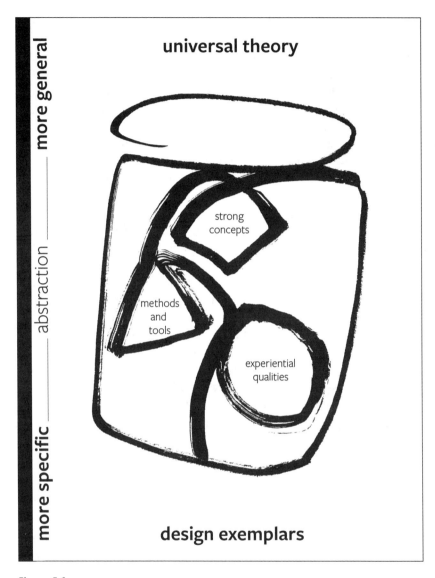

Figure 5.1
From design exemplars to universal theories—and various mid-range conceptualizations in between

Why a Soma Design Theory?

Why do we need a somaesthetic design theory? It might seem contrary to what has been discussed so far, as we have argued that the only way to really "know" what soma-based designs are is to experience them through a first-person perspective—both as a designer and a user. The experience is somatic and aesthetic, touching on our somas, our aesthetic sensibilities, emotions, and values. The knowledge and understanding is tacit, culturally and contextually bound. It is grounded in experience and first-person somatic reflection. It cannot be reduced to some objective rules or design patterns that can be replicated over and over and that will always generate the same somaesthetic experience: that would be impossible. Given this view, what is the design knowledge we can bring forth, and what potency will it have in generating viable designs? What is a theory, anyway? We are grappling with epistemological questions that are ancient. We need to question what it means to know something that you have learned through your senses and that remains tacit, unarticulated, filtered through your subjective experiences.

In chapter 1, we compared this to another aesthetic practice: music (Kosmack Vaara 2017). We discussed that musicians will train their tacit knowledge for years, engaging with their instruments until those instruments are ready-to-hand (Merleau-Ponty 1996), allowing musicians to dynamically shape aesthetic expression as they play. They also learn

- a repertory of music pieces,
- a terminology to describe them,
- a set of genre-specific concepts,
- music scores, and
- a terminology for speaking of the temporal and emotional gestalt the composer aimed for.

Musicians need to make all this knowledge readily available the moment they play music. When a group of musicians wants to come together in their expressions, they might engage in visual imagery to help shape the aesthetic expression: "Satie[2] urged the pianist in one of his compositions to play 'like a nightingale with toothache.' This might seem humorous, but emotional imagery is commonly used to describe a shared sense of what is supposed to happen in the performance of the music" (Kosmack Vaara 2017).

Let us for a moment return to the concepts introduced when we discussed Sheets-Johnstone. Her emphasis was on seeing movement as primary and language as secondary. Language is only an impoverished way to communicate our somatic experience, because the knowledge is tacit; instead, movements form kinetic bodily logos, meaningful in themselves. As Parviainen (2002) writes about dancers, the way they know is "not disconnected from language, yet their bodily knowledge is grounded on a tacit and nonverbal dimension of knowing." Musicians know a whole range of kinetic bodily logos, both from their own experience and from watching others—not the least their teachers. That is, language and verbalizations are important to our inquiry and design work, because they facilitate the sharing of tacit knowledge and experiences. Depending on which concepts we use, the labels we put on our emotions and experiences, we will perceive and appreciate our experiences differently. But our understanding may also take the form of kinetic bodily logos that are not necessarily given a "label" but are still known to everyone sharing expertise in that aesthetic practice.

Similarly, soma design is also an artistic practice. If you have shaped a soma interaction—as designer or user—then various kinetic bodily logos, articulations, and conceptualizations will start to make sense to you. You will be able to connect your tacit understanding to the accounts other designers provide. In the same way that the world is inherently meaningful to you through your own movement and through sensing the movements of others, these theories and concepts will no longer be vacuous words written on a paper or movement patterns that you cannot discern. Once you have obtained the tacit knowledge and can discern the logos, you can engage in a more informed practice. This enables discussions with your coworkers on a design team. It enables a more informed and acute aesthetic sensibility. These conceptualizations help you shift between first-person and third-person perspectives of yourself and the interactive experience you are partly shaping. Or, in Schön's (1984) terms, by reflecting on your practice and experience, you can bring knowledge from one situation to the next, even if it does not generalize into simple rules that can be applied irrespective of context and available resources. The combination of your tacit understanding and the conceptualizations you use to describe them forms your knowledge, your theory.

As with any theoretical stance, the conceptualizations we bring forth will have their limitations—and they will also be limiting. They serve as a lens to spotlight certain aesthetic processes, spurred by certain designs and not others. They allow you to put words to some of your somatics, emotions, movements, bodily rhythms, and engagements with designed artifacts, but not to others. They will let you probe and feel the affordances of the interactive digital materials in certain ways and not others. This in turn affects which design spaces we open and which ones we do not even consider. Design theory is not innocent or "objective" in that sense; it is a creative practice, not a study of what is in the world already.

An informed aesthetic sensitivity will contribute to engaging in the "highest art of all," living that "better life" that Shusterman speaks of. It makes you open to new contexts, new situations, in which you can appreciate the aesthetic potential offered—whether you are a designer or user. The more body-aware and experienced you are, the more you can discern and appreciate different soma experiences.

Four Criteria

But what is the difference between a general theory of aesthetics or human behavior (such as the somaesthetic theories of Shusterman or the primacy of movement theory from Sheets-Johnstone) and a theory that speaks more specifically to a soma design practice? I propose that four criteria distinguish soma design theory from other theories, as well as differentiating it from other design programs: sociodigital materials, interactivity, a perpetual state of being designed, and somatic experiences.

Sociodigital Material

First, our conceptualizations should not speak only of the somaesthetic experience without also including a description of the design elements that were able to spur that experience; otherwise, we end up with a theory belonging in philosophy, psychology, neurology, or sociology rather than interaction design. Interaction design is always the study of the sociodigital material: the coming together of people with designed interactive artifacts and the behaviors and experiences generated in the combined material of people, practices, tools, and designs. Soma design theory will always depend on the affordances of the technologies and materials used to shape the designs.

Interactivity

This leads us to our second criterion: conceptualizations should speak of the *interactive* behavior rather than static appearance of the design, as this is what constitutes a dynamic gestalt, unfolding over time between user and system. The interactive behavior should be seen as a process of designing, as the interactions do not exist outside their use. As the behavior is being used, it continues to be "designed" by the interpretations and choices of the end user, filling it with meaning, movement, and interactions (Redström 2017; Stolterman 2008).

The meaning-making process resonates with the kinaesthetic, dynamic possibilities arising in the context of use, creating for kinaesthetic bodily logos inherently meaningful to us in their context of use. Wiggling your tail does not make sense unless you wear Svanaes's Tail, but once you do, it makes immediate sense, creating for kinaesthetic bodily logos of relevance to the context. As you practice with the tail, like the actors had to practice, it will allow you to be more expressive in your movements. Our conceptualizations need to reflect this ongoing process of meaning-making in interaction; the system is continuously being designed in and through its use.

In a Perpetual State of Being Designed

The way we frame design knowledge can range from pointing to some *specific design* through describing a larger *design research program* or whole *paradigms* of interactions, as discussed by Redström (2017). Regardless of where on the scale we put an articulation of design knowledge, that articulation will always be a provisional theory (Gaver 2012). Designs in use respond to their user, shifting in method and purpose. As our design material changes, as the maturity of design and use grows and changes. As our societies integrate interface paradigms (such as the desktop) into the societal discourse and practices, these theories will be modified or made obsolete. In addition, whether we are talking about a specific design, a design research program, or a whole paradigm, all are in flux, mutually constituent entities, forever frozen in their form. We are designing them as we go along. Bringing forth a design research program is a design activity, much like how a specific design is continuously designed through its use.

Whether we focus on a specific design or on a whole design research program, these articulations help us see design possibilities. As designers and users, we can borrow, interpret, steal, and transform ideas from either specific designs or from whole design programs to make them part of our own design/use repertory.

What we are looking to capture in the sections that follow are some of the core ideas of these designs or design research programs based on how they have been presented in the literature so far. Some of those core ideas may have the potency to cut across particular use situations and perhaps even application domains so that we can reuse them repeatedly. Others will be unique—interesting in themselves—and thereby relevant to know of as they form part of our canon, creating reference points in the design space, even if we might not want to replicate them. Depending on how the design knowledge is framed, it will have different potency. A design research program might bring forth a design method, for example, which helps to direct the orchestration of a design process. It can be an exploration of the essential aesthetic properties of a material; it can also prompt several strong concepts, describing the behavior spurred by certain design elements in the design; or it can produce some design experiments (in the *basic research* sense of an experiment) that will be inspirational, even when they are not fully fledged products (Buchanan 1992).

It is important to note, though, that simply applying a method or introducing a strong concept will not guarantee success. There always must be a designerly exploration, a team of trained designers, to interpret and make sense of ideas vis-à-vis the design setting at hand.

Soma Experiences

The three criteria we have discussed so far can be applied to any interaction design theory. Our fourth criterion, therefore, addresses the specifics of a *soma* design theory—capturing or engaging with the unique aesthetics of somatic engagement in interaction.

As discussed by Bardzell and Bardzell (2015), the humanities have a long history of engaging with aesthetics of cultural artifacts. For instance, when critiquing a piece of music, the listener can draw on a whole history of concepts and ideas, together forming aesthetic theory. Humanities scholars look not to capture the experience in the one and only possible way, but to contribute their interpretation, their assessment, filtered through their own experiences, engaging with the art piece or designed object over and over again. Ultimately, soma design will have to start forming its own language, perhaps initially borrowing from other art forms, but ultimately aiming to provide rich, thick, evocative, interpretative descriptions of the aesthetics of soma-based design.

But as Redström pointed out, the concept of aesthetics can be used in many ways—not only in the context of a humanistic tradition. Designers may want to engage with aesthetics more as a verb—as something achieved in the design process. Aesthetics in this sense will not be a property of the design or an interpretation against the backdrop of the humanistic tradition, but an active, somatic engagement (by both designers and users).[3]

Following Shusterman's definition of somaesthetics, a soma design theory must be a project of improved sensory appreciation through a lived, sentient, purposive body. Because the aim of this book is to engage interaction designers in the exploration of soma design, we are going to focus on creative, form-giving engagements with digital (and other) materials.

As interaction designers, our goals are to transform, alter, and sometimes improve somatic experiences through orchestrated engagements with designs.

To achieve this, we must never forget that our digital and technological materials are only half of our design material: the other half consists of our own somas and those of our users. Our materials are, in fact, sociodigital. In a soma design process, we engage with and improve on the aesthetics of our own somas: our bodies, our subjective experiences, feelings, values, meaning-making, and movement-based engagements. Only when we improve on our appreciation skills can we create novel somaesthetic experiences facilitated or scaffolded by our designs. Ultimately, our aim must be to enlist our imagined users in the somaesthetic project, engaging with their appreciation skills.

As designers, we are not only examining the aesthetic potential of the materials and improving on our own somas, we also put these together into whole interactions. We orchestrate whole experiences. Our somaesthetic design theory therefore needs to speak of how somaesthetics will shape the dynamic gestalt, the orchestrated interaction, arising between user and system as the interaction unfolds.

In my view, soma design is a holistic approach to aesthetics in design. It is a way to examine and improve on all connections between sensation, feeling, emotion, and subjective understanding and values (Khut 2006). Somaesthetics engages with bodily rhythms, touch, proprioception, and bodily playfulness, but also with our values, meaning-making processes, emotions, and ways of engaging with the world. It is individual, as well as social. It deals with self-care, as well as empathy with others. It has to do with movements and bodies, but addresses the whole self, body and mind, as one. In that sense, to me, soma design is relevant to any design process engaging with aesthetics.

In summary, our soma design theory must speak of the aesthetic potential of the sociodigital materials and the creative process of shaping these into dynamic gestalts, orchestrated experiences. Aesthetic interaction experiences are achieved in the meeting between user/designer and design; they are not properties of the interactive design as such. They cannot be isolated and injected as an add-on to a design.

Fulfilling the Four Criteria: The Homo Explorens Example

Descriptions of soma design knowledge contributions fulfilling the four criteria can be found in my six first-person accounts in chapter 3, as well as in the work by me and my colleagues on Soma Mat, Breathing Light, and

Sarka, discussed in chapter 4. Ahead, I take one of those encounters—the Mediated Body and Touchbox by Mads Hobye—and show how it exemplifies the four criteria.

First, note how Mediated Body, Touchbox, and Hobye's other designs presented constitute facts in our soma design theory. They embody the somaesthetic engagement Hobye and his colleagues wanted to scaffold.

In his academic account of these designs, Hobye provides a conceptualization of what unites all his designs in the form of what he names the *Homo Explorens manifesto* (Hobye 2014). According to Hobye, Homo Explorens "extends the Homo Ludens view of humans as playful creatures with the perspective of exploratory interaction" (ibid.). Hobye builds art installations that encourage users to explore and play together in gentle, poetic manners, without a strong orchestration of the experience but instead aiming for users to create their own stories and explorations together. An artist's manifesto is a declaration that ties together the artist's project by declaring the values and aesthetics that drove it. It is also an invitation to join in the exploration of those values. In that sense, the Homo Explorens manifesto invites designers and artists to join, to engage with these values and politics.

To explain what it means to create somaesthetic Homo Explorens engagements, Hobye points to a tension between poetic social play and overly strong narratives, the latter of which are meant to be consumed rather than invite exploration. Hobye aims for the former, a particular somaesthetic experience: an open-ended, playful, bodily, social engagement that goes beyond examining what the system does and instead invites prolonged social play. He aims for tender, poetic experiences, using designs to lower the barriers for touching others and engaging in social play. The open-ended, poetic, gentle, and subtle interaction space did not provide a fixed narrative, but a space where participants can express their own stories. Participants who enter this space have to engage personally, with some risk, breaking taboos of touch or intimacy with others. Löwgren and I discussed the elements of this interaction that made it evocative and seductive:

> The touch-sensing technique used was intentionally designed to require bare-skin contact between Performer and Participant. Moreover, the way Mediated Body is "played" by the Performer is that a stranger is approached and invited to explore the experience. These two elements in combination lead to a situation where the boundaries of social norms are transgressed and the Performer and Participant enter a zone of "social play," performing actions in public view that would normally constitute unacceptable behavior for a first encounter between

strangers (akin to the oft-cited concept of the magic circle in games [Huizinga (1944) 2003)]. In other words, the Mediated Body and the way it is framed performatively makes it possible for two strangers in a public place to stand within personal and even intimate space (Hall 1966), touch and stroke each other's bare skin and maintain prolonged eye contact—all the while being engaged in exploring a haptic soundscape that they share but that the bystanders cannot hear. (Höök and Löwgren 2012, 23:14)

In Hobye's (2014) thesis on this topic, he presents a range of successful art installations that (often) engage participants in this poetic play. He also lists some installations that failed in the sense of successfully addressing this particular somaesthetic engagement (even if they might have been fun and engaging in other ways). That is, he probes the limits of the design program, showing what falls inside and what falls outside.

His accounts of the designs include descriptions of the settings in which they were deployed. He provides accounts of people engaging with the designs—showing us how the interactions unfold. Including the successful as well as the failed designs shows how the sociodigital materials, as well as the context, must come together into whole orchestrated experiences in order to achieve social, poetic play. Taken altogether, this defines the particular somaesthetic experience he aimed for: the Homo Explorens experience.

In summary, Hobye's Homo Explorens designs fulfill the four criteria defined earlier: they are expressed in sociodigital materials, engage participants in interactions unfolding over time, change with how they are used (being perpetually designed), and engage participants in (particular forms of) soma experiences.

Forms of Articulations in a Soma Design Research Program

With the four criteria in mind, our soma design theory may consist of many different forms of articulations. A manifesto such as Homo Explorens is one way of articulating and pinpointing a specific soma experience; the specific designs are another. Each articulation captures different aspects of the design knowledge. Soma design knowledge can be in the form of

- prototypical design exemplars (facts), experienced first-hand or described through first-person (autoethnographical or phenomenological) accounts of use (as in chapters 3 and 4);
- tactics/methods for shaping soma designs (as in chapter 4 and upcoming in chapters 6 and 7); or

- conceptualizations proposed by soma design researchers when trying to draw our attention to different aspects of their designs—such as strong concepts, experiential qualities, manifestos, or annotated portfolios.

Adding to the prototypical design exemplars in chapters 3 and 4, let us now turn to some of the conceptualizations of various soma design experiences put forth in our field. The conceptualizations will be explained through brief accounts of artifacts that embody the concept.

I divide the conceptualizations into two sets: first, we discuss some of the bodily processes that technology can tap into or support: biofeedback loops, affective loops, social play, somaesthetic touch, kinaesthetic mimicry, and somaesthetic appreciation (from chapter 4). These conceptualizations are generative strong concepts or manifestos, bridging technology and bodily processes to create for the dynamic gestalt.

Second, we can also imagine somaesthetic resemblances between a whole range of design exemplars relating to the aesthetic "feel" they engage—that is, their experiential quality (Ståhl, Löwgren, and Höök 2014). We will discuss some somaesthetic qualities such as suppleness, evocative balance (for lifestyle applications), and machine aesthetics.

Strong Concepts

Biofeedback Loops In the encounter with the BrightHeart app, we learned about one of George Khut's biofeedback artworks—but this is just one of the many different art projects he has engaged in during the last twelve years.

Khut describes his biofeedback artworks and mobile apps as "engaging in audio-visual interfaces for exploring psycho-physiological self-efficacy" (Höök, Jonsson, Ståhl, Tholander, et al. 2016). These heart-rate- and brainwave-controlled artworks borrow from clinical biofeedback methods in medicine, in which electronic monitoring of moment-to-moment changes in a subject's physiology are fed back to the user so that he or she can begin to sense and eventually influence the behavior observed. Khut's works frame the biofeedback loop as an intensely aesthetic process of learning by doing and sensing, in which agency and self-efficacy emerge through processes of feeling into and feeling through the biofeedback sound and light displays.

George Khut brings a particular aesthetic to the table, an aesthetic sensibility grounded in his particular artistic expression, but aspects of the same experiences can be seen in other design work. For example, my group worked with a design we named *Affective Health* (Sanches et al. 2010). In short, based on biosensor data such as arousal, determined from galvanic skin response and pulse, and on movements, based on accelerometer data, the system mirrors this data back to you in real time on your mobile device. Like in the BrightHearts app, you can see bodily responses in real time and learn to regulate your responses. You can also see patterns of data and engage step-by-step learning to determine how different contexts and social encounters trigger these responses. Our work was influenced by Khut's.

Designing with biofeedback loops is therefore a somaesthetic strong concept that has a generative potency. We can imagine many different settings—individual uses, as well as social settings—in which a biofeedback loop can be an interesting aesthetic to engage with.

Affective Loops In my own work, together with Petra Sundström and Anna Ståhl, we worked on a concept similar to biofeedback loops, which we named *affective loops* (Höök 2008; Sundström 2005). Here, the system not only mirrors users' biorhythms but also possesses some agency of its own, persuading or engaging users to partake in emotional-bodily processes induced by the system. As described by Petra Sundström (2010, 10): "To allow for Affective Loop experiences with or through a computer system, the user need to be allowed to express herself in rich personal ways involving our many ways of expressing and sensing emotions—muscles tensions, facial expressions and more. For the user to become further engaged in interaction, the computer system needs the capability to return relevant, either diminishing, enforcing or disruptive feedback to those emotions expressed by the user so that the she wants to continue express herself by either strengthening, changing or keeping her expression."

The idea for affective loops originally came from performing a user study with an interactive, sensor-enabled doll named *SenToy*, built by Ana Paiva's group in collaboration with my own research group (Andersson et al. 2002; Höök et al. 2003; Paiva et al. 2002. SenToy was a tangible doll that fit nicely in your lap, with sensors inside its body to allow users to perform different gestures with it. The gestures influenced the emotions and actions of the user's avatar in a game. The effort of performing the gestures and their shapes mirror the typical experience associated with six different emotional processes: happiness, sadness, anger, surprise, gloating, and fear. For example, the movement for expressing anger is energetically shaking the doll back and forth. The experience of performing this gesture resembles the inner experience of anger. In fact, when you perform the angry gesture as part of playing the game, you sometimes become completely immersed, through the gesture, to such an extent that you feel the anger. (Obviously, you know that you are playing a game and that you are not angry for real, but you feel very much as if you are your avatar.)

But what caught our interest when performing a user study of SenToy was more than how different gestures created immersive experiences. We also found that users were influenced by the gestures the avatar in turn performed on the screen. The avatar would, for example, express happiness after successfully attacking an opponent in the game, waving its arms in a gloating gesture. This was sometimes imitated by our users, who waved their arms in the air in response, almost as though greeting their avatars or acknowledging their identification with them.

The interaction between how the user gestured with the doll, how the avatar portrayed the user's input and subsequently responded to the next action in the game, and users' imitation of the avatar behavior, going back and forth between user and avatar, became a strong, immersive, interactive loop. It (sometimes) lets the user transform into a single unit with his or her avatar and its emotion processes.

Affective loops are a somaesthetic strong concept, alongside biofeedback loops. As such, it has generative potency. We can imagine many different settings—individual and social settings, and games as well as other design contexts—in which it makes sense to think of interactions as affective loops.

Somaesthetic Touch   In one of Canadian media artist and scholar Thecla Schiphorst's (2009a) explorations, she similarly engages with touch—but not through touching the bare skin of another person, but instead touching interactive materials, spurring evocative experiences. Her idea is to build interactions that help us cultivate our own appreciation of touch. She bases her exploration on Gibson (1966), who described active touch as "the detection of the impression made on a perceiver while he is primarily engaged in detecting the world." Touch is associated with intimacy and empathy. We know that grooming elicits positive hormonal reactions, releasing oxytocin into our blood streams, a hormone that calms us down and enables trust.

To explore touch in design, Schiphorst built a set of interactive sculptures she named *soft(n)*. The ten soft sculptures use sensors to pick up on how users touch, hug, and manipulate them. They respond with different vibrations, lights, and sounds depending on how they are touched. When thrown in the air, they make childlike "wee" sounds. When "sleeping" as a result of not being touched for a while, they emit wheezing sounds. The ten objects are wirelessly connected to one another, allowing both light and sound to travel, like patterns, through all ten objects. They will be "sighing, humming, shaking-shivering, and a shared 'glow-on': moving light patterns that communicate the interrelationship of the group" (Schiphorst 2009a, 234).

Soft(n) is a design example of Schiphorst's four aims for somaesthetic touch:

> 1) Experience, which frames questions of cultivating embodiment, sensory perception and links to techniques of somatics; 2) Poetics of Interaction including meaning-making and open interpretation, which explores perception and cross-modal relationships between touch and other sensory expression; 3) Materiality, which emphasizes the importance of the physical body as well as the physical material, texture, shape, and form that support experience within the installation; and 4) Semantics of Caress, investigating the meaning of touch as applied to tactile interaction (how can models of meaning be applied to a computational model for interaction). (2009a, 229)

These four aims clearly connect to the soma ideals we have been discussing so far. Their focus on experience as a route to better appreciation skills follows Shusterman's ideas of cultivating our aesthetic perceptions. The poetics of interaction follow the ideas of sensual engagement, not overwhelming us with stimuli, but also allude to Aristotle's poetics: the orchestration of an experience. Schiphorst refers to materiality as a moldable combination of bodily sociodigital materials. Finally, more specifically addressing touch, she speaks of the meaning-making processes concerning touch and how to model those in our computer systems.

There are many overlaps between somaesthetic touch as Schiphorst engages in it and the Homo Explorens manifesto by Hobye. But Hobye is looking for poetic social play, whereas Schiphorst is more generally engaging with touch as a moldable aesthetic appreciation process that you can improve on.

Kinaesthetic Mimicry   The most advanced genre of movement-based digital interaction is games. From an analysis of a wide range of movement-based games, Isbister and DiMauro (2011) found that kinaesthetic mimicry helps explain what works and what doesn't.

By *kinaesthetic mimicry*, they mean imitating movements from the real world—but with an alternative meaning. For example, the game control could be used to mimic a steering wheel to drive through the game world, or it could be held in front of a player's nose to simulate an elephant trunk. Through mimicry, players quickly grasp how to manipulate game controls.

Isbister and DiMauro could discern which movements evoked more engagement and generated more fun for the players. For instance, they found that full-body movements made games more fun for players. Moving our whole bodies feeds back into our experience (as discussed for affective loops). But what is interesting in Isbister and DiMauro's work is their analysis of exactly which full-body movements are engaging. By using a Laban movement analysis (turn to chapter 6 for a longer explanation of this framework), they show that mimicry movements designed to achieve an emotional experience are much more engaging:

> In our experience, performing the Boogie Superstar movements (such as swinging both arms in front of the body, back and forth, to a tight rhythmic metronome), felt mechanical and constrained, whereas the dancing in the other two games felt more silly and joyful. We believe the Laban Effort dimensions help illuminate why this was so. Dancing while playing Boogie Superstar does require performance of movements that could be part of real-life dance, but the tight tempo constraints and repetition do not feel like real improvisational, casual dancing, and don't seem to generate the same buoyant state in the player. Thus it may be important for designers who are aiming for kinaesthetic realism to have particular physical and emotional end states in mind to aim for, which are derived from certain qualities of the movements they are trying to imitate with the movement mechanics. (Isbister and DiMauro 2011, 70)

Kinaesthetic mimicry is therefore a helpful tool in innovating movement design, but it needs to be crafted carefully to correspond with the emotional experiences those movements spur.

Isbister and her group have designed several games that capture kinaesthetic mimicry in different ways (Márquez Segura and Isbister 2015). One of them, Yamove, is played as follows: "The game is played by two teams of two dancers. Each dancer puts an iPod touch device on her wrist, using a special holster. ... During a round, a dance pair performs moves that they improvised together. They can do anything so long as they do it in synch. ... They are scored on synchrony, as well as on how much they move (intensity) and on whether they mix their moves so they are not doing the same thing all the time (creativity)" (ibid., 215). Here, the kinaesthetic mimicry happens between the two players.

Bodily mimicry between people is contagious (Hatfield, Cacioppo, and Rapson 1993). As discussed in chapter 2, Alan Kay mentioned that he was inspired by kinaesthetic mimicry when designing the desktop. He noted that if you suppress or distract your language-oriented thinking, you can learn movements extremely quickly based on imitation. Once the bodily moves are learned, you can start engaging in other processes. For example, you can speak, reason, or even meditate while bicycling, even though bicycling is quite a complex and demanding task.

Mimicry is also contagious in that it spurs emotional processes. Standing in a crowd, dancing, cheering, and praying can all be strong emotional processes. Yamove is not the only game that has picked up on this. For example, in Ghost in the Cave (Rinman et al. 2004), depending on how a crowd behaves (as picked up by a motion-sensitive camera), a shark displayed on a large screen in front of the audience will swim toward a cave in which a ghost can be captured. If the crowd moves vigorously, the shark swims faster, and so on.

Concepts like biofeedback loops, affective loops, and kinaesthetic mimicry overlap—but this should not be seen as a flaw. Instead, they are different lenses, highlighting different aspects of a design. Each engages the body differently, involving, respectively, the parasympathetic nervous system, affect and emotion, or full-body movement. Each engages users in its own manner, providing users with more or less control, emphasizing individual or social use—but they can also be combined. If we analyze, for example, SenToy or Hobye's festival installations, they have both mimicry and affective loop elements.

Experiential Qualities

Although strong concepts are defined by the idea of generativity (their ability to help generate ideas in a given design situation), experiential qualities are slightly different. An experiential quality is a feeling arising in the interaction between user and system. It is harder to take a given experiential quality and generate a bunch of ideas. Instead, you must craft the interaction step-by-step to know if you have achieved the feeling you wanted to craft.

When put together in just the right way, the tools and approaches discussed earlier can work together to create specific experiential qualities. In the following sections, I describe three qualities that have been proposed as successful soma experience designs, but these are only a few examples in an almost infinite space of potential somaesthetic experiences. In particular, machine aesthetics illustrates what we might do if we want to be inspired by a particular art style.

Suppleness Suppleness has been proposed as an experiential quality (Isbister and Höök 2009). When I worked with Katherine Isbister, we noted how some designs we had been involved with, separately or together, had a similar feel to them. We discussed all the failures we had experienced on the way toward designs that worked. It was clear to us that even very small design decisions could easily break the particular smoothness we were after. We named this quality *suppleness* and framed it as follows:

> *Subtle Social Signals:* Rich human communication and interpretation strategies (e.g., emotion, social ritual, nonverbal communication, kinaesthetic engagement). Supple interfaces are working beyond the cognitive/rational level of the standard GUI interface, both because of the use contexts they operate in (potentially emotionally charged, social and leisure situations), and because of the input modalities they may make use of (such as gesture, facial expression, biosensor data). A supple interface is one that enables and possibly enhances these subtle social signals. In a sense, a supple system is doing a sort of social/emotional "dance" with the end user.
>
> *Emergent Dynamics:* Taking into consideration subtle communication dynamics that require new thinking about system adaptability and feedback. For example, increased legibility of system moves to help users actively co-construct practice and meaning and push system boundaries in interesting ways. A supple system fits smoothly and gracefully into my social and situational context as I interact.
>
> *Moment-to-Moment Experience:* Privileging the quality of moment-to-moment experience both in terms of design and in terms of evaluation of success of design (e.g. a focus on engagement, pleasure, rapport). This requires flexibility in establishing the exchange between user and system. (Isbister and Höök 2009)

The SenToy doll described earlier had this kind of smooth feel to it——or at least, it had that feel until we changed it. Because the sensors and wires inside SenToy were easily destroyed by the more vigorous shaking of the doll, we decided to put a skeleton inside the doll to keep all the sensors in place. The skeleton was hard and heavy, which in turn required rigid, hard movements. It removed the floppy feeling of the doll. The emotional "dance" experience was broken as the motions lost their suppleness. Users no longer felt at one with the doll.

As a somaesthetic experiential quality, suppleness might be hard to understand without a first-hand, tacit experience—but you immediately know it when you experience it in an interaction. The quality therefore serves an evaluative role in your design project. If you know that it is this emotional/social dance you strive for, then you will be able to make choices among different design alternatives.

Suppleness is not the only somaesthetic experiential quality, nor is it required for every sort of soma-based interactive experience. It is one in a repertory of experiences we might want to engage in. Let us move on to describe yet another such experiential quality: evocative balance.

Evocative Balance   Sometimes when interacting with a design, the experience feels familiar to us. It touches on soma experiences that we somehow recognize, even if the setting is novel. For example, in certain Feldenkrais exercises, like when rolling like a baby (as described in chapter 2), the feeling is familiar to you; your body remembers it. But it is also different because you are doing it with an adult body, in an unfamiliar setting, performing the movement extremely slowly, rediscovering parts of your movements you might have forgotten, and thereby altering your ways of being in the world.

When we design for emotional engagement, we can draw upon such familiar experiences that touch on movement and emotion in an integrated manner. In my lab, we were designing several different life-logging systems, which gathered and displayed many forms of data regarding the user's habits. We found that we had to be very careful with the way the data was provided, intentionally designing this sense of familiarity with the past movement-emotion-experiences. We had to portray data collected about the user in a form that serves as a reminder, a way to transport yourself back to the situation in which that data was generated.

Anna Ståhl, Jonas Löwgren, and I framed this emotional, movement-based familiarity in design as follows: "Affective interaction has the experiential quality of evocative balance if the user finds the data to be familiar, recollecting lived experience, and at the same time suggestive and open for fruitful interpretation. Drawing on the dual meaning of the word 'to evoke,' evocative balance is experienced when the design evokes the past and evokes the new in a dynamic interplay" (Ståhl, Löwgren, and Höök 2014, 47). Apart from feeling familiar and recognizable to us, we emphasize that the interaction also needs to be abstract or ambiguous enough that we can layer novel interpretations and experiences on top of it.

Evocative balance allows designs to encourage user memories, without having to adhere to some objective truth about the past, but instead allowing users to create their own past (as discussed in chapter 4). A photo from the past might sometimes be too crude, too closed in its interpretation, and not allow us to remember the feeling of the time or to put a new interpretation on top of it. The balancing act lies in becoming not too photorealistic, but also not too abstract.

As we shall discuss in chapter 6, touching on a sense of familiarity in the somaesthetic experience is one path to design. Another is to defamiliarize, make the movement strange, in order to juxtaposition it against our habitual, everyday experiences. As design tactics, both paths are interesting and may lead to a design that has this evocative balance somaesthetic experiential quality.

Machine Aesthetics   In the *Metaphone* project presented in chapter 3, an art style called *machine aesthetics* guided the design process. As discussed by Gross, Bardzell, and Bardzell (2013), an art style is a holistic or gestalt phenomenon that permeates the whole interaction. Art projects in a particular style will resemble one another: they will be characteristic of an "author, period, place or school" (ibid.). Typically, these art styles are not articulated or discussed until years after they have been formed and often are not considered a particular style at the time. Gross and colleagues proposed that art styles could be used to understand and analyze styles in interaction design. As they point out, "Style is an important tool for understanding and communicating the creative design processes that generate experience-focused tangible interactions" (Gross, Bardzell, and Bardzell 2013, 281). Although they focus mainly on how an art or interaction design critic can use a particular style as a lens when analyzing products, we are more interested here in how we can draw upon art styles in our creative design processes.

The *Metaphone* project drew upon an art style from the beginning of the last century. When industrialism swept through Western society, artists and craftspeople started questioning their roles and the authenticity of their own work. Machines could mass-produce products; perhaps machines could also produce art? A whole range of machines were built that generated art. After a while, a style crystallized. Machine aesthetics can be described as exposing the inner aesthetics of technology—its mechanics or algorithms—by turning the machine inside out. That is, no casings or other means of hiding the technological details of the built system are used. Exposing functions and operational properties of the design become core values of machine aesthetics. In a sense, it is an antistyle: the raw machine is exposed without any beautiful casing or other finishing layers. But of course, this becomes a style in itself.

The *Metaphone* is not a replica of the earlier art machines, but it presents a new take on machine aesthetics in that the machine feeds off user data. To achieve the machine aesthetics feel, the *Metaphone* did not have a casing, the soundscape was generated from the same data as the drawing, cords were sticking out, the whole machine was shown inside out. The only part that was perhaps not openly shown was the execution of the code. Otherwise, all the workings of the machine were openly shared; nothing was hidden from view.

As described in my encounter with the *Metaphone*, the machine aesthetics lead to a slightly creepy, unsettling experience. The *Metaphone* machine conveyed a somatics of its own—a machine-like way of being in the world, foreign to my human ways. As it fed off my biodata, it had resemblances to the biofeedback or affective loops described earlier, but it was acting more on its own, doing its own thing, being a machine acting in its own machine-like ways, creating its art. But like the other encounters, it engaged with bodily rhythms and movements. The materials of the interaction came together in a strange, bewildering, evocative somaesthetic experience.

Cocreation and Generative Power?

We now have some conceptualizations that reside on the intermediary level of knowledge: Homo Explorens, biofeedback loops, affective loops, social play, somaesthetic touch, kinaesthetic mimicry, somaesthetic appreciation (from chapter 4), suppleness, evocative balance, and machine aesthetics. From chapter 3, we also learned of pliability and the extended lived body. These concepts allow us to distinguish between different soma designs and engage in a more informed discussion.

Another way we can communicate tacit knowledge is through design methods—which we will turn to in chapter 6. But before we do so, let me briefly comment first, on the role of the user versus the designer, and second, on how to understand the potency of a somaesthetic design theory.

User or Soma Cocreator?

What does it mean to be a so-called user of a soma-based design? As argued by Shusterman, we can be sleepwalkers, shuffling through life without listening to our senses, without appreciating the qualities of our movements, without deepening our experiences. Or we can choose to train our senses to be more acutely aware of our surroundings, discerning the pleasures and displeasures, pains and potentials somatically. Does this mean that an untrained user might totally miss out on the experience and unique qualities of the soma design interactions? At some level, the soma qualities of course will be perceived, but as I have argued throughout, aesthetics is a process, a way of perceiving, of attending. Without that attention, much will be lost.

As many have argued before me, designers need to train their aesthetic sensibilities, engage in form-giving processes, gain tacit knowledge of the materials at hand, and thereby learn how to shape the aesthetics of the interaction gestalt (Lim et al. 2007). Likewise, we might argue that users, too, must bring their aesthetic sensibilities, their training and understanding, into the cocreation of the interaction gestalt during use. The interactive system may encourage and scaffold their experiences, but ultimately the interaction gestalt depends on users' somaesthetic appreciation abilities and attitudes.

To avoid confusion, I will continue to use the word *user* throughout the text, but I would have preferred to use *participant* or *soma cocreator*, or even *designer*, which are all closer to what is required of the user. This active stance is important: it rules out a naïve understanding of bodily experiences as landing on our senses as stimuli, immediately generating particular responses, without any prior training, experience, or tacit knowledge.

Potency of the Soma Design Program

All the conceptualizations (strong concepts as well as experiential qualities) discussed thus far speak both of the system and of user behavior and the interaction that may arise between them. They all attempt to capture a specific dynamic gestalt, a specific interaction experience that unfolds over time. In some cases, they seem to have the potency to move across design situations and even design domains—as when, for example, Khut moves his biofeedback loop systems from an art setting into medical care settings with children (Khut, Morrow, and Watanbe 2011). But even if the conceptualizations share certain properties, they are not interchangeable. They emphasize different somaesthetic experiences, different possible interactions.

The conceptualizations introduced herein vary, for example, in how much agency they place in the interactive system, ranging from mirroring user behavior to actively nudging, influencing, persuading, or even taking control over the interaction. This in turn puts different requirements on the (digital) materials, modalities, and interaction techniques that may be used to achieve a particular dynamic gestalt.

In social situations, these designs seem to succeed when they thrive on the empathic feel we have for others and how easily we align our expressions with others when present in the moment (Mentis, Laaksolahti, and Höök 2014). *Coexperiencing* (Forlizzi and Battarbee 2004), acting together, pulls the participants into the experience, unfolding together with the system. The system can serve an excuse to engage in intimate interactions (as in the bare skin interaction of the Mediated Body or Schiphorst's soft(n) system, exemplifying the somaesthetics of touch) or as a trigger of joint synchronized behavior (as in Ghost in the Cave).

Outside the social realms, in individual use in which the system mirrors somatic processes, engagements vary from those that help users to turn inward, directing their senses away from the surroundings (as in biofeedback loops), to those that spur strong bodily engagement spreading over the assemblage of subject and interactive design (as in the affective loop examples). An interesting development here is found in those interactions that are slightly scary, as in the machine aesthetics experience of the *Metaphone* (Šimbelis et al. 2014) or the concept of "uncomfortable interactions" (Benford et al. 2012). Both rely on the sense of the computer/machine being foreign to us, pulling us into its somatics, its inner workings, rather than probing our own somatic experiences.

Most of all, the emphasis on poetics, subtleness, careful design, and honing your somaesthetic skills (for designers as well as users) runs like a thread through all somaesthetic design work. In chapters 6 and 7, we will discuss some of the tactics—the how-tos—that may be useful in obtaining somaesthetic tacit knowledge.

III How

6 Training Somaesthetic Skills

In chapter 5, I offered some building blocks for a theory of soma design. I suggested four criteria that characterize soma designs: (1) sociodigital material, (2) interactivity, (3) a perpetual state of being designed (because these designs are changed by their interactions with users), and (4) the production of somaesthetic experiences. I suggested that soma designers will draw on strong concepts, including biofeedback loops, somaesthetic touch, and kinaesthetic mimicry, to produce characteristic somaesthetic experiences or feelings, particularly a sense of suppleness, evocative balance, or a certain machine aesthetics. In short, chapter 5 gave us the beginnings of a vocabulary that will be useful to designers trying to capture, discuss, or develop their soma designs.

But in soma design, because we are designing for the gestalt of body and mind, we need another kind of vocabulary as well: a felt experience of somaesthetics. In other words, learning about your own soma is a prerequisite to designing with it. Some people, such as dancers, athletes, yoga practitioners, or others, have spent years developing a sense of body awareness that is useful in soma design. However, you do not have to be an expert to practice soma design. We are all beginners when we enter into some design arena—and as Thecla Schiphorst says, "our bodies are generous with tips"[1] if we just listen to them. In this chapter, I discuss five techniques for training your somaesthetic appreciation skills: focusing on change and interest, disrupting the habitual, Laban movement analysis, autoethnographies, and engaging with other somaesthetic connoisseurs.

Change and Interest

When I described Soma Mat, Breathing Light, and Sarka, I observed that directing and maintaining your attention on some specific experience can be difficult. We discussed two different cognitive processes that Shusterman

(2008) has developed from William James (1905) to make it easier to direct and maintain focus: change and interest. By *change*, Shusterman refers to the importance of subdividing bodily experiences into more specific areas or functions and then engaging in activities that shift focus from one area to another and back to provide a more nuanced and rich perception of fine-grained movements. The notion of *interest*, on the other hand, deals with finding means to achieve sustained attention toward a specific body part.

Shusterman has devised a set of six tactics to help guide this process, relying in part on Feldenkrais technique. As mentioned in chapter 2, a typical Feldenkrais lesson consists of probing questions offered by the instructor. You are not supposed to answer them, but rather use them to guide your attention to different parts of your body and bodily processes. In a typical lesson you will engage in very slow movements, such as breathing slowly all the way down into your legs or slowly rolling your whole body from one side to the other. When you engage in those movements, you are again asked to probe your experiences, through questions such as, "Can you feel movements in your legs as you breathe?"

Lee, Lim, and Shusterman (2014) have applied these six tactics to design. To provide heightened attention to and interest in the body, they suggest the following:

1) *Questions:* Asking questions about different aspects and relations of what we perceive.
2) *Division into parts:* Subdividing the body and directing our attention to each part, one by one.
3) *Contrasts of feeling:* Discriminating the different feelings in one part of the body from those in another.
4) *Associative interests:* Making the noticing of what we are trying more precisely to feel key to something we care about.
5) *Avoiding distracting interests:* Warding off competing interests to what we are trying to attend to and feel.
6) *Pre-perception:* Preparing our attention to notice what we are trying to discriminate in what we feel (ibid., 1056)

This process relies a lot on shutting out the outside world, warding off possible distractions—for example, through closing your eyes, lying down on the floor, and making sure everything is quiet around you. The aim is to listen intently to only some of the activities and movements in your body, rather than overwhelming yourself with stimuli and interactions. This is a demanding activity, so in most situations, you can only expect to engage for half an hour to an hour. It is also exhausting. It consumes your energy and capacity to focus, which means that you need to plan for a slow awakening after one of these exercises. Prepare for a slowness in coming "back" to the world, interacting with others, and in starting to work on your design thinking.

The questions posed help you direct your attention and interest so that when being asked to feel, for example, your own breathing, you attempt to focus entirely on that process alone. By contrasting different parts of your body, you can start discerning small differences; this is what Shusterman refers to as *change*. Sometimes you will notice, perhaps, how your left-hand side is different from your right-hand side—for example, how your left lung is smaller than your right lung. But you can also start noticing how different body parts are connected. When slowly moving your left shoulder toward your right hip, you start feeling how your inner organs are connected to this movement, how the fascia of your body connects your neck, your spine, your hips, your legs, and how movements across your middle line create symmetries and asymmetries. This connection awakens interest in aspects of your own body you may never have noticed.

The process provides for precise experiences, pinpointing particular movements, muscles, body parts, and how they connect. In my experience, it is also a process of discovery, joy, and aesthetic appreciation. We rarely attend to our movements this carefully. In fact, there are many movements we hardly ever perform because we are stuck in certain habitual motions. To me, the experience is fascinating, playful, and often feels like entering a whole different place outside my everyday experiences.

These exercises create empathy with yourself, in the sense of an intimate, profound, emotional experience of your own soma, your pains, your joys, your sense of being alive, breathing, living. This is not purely an internal, self-absorbed process, however. As I mentioned in chapter 5, this empathy with yourself translates into empathy with others, too; in many ways, focusing on your own soma is a preparation for intersubjectivity.

This focus on change and interest also cultivates honesty of a particular kind. Although language is good for making quick assessments and for generating and expressing ideas in rapid succession, it is not always anchored in the realities of our somatics. We can speak of experiences we have not had, we can lie, and we can talk past each other. But if we engage in the same movements, in the same room, together, then the connection to our somatic experience becomes readily available to us. Given these precise, discernable experiences, pinpointing certain feelings, cultivating empathy and honesty, it becomes easier to share and discuss such experiences in the design team, articulating concepts and ideas.

There are also empathy exercises that we can engage in. Professor Shusterman introduced an exercise involving breathing together in one of our workshops. As we laid down on the floor, he gently put one hand on my ribcage (see figure 6.1). Through his arm, he could feel my breathing. I could also feel his breathing through the movements of his hand on my ribcage.

Not everyone will have the same experience. In fact, sharing experiences like this also helps remind us how our experiences and bodies differ.

Disrupting the Habitual: Estrangement

Another method frequently mentioned by experts in soma-based design is to slow down or *disrupt* a habitual movement to be able to discern small changes, to note how the movements relate to your emotional experiences, to enjoy or feel pain, to be engaged (Bell, Blythe, and Sengers 2005; Schiphorst 2007; Wilde, Vallgårda, and Tomico 2017). Defamiliarizing habitual movement patterns is a core principle in many somatic practices, based on the rationale that only by bringing to the surface what has become

Figure 6.1
Professor Shusterman and I breathing together

automatic and tacit can we change deeply ingrained, habitual patterns of movement. Often this is achieved by providing constraints to the habitual pathways in a movement pattern, but it can also be as simple as interlacing your fingers in a nonhabitual way—putting the other thumb on top, for example. Let us engage with this situation for a moment:

> Sit back and interlace your fingers, then try doing it the non-habitual way, putting the other thumb on top. Let yourself feel where your fingers are, how your fingers touch one another. Can you feel every finger? Can you feel the palms of your hands touching one another? Are your palms soft or hard? Do you feel any pain anywhere? Do you like your hands and fingers? Now imagine designing a system where empathy with someone else is core—can you bring anything from that feeling of your two hands touching into design?

In terms of movement-based interaction design, this awareness and playful approach to repatterning movement enables us to explore new kinds of meaningful movements in a structured way by drawing on techniques that have already been developed and refined in somatic and dance practices.

As another example, let us turn to an exercise from the Body Weather practice.[2] The Body Weather practice was invented in the 1980s in Japan by choreographer Tanaka and an international group of dancers (Hug 2016) and was introduced to the HCI community by Loke, Khut, and Kocaballi (2012). In one exercise, Loke devised a workshop on soma-based design: all participants were asked to stand in a line, shoulder to shoulder, with a thread passing through their mouths, joining the whole line from the first participant to the last. Participants were asked to close their eyes and walk together, very, very slowly, based on their connections through their shoulders and mouths, without losing contact with their neighbors (see figure 6.2). After the exercise, participants were asked to articulate their experience, sharing any insights into or discoveries about walking.

Walking is a movement most of us do every day. We get used to walking in a particular manner. By disrupting that experience for the workshop, forcing participants to question every part of that movement, Loke allowed participants to engage walking in a playful new way, to see it with fresh eyes, create a "body with altered perception." When my colleagues and I took part in this workshop and this exercise, we were reminded of differences in height, attitude, and movement, of all our different bodies. In the workshop, this created a sense of intersubjectivity and empathy.

In both the strategies introduced thus far—change and interest, and disrupting the habitual—the experience does not end with the exercise; putting the experiences into words completes them.

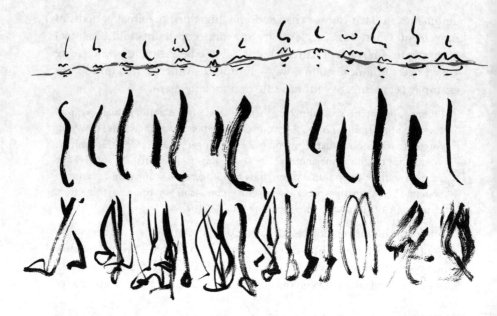

Figure 6.2
Standing shoulder to shoulder, walking slowly, with a thread through the mouth connecting all participants

In our work with Soma Mat, Breathing Light, and Sarka, for instance, we often started our joint design sessions by talking about what we were feeling, then did a bodywork lesson, such as Feldenkrais, and then returned to talking about what we felt after that lesson. Only after that could we dive into our design work. This allowed us gradually to share a vocabulary grounded in the joint experience of our bodywork exercises. Note that doing the same movement, in the same room, at the same time, does not mean that everyone has the same experience. In fact, I was surprised at how often we had entirely different experiences of the same lesson. But through sharing the experience and empathetically trying to understand what others had felt, we could approach a common language and develop intersubjectively constructed meanings (Schutz 1967) based on kinaesthetic empathy (Fogtmann, Grønbæk, and Ludvigsen 2011).

Laban Movement Analysis

Similar to how music has its notation system, Rudolf Laban developed a notation system for movement (Davies 2006). These notations not only capture the different shapes of movements but also provide a description of the experience involved in performing them. Laban movement analysis (LMA) has five different parts. Here I will focus only on one of them, *effort*, to simplify the description (to really grasp LMA, you need to study it carefully, maybe even taking a course at the Laban Institute).

In table 6.1, we list the four different motion factors of effort and their dimensions. These are then used to construct the notations in figure 6.3a. In figure 6.3b, we show the effort graph for inserting a light bulb (if the bulb is one of those that you screw into place). The movement is sustained (you must continue screwing the bulb in with an even movement), light (otherwise you would break the bulb), direct (it is aiming toward a particular place where the bulb needs to fit), and bound (as the movement has to be controlled and restrained). These dimensions give a good description of the effort needed to insert a light bulb.

LMA is valuable for how it explicitly bridges the first-person experiential with connection to the external environment and how we relate to others. LMA also includes somatic exploration of the body's developmental patterns, personal movement signatures, proxemics,[3] and cultural movement patterns that influence our own and larger group patterns of movement style.

In design work, LMA has been used to create computer models of a practice, which can then be used to understand what the experience of a movement is (Fagerberg, Ståhl, and Höök 2004; Françoise et al. 2014; Levisohn and Schiphorst 2011; Loke, Larssen, and Robertson 2005).

Autoethnography

Another, very different, way to understand the experience of movement is *autoethnography*, which allows the researcher to dive into the details of an experience he or she has had. Such accounts usually focus on the details associated with the experience, but they also let the author express his or her thoughts and feelings about what happened. The researcher also reflects on how the experience links to the cultural, social, and political context (see, e.g., Ellis, Adams, and Bochner 2011).

In the design field, autoethnography has been used to inspire design, as in my own study of my horseback riding experiences, discussing how those experiences could be translated into design (Höök 2010). The method I employed was inspired by ethnography. I took plenty of notes, I videotaped what was possible to videotape, but I also spent quite some time returning to the experience, reliving it, trying to note as much as I could of my

Table 6.1

The dimensions of effort according to Laban, as described by Zhao and Badler

Motion factor	Dimensions	Examples
Space: attention to the surroundings	**Indirect:** spiraling, deviating, flexible, wandering, multiple focus	Waving away bugs, surveying a crowd of people, scanning a room for misplaced keys
	Direct: straight, undeviating, channeled, single focus	Threading a needle, pointing to a particular spot, describing the exact outline of an object
Weight: attitude to the movement impact	**Light:** buoyant, weightless, easily overcoming gravity, marked by decreasing pressure	Dabbing paint on a canvas, pulling out a splinter, describing the movement of a feather
	Strong: powerful, forceful, vigorous, having an impact, increasing pressure into the movement	Punching, pushing a heavy object, wringing a towel, expressing a firmly held opinion
Time: lack or sense of urgency	**Sustained:** leisurely, lingering, indulging in time	Stretching to yawn, striking a pet
	Sudden: hurried, urgent, quick, fleeting	Swatting a fly, lunging to catch a ball, grabbing a child from the path of danger, making a snap move
Flow: amount of control and bodily tension	**Free:** uncontrolled, abandoned, unable to stop during the movement	Waving wildly, shaking off water, flinging a rock into a pond
	Bound: controlled, restrained, rigid	Moving in slow motion, tai chi, fighting back tears, carrying a cup of hot tea

Source: Zhao and Badler 2001

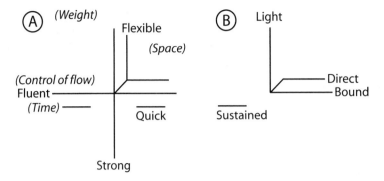

Figure 6.3a, b
(a) Laban's effort graph; (b) an example effort graph for inserting a light bulb

body posture, how each limb felt, my direction of gaze, my thoughts and feelings. The study was based on seven horseback riding lessons. The videotapes were made both by the riding instructor, Christian, and by cameras placed next to the paddock where the riding happened. The instructor also watched one of the videos and made comments on it that I used in the analysis. All of what was said in the videos was transcribed, and snippets of video were cut out and analyzed in detail. I wrote down detailed accounts of the riding experience after each of the seven lessons. These notes were juxtaposed with the written transcripts of the videos.

My study of myself horseback riding made me more sensitive to my own practice—more articulate, better able to discern some of what is going on between the two agents: myself and the horse. It helped me shape my practice, going back and forth between first-person immersion in the experience and third-person views of my own body.

But, as we shall come back to in the next chapter, it is not enough to learn more about the practice you are designing for. You also have to translate that experience to design. Design is rarely in a one-to-one relationship with the practice you study. In most cases, the aim is to change the existing practice, or to be inspired by the current practice to arrive at something entirely novel (Ljungblad and Holmquist 2007). In the case of my horseback riding study, my aim was not to create technologies that would support horseback riding, but to inspire design on a more generic level. I aimed to extract some of the qualities that make horseback riding so engaging so that we could reuse them in other design situations. I emphasized, for example, the pleasure of rhythm as it is communicated through the horse's gaits. Later, Elsa Kosmack Vaara (2017), one of my coworkers, explored rhythm as an organizing principle in the temporal gestalt of an interaction.

Although my study of horseback riding was interesting and provided evocative ideas for design, today I would recommend engaging with autobiographical design methods (Neustaedter and Sengers 2012) rather than autoethnography. Ethnographies in general tend to make us stuck in *what is* rather than *what could be*. The active creative element in an autobiographical design provides a better path to design.

Somatic Connoisseurship

Horseback riding happened to be a practice I already knew. But how do you approach a practice that you know nothing of? Schiphorst (2011) proposed that involving a "somatic connoisseur" in your design process is a way out of this dilemma. A somatic connoisseur is someone who is skillful in an embodied, movement-based practice and who guides, mentors, and shares his or her insights with codesigners and participants, guiding collaborators in what to attend to, how to move and feel. Many soma-based design situations will require years of training in the practice to achieve proficiency, but with the guidance of an expert, we can get help to train our experiential acuity, including observation, discernment, synthesis, empathy, and focus. Somatic connoisseurs may be our codesigners, or they might be experts in the practice we draw upon, but not experts in the digital materials engaging researchers in interaction design.

The situation is similar to a participatory design method (Ehn 1993) in which we involve the experts or future users of a technology in our design process as their contribution will help us to not only shape relevant technology but also arrive at solutions that are ethically and politically relevant to and respectful of their (future) practice. It differs from participatory design, however, in its emphasis on somatics and how the sharing of expertise requires communication of tacit knowledge through performing the activity together. Somatic connoisseurs will share their insights through inviting the design team to engage in the practice together, leading them through the experience, pointing to salient properties, and facilitating first-person experiences. Like participatory design, this process is not a quick, user-centered design engagement; it may take quite some time to develop. As discussed in chapter 4, when we designed Soma Mat, Breathing Light, and Sarka, we engaged in weekly Feldenkrais exercises for a couple of years in parallel to our design work.

Many Roads to Aesthetic Appreciation Skills

Just as musicians, writers, or other practitioners and consumers of art forms will have a richer experience when they train their aesthetic perceptions, so too will those training in soma techniques. In this chapter, I have listed only a few techniques for tuning one's somaesthetic perception skills. What is important here is that cultivation of somaesthetic senses prepares the designer for creating richer, more productive, and generative experiences in his or her designs. In the next chapter, we will explore tactics to put these somaesthetic senses to work.

7   Soma Design Methods

What does it mean to look upon our own bodies as a design material? In the preface, I mentioned that design shapes us, both figuratively and literally. The design of a violin will shape the violinist's muscles and nervous system reactions. Once mastered, the violin can become part of the violinist, making the craft become seemingly effortless and putting the focus on creating a musical expression. Likewise, the computer mouse shapes the computer users' muscles and nervous system reactions. Once we have mastered it, we can shift our focus from explicitly thinking of commands to making them part of our repertory of bodily acts; we can drag-and-drop effortlessly (following Alan Kay's ideas), freeing our focus from computer commands to the content of our tasks.

In this way, our somas not only shape our designs but also serve as a design material, to be shaped and influenced by the designs we create. In chapter 6, I focused on how to train your soma aesthetic sensibilities in a structured manner, turning attention inward, toward your own somatics, to equip yourself to appreciate the somatic impact of your designs. In this chapter, we will focus on tactics and methods to turn outward, to create designs that rhyme and resonate with the soma, to use the soma itself as a design material and create designs that in turn shape the soma through interaction.

The chapter is divided into three sets of methods: (1) ideation methods, (2) engagements with the experiential and aesthetic potential of the digital and technological materials, and (3) evaluation approaches for soma designs once they start to take shape. I end the chapter with a comparison with well-established HCI methods, such as personas or brainstorming methods.

Soma Ideation Design Methods

Most user-centered design projects are enacted from a third-person perspective: observing, interviewing, and testing on users, but not stepping into their shoes. In contrast, the first-person approach uses the designer's *lived body* as a resource in the design process (Svanæs 2013). Although we might bring in users to test our ideas as they take shape, the designer's first-person perspective will take precedence. In the next sections, I outline three first-person ideation methods useful in soma design: slowstorming, aesthetic laborations (or *A-labs*), and two approaches to embodied sketching. Each of these methods entails engaging with your own movement as a moldable material. They also emphasize discovery of felt experiences we might want to hone and further refine in our design work.

Soma Slowstorming

Early in our work with the Soma Mat, Breathing Light, and Sarka, we learned an important lesson that changed my own understanding of how to brainstorm.

Most brainstorming methods in use today focus on bypassing our inhibitions—helping us to remain energetic, open, positive, nonjudgmental—to generate many ideas quickly. This often entails a particular process: First, you fill your mind with various insights based on statistics or user behavior, close encounters with what is already out there, experiences of a practice if there is one, and so on. Once you have all of those components fresh in your mind, you set up a situation that allows (or even forces) you to be a bit silly, proposing crazy ideas, rapidly churning out whatever comes into your mind. The aim is to open the design space to all sorts of alternative solutions and, most importantly, to relax your inner critic, be looser in your thinking, and allow unexpected associations to spring up. By having such a flexible mind, you can go beyond the first obvious solutions and instead rethink the whole problem space (this is often referred to as *design thinking*).

In a typical brainstorming session, ideas are thrown out in rapid succession, one person taking up someone else's idea, changing it, turning it around, shifting perspectives. It needs to be done in a rapid manner to put many ideas and perspectives on the table without much critical reflection. Only later do we allow ourselves to be critical, discarding some of these ideas and developing others.

But as we discussed in chapter 4 in the description of the design journey resulting in Soma Mat, Breathing Light, and Sarka, an interesting result of engaging in Feldenkrais exercises before brainstorming was that we became a bit slower in our movements and reactions. Ideas formed more slowly, in a more thoughtful manner. To me, they felt more honest, closer to my own heart and desire. The interactions envisioned became delicate, sensitive to our bodily processes. I felt a strong sense of empathy for myself and for others. I still had a sense of a flexible mind and a relaxed inner critic, but the process was grounded in a qualitatively different somatic reality. I could more easily *feel* the imagined interactions as ideas formed in my mind.

As we continued to slowstorm with different groups of people, these experiences and considerations reappeared every time. One of the participants, from a big design firm in Stockholm, talked about how this method had transformed his whole view of how to do design, making him less aggressive, less competitive in putting the best ideas on the table before anyone else, and more reflective and honest.

We also noted that if we did not engage in Feldenkrais or some other movement-based exercise before working on our design, we quickly lost track of what our aims were. The tacit understanding, the meaning, was lost. It was not enough to label the experience we sought and then refer back to that label when making design decisions; we had to revisit the physical, somatic reality of the experience regularly, transporting ourselves into the experience: a surprisingly slow process. This is perhaps where my own insight first took form: soma design is a qualitatively different process from those involving symbolic processing.

When engaging with the sociodigital materials after one of these Feldenkrais exercises, the interaction had to be made with care and thoughtful engagement. When playacting interactions with semifinished prototypes or raw materials, you have to go deep into the experience, letting it take time, feeling what is there, repeatedly.

In short, slowstorming involves first engaging deeply with your own somatics—for example, through a particular body practice—and then generating ideas, engaging thoughtfully, slowly, and repeatedly with materials, envisioning the dynamic gestalt of the interaction.

A-labs

The importance of closing your eyes, turning inward, experiencing through all your other senses, and putting words to those experiences is explored in Cheryl Akner-Koler's (2007) aesthetic laborations (A-labs) method. This method focuses on aesthetics and haptic experiences—not necessarily only digital, interactive materials, but also other materials.

Laboration is a Swedish word denoting experimental work in a laboratory. Akner-Koler uses it in a metaphorical sense to describe an interactive, embodied experiment performed together with others. The idea is to invite aesthetic reactions and reasoning, creating a forum for playful dialogue and impulses (Akner-Koler 2007, 60).

To explain A-labs, let me provide an account of an A-labs process that I participated in myself. Back in 2008, we asked Akner-Koler to help us choose among different materials to cover vibrating motors in one of our projects.[1] Depending on whether you put fur, cloth, plastic, or wood on top of the objects, the resulting experience would be quite different. Akner-Koler generously organized a workshop for us on this topic. In the workshop, we were divided into groups of three. In each group, a blindfolded participant touched and felt the vibrating objects through different materials. A second participant interviewed the blindfolded person, following a protocol of questions, narrowing down to precise descriptions of what those materials felt like step by step, while the third participant took notes.

When blindfolded, I remember being given materials covering the vibrating objects, exploring them haptically on different parts of my body: on my head, on my cheeks, on my chest, hands, and arms. Because I did not know which material I had been given, all sorts of nonvisual experiences came to the fore. A particular material-object combination could feel big and sensual when resonating through the cavities of my upper body, but annoying and disturbing when touching sensitive parts of my face. I realized, in a haptically/physically grounded manner, how many small design decisions in choice of movement, material, and vibration speed and intensity would determine the aesthetic experience.

Akner-Koler defines A-labs as a process in which you stimulate perception, inspire playful interaction between professionals from different disciplines, lead people to encounter sensual complexity, and consider how experiences can be transformed over time. The A-labs have a particular focus on haptics and material encounters. In the A-labs I took part in, the outer properties sometimes came as a surprise when removing the blindfold. For example, a material that "felt" like it was brown turned out to be green. A material that I experienced as a typical wall-to-wall carpet looked quite different without the blindfold—more like the felt on a pool table.

Akner-Koler does not want the laborations to be strictly regulated processes, following set rules. Instead, she asks lab leaders to articulate somewhat ambiguous directives to help participants rely on their own senses. In her work, she notes that this open explorative method sometimes frustrates those participants who are goal-oriented problem solvers. But she insists that by going back and forth between more focused, structured explorations and fuzzy, open-ended inquiry, aesthetics may take form more vividly.

In the design process, A-labs are helpful for making choices of materials or feeling some interactions.

Embodied Sketching

After brainstorming and choosing preliminary materials, a next step can be to start sketching and experiencing the interaction as it unfolds over time.

As discussed by Márquez Segura (Márquez Segura 2015; Márquez Segura et al. 2016; Márquez Segura 2016), *embodied sketching* is an umbrella term to describe ideation activities leveraging the participants' in-the-moment, in situ experiences. For example, in Bodystorming, designers perform brainstorming in the location where they expect a system will be used (Oulasvirta, Kurvinen, and Kankainen 2003). If you are designing for a public setting, then you brainstorm in that public space. Once in that space, you act out your ideas, almost as in theater. This usually reveals quickly what works and what does not.

Embodied Sketching of Core Game Mechanics   As performed by Márquez Segura, it is similar to Bodystorming in that you place yourself in a situation that resembles the design context you are aiming to address. In a sense, you are approximating the body motions and interactions you might design. Marquez and colleagues have used this method mainly to design movement-based, colocated games. Participants are asked to improvise using fake or semiworking technology, acting out various movement-based interactions according to certain game rules. The workshop leader will watch how the events unfold, encouraging improvisation. When something interesting happens between participants, the workshop leader quickly picks up on it and builds on it. He or she might add some novel rule to the game or prescribe that a certain movement be performed as part of the game play. The workshop leader may also take on the role of the not-yet-existing technology to help uphold the pretense. In this way, the designer can watch the unfolding consequences of different design choices.

Note how this method relies on playfulness, pretense, act-as-if reasoning, and moment-to-moment unfolding of events. Although these situations are videotaped and analyzed in detail afterwards to make sure the fun is kept in the final game choices, the method does not invite the same slow, inward-looking process as slowstorming. It instead allows the designer to see faster movement-based interactions in situ, assessing which ones seem to engage participants and which ones do not. However, the process is similar to slowstorming in its attention to experiential awareness. The design process begins not in the designer's mind, but rather *in movement*; then the designer builds on those movements that seem to spur joy and playfulness. Only after identifying those joyful, playful engagements is the technology built to support them—not the other way around. This tactic requires a workshop leader with a trained eye for detecting movements, experiences, and, in this case, rules (or core mechanics) for games, as well as a good sense of technological affordances.

Move to Be Moved   When we move to create design, we feel the design taking shape. The dynamic qualities take form and we can experience them. This is why Hummels, Overbeek, and Klooster (2006) argue that industrial designer training should incorporate movement skills. They show that instead of sketching with pen and paper, sketching can be done through movement. Videos of designers moving can be used to extract shape, as well as dynamic qualities in interaction. Because movement is inherently meaningful to us, Hummels and her colleagues argue that incorporating movement as part of our design process helps us access that meaning. They see interaction design as a kind of choreography, putting together a sequence of events into a dynamically unfolding experience. In fact, they argue that *only* movement can capture the dynamic and temporal complexities of interaction; by sketching our ideas through movement, they say, we can reflect in action, just as sketching on paper can be a process of reflection for designers.

To sketch efficiently through movement, Hummels and colleagues have devised various tools based on the concept of *tinkering*: they draw on dataflow-modeling programs, sensor technology, playacting, and physical modeling. To accelerate the process, they have devised half-finished designs that can be easily put together as prototypes. All this allows for physical engagement from the earliest moments of the design process.

Digital and Technological Material Encounters

Most design situations are dialogues among feeling the material, imagining possible interactions, sketching (in various forms—including sketching in movement), reflecting, feeling the materials again, and so on (Schiphorst 2007). In that process, the designers will rely on any prior design situations they have engaged with—their design *repertory* (Schon 1984).

One of the key activities for soma designers, then, is to set the scene so that the design ideas can thrive off the affordances and experiential qualities of the digital (and other) materials, the imagined use context, and our own somatics and aesthetic sensitivities. This requires cultivating deep knowledge of the materials at hand as most digital interactions can be shaped in myriads of ways.

Crafts and Materials

Today more than ever before, a whole range of novel interactive materials are coming onto the stage, enabling a huge space of potential designs. To take advantage of that, we must reconnect with the history of industrial design, all the way back to Bauhaus,[2] and with traditional crafts. Design and craft have always been about form-giving through movement and obtaining tacit knowledge. They have required a deep material connoisseurship (this is why chapter 6 emphasized cultivating the aesthetics and connoisseurship of the soma). But now, with new digital materials, we are designing with materials that *change with use*, even as they change us. These materials offer affordances beyond what you can touch and feel with your hands, but still require engagements with and through your body. As designers, we have to learn about the affordances of sensors, actuators, wireless connectivity, data and data analytics, interactive textiles, visualizations, screens, and so on. Some materials in that list are extra hard to touch and feel. They might require tools that make them accessible to us to be experienced.

On the one hand, as discussed earlier, digital material is very plastic: we can design almost anything. This led Löwgren and Stolterman (2004) to talk about it as the *material without properties*. But as Vallgårda and Redström (2007) noted: "Such a perspective ... makes it difficult to understand how this material relates to other materials we use in design, as it almost seems to exist in isolation on its own premises." At the same time, the reality of the computation is undoubtedly present once the interaction gestalt has been shaped.

Many design researchers interested in somatics have a background in dance, art, or movement practice, coupled with a deep interest in digital materials and interaction design. Only a few, however, are computer scientists. The effects of this can be seen in the work we have reported on so far; though providing promising starts, a stronger engagement with the actual, physical materials of sensors, actuators, wireless communication, algorithms, and data analytics would enhance the work. This lack of deep experience with digital materials is unfortunate because material properties are key to our design processes. We need to feel and exploit all their somaesthetic potential—a mandate made even more complicated by the fact that digital materials are not a stable, once and for all, given set of algorithms, programming languages, or technologies in the way that (some properties of) wood or plastic might be. Instead the digital possibilities to shape functionality and aesthetic interactions are undergoing rapid development and constant change.

As these computational materials have only existed for a few decades, we lack a long crafts tradition that we can rely on. Instead, we have to approach them with an open mind. In our experience, not very surprisingly, the best way to approach a somaesthetic design has been to work in multidisciplinary design teams who together approach the technical materials in a "designerly" manner (Cross 1982). A designerly approach to "ill-defined problems" produces a wide range of semifunctioning prototypes instead of a process that attempts first to define the problem and then solve it. Instead, after producing many design ideas, exploring the material properties and their aesthetic potential, we can map out the problem space in a different manner, one that helps us to see the potential.

In chapter 5, I introduced Schiphorst's soft(n) sculptures. In her description of her design process, Schiphorst emphasized how her team touched and felt the aesthetic potential of the various materials they considered for the sculptures. In an earlier publication, she writes of the need to engage with the "palpability of the invisible" (Schiphorst 2007). By *palpability*, she is referring to what is perceivable, easily observable, and felt. As we engage with the materials that will form a design, we need to actively engage with all of our senses—touching, feeling, and moving. But computation is, in a sense, invisible until we have put it together, programmed it, and shaped it into that whole, orchestrated, dynamic gestalt. We therefore must find ways to make the computational material reveal itself, making it visible and palpable in our design processes.

Soma Design Toolkits

Vallgårda and Redström (2007) proposed creating composites of digital technology and other materials, such as wood or paper, to characterize and work with the properties of the digital material. By creating composites, they manage to expose properties of the digital material, as well as put the material into a physical form that can be handled.

In my research group, Petra Sundström and Jordi Solsona proposed a similar but more lightweight method they named the Inspirational Bits (Sundström et al. 2011; Solsona Belenguer et al. 2012; Solsona Belenguer 2015). Their idea was to create (in a quick-and-dirty manner) functioning, one-function systems that would expose and make one or several of the dynamic properties of a digital material palpable to the whole design team. They built many different Inspirational Bits, exploring, for example, the properties of the Bluetooth connection protocol (Sundström, Taylor, and O'Hara 2011), radio-frequency identification (RFID), accelerometers, and radio (Solsona Belenguer et al. 2012). One of the bits, RadioSound, makes the invisible landscape and reach of radio signals palpable by converting them into sound. RadioSound consists of two sensor nodes, one of which is equipped with a small speaker emitting a single tone. The tone increases with increased signal strength between the two nodes. To explore the reach of radio signals, you can, for example, put one node on each ankle and then walk around, listening to how the volume changes as one leg approaches the other or how the signal is affected by other materials, walls, and furniture. With RadioSound, the invisible landscape of radio signals is made tangible. Similarly, with the BluePete game, the team playfully explores how Bluetooth devices connect to one another. When playing the hare you have to "hide" so that the other players, the wolves, cannot see your Bluetooth connection. If they do, they gain a point. You also gain points from finding open Bluetooth signals, such as those from printers or other devices, discovering the invisible Bluetooth-landscape. In this way, the design team may more easily feel, for example, the slowness in the pairing of two Bluetooth-enabled devices. Once two Bluetooth units are connected, they can send data rapidly, but the initial pairing takes time. This in turn enables or disables different aesthetic potential. We can imagine designing an interaction that requires slowly moving closer and closer to a Bluetooth device until the pairing is done, then faster interactions once the connection is set.

Although building Inspirational Bits might be a costly and roundabout way of doing design grounded in the material properties, nowadays there are various toolboxes for embedded programming and visualization of wireless connectivity that speed up these kinds of quick-and-dirty explorations. Those toolboxes (as well as the compositional materials from Vallgårda and Redström) must be approached with care: their inbuilt form factors will otherwise entirely determine the form of our designs. Although toolboxes such as the Arduino platform have made embedded programming accessible to nonengineers, the physical form and limited functionality of the actual board has enabled certain form-giving processes and not others.

Digital Materials with Soma Potential

Many new forms of digital materials are being shaped right now. Together, these technological developments are moving interaction design into novel contexts, such as, to name just a few, interactive sex toys (Bardzell and Bardzell 2011), kitchen appliances, or gardening tools. These contexts entail obvious somaesthetic concerns. When shaping technologies for the intimate spheres in our lives, somaesthetics ideals could guide and alter what we envision. There is always a dialogue between the development of new technologies, computer architectures, connectivity, and so on, and the perceived needs we imagine they will meet. Let us just briefly touch on some of technologies that seem particularly interesting to soma design and that could shape and be shaped by somaesthetic ideals.

Data as a Design Material   More and more interaction is shaped by data-driven models enabled by the masses of data that can be obtained from web pages, social media, mobile devices, and sensors integrated with all sorts of practices and machinery. Data-driven design has enabled tools such as natural language translation, facial recognition, and movement recognition. These tools in turn are changing in relation to the application demands. Interactive machine learning and other emerging technologies will accelerate these developments further yet.

Shape-Changing Interfaces   As we have seen, somaesthetics-interested designers are already engaging with movement recognition, wearables, interactive textiles, wireless connected biosensors, and handheld devices for gaming and other purposes. Recent trends in material science enable technologies with even more potential for somaesthetic interactions. For example, shape-changing interfaces (Coelho and Zigelbaum 2011; Grönvall et al. 2014; Rasmussen et al. 2016) make it possible to dynamically change the form of anything, from furniture (Grönvall et al. 2014) or walls (Vallgårda 2014) to the texture and shape of your smartphone (Juhlin et al. 2013). The kinaesthetic properties of shape-changing interfaces will interact in interesting ways with soma design. Imagine sofas subtly redistributing your weight when you have been sitting for too long or changing the texture of objects in response to how you touch or caress them.

Light Communication   Another particularly interesting "material" is light communication, which has enjoyed renewed attention with the proliferation of LED lights. Light communication, in which data is transmitted via LED lights blinking faster than the eye can see, may soon replace radio-based wireless communication in some contexts (Varshney et al. 2017). This invisible blinking allows LED-enabled objects, such as lamps in the home or children's toys (Corbellini et al. 2014), to communicate whenever they are "in sight" of one another. Again, the kinaesthetic properties of their interaction can be exploited by soma design (Windlin and Laaksolahti 2017).

Autonomous Systems Another development for which somaesthetics should be an obvious concern is in the design of both autonomous and semiautonomous technologies. They have already entered our everyday lifeworlds through robotic lawnmowers, vacuum cleaners, and children's toys.

Biological Materials On the horizon, we note explorations into entirely different technologies. For example, the blending of life sciences and material science allows us to "program" with biological materials.

Evaluations: Involving Others

Although the first-person perspective and designerly judgment and movement reside at the core of the design process, sooner or later the design will meet other users. During the design process, we might also want to involve others to make sure we are on the right path.

Before discussing some of the evaluation methods I have worked with, I briefly would like to untangle some of the underlying assumptions of why we perform user studies. In academia, and in HCI in particular, user studies serve the role of "scientific proof." The aim is to back up claims about how the system works and what kind of experience it delivers. By bringing in users who report (or somehow show) that they "feel" what the design aimed to deliver, we believe we have enough evidence to claim that our design works as intended, that it delivers the experience we said it did. For somaesthetic design work, this becomes complicated for several reasons.

The argument throughout this book has been that we (both designers and users) can train our somaesthetic appreciation skills. In fact, this happens even when you are not deliberately engaging with it as some "task" or with a conscious intent of doing so. In a Feldenkrais lesson, for example, your soma will register the lessons even if you do not think it has happened. And overall, the advice for most of the practices we have discussed is to accept yourself, where you are, your pains and worries, and not be so harsh on yourself. Compassion, playfulness, enjoyment, and the amazing plethora of somaesthetic experiences we can engage in are key guiding design values.

Even so, successful engagement doesn't always happen. Users must be willing to engage. They come to these experiences with different backgrounds, different skills and needs, different somas. It is not always the case that some uniquely crafted somaesthetic design is accessible or interesting to everyone at every moment. The design's aesthetics might bore you, or you might be in a stage in life in which you are not willing to engage at all. In a sense, evaluation of somaesthetic design is as problematic as, say, user studies of art (Höök, Sengers, and Andersson 2003). What would it mean to perform a user study of a theater performance? What is good art? Is it a statistical average of what your users think?

Let us imagine being in the middle of a somaesthetically informed design process for, say, a movement-recognition system that allows users to control the volume of the radios in their homes. The system might "wake up" through some unique gesture, perhaps when the user turns his or her face toward the device. Then, by raising an arm or perhaps making a small, rhythmic shoulder movement upward, the volume is raised. Let us imagine that we have designed this interaction through a somaesthetic design process and that the shoulder movements, as well as the look and feel of response device, are carefully crafted to engage users musically, rhythmically, emphasizing movements that are unusual in our everyday life but bring pleasure and maybe even health effects. Now we reach a point in our design process when we need to test our design. We place our prototype in people's homes for a longer time period to see whether it will bring the kinds of pleasure we intended as designers. But given the infinite variation in life, the plethora of kinaesthetic everyday experiences, how can we know whether it brings those intended pleasures? Some days our study participants might attend to the system in the way we intended: feel it, engage with the experience, and appreciate the beauty it brings to their lives. Other days they might hate it as it gets in the way of their busy lives; it might seem like an annoying extra burden to have to gesture in the middle of taking care of kids, dogs, and visiting guests. Some participants may never appreciate it. Some may have pains or bodily limitations or prior somatic experiences that make it hard or impossible to engage in anything but negative experiences when performing these gestures. Or they might not be open to engaging in the somaesthetic experience staged through the device at all: they might expect technology to minimize movement, as do remote controls or most other machinery we use in our homes. After extended use, the gestures might give some participants shoulder pains. And so on. Some participants will recognize and engage with the aesthetics of the interactions; for others, other aesthetic forms will be closer to their tastes and more appreciated.

What do we learn from this study, really? As a piece of empirical evidence of the design validity vis-à-vis the design aims, it will not tell us much, unless certain tactics or qualities are integral to the evaluation method. First, rather than seeing user studies as providing objective evidence, they need to be set up with the same somaesthetic concerns governing our design process. We need to value and engage with our participants' first-person perspectives and tastes and probe their somaesthetic appreciation skills. The truly objective answer to whether a design meets our aesthetic aims will not be found in generalizing user feedback, trying to find objective proof or data.

Don't get me wrong here. Somaesthetics is a reality that we recognize and feel once we have trained our designerly judgments and somaesthetic sensibilities. It is not "unclear" to you when you engage with an interaction. You know when it touches your soma. It is a reality, but a reality you can only probe through your own somaesthetic sensibility. To me, to get around the feeling of "studying people using my technology and trying to extract objective proof about their experience," it has been helpful to think of participants as collaborators, helping us to further refine and shape the somaesthetic experience in the design.

Second, a key insight from our design work with the Soma Mat, Breathing Light, and Sarka concerns the volatile and impalpable nature of human experiences—more specifically, the experiences of one's own body. The problem is twofold: First, it concerns the ability to get access to the sensations of the body, to turn your direction attentively to them, to discern them, and to have the skills to interpret and make sense of those sensations. Second, it is not trivial to then articulate and share these experiences with others. We had problems in articulating the experience we sought for our prototypes and had to spend a whole year learning Feldenkrais before being able to design for it, so how can we expect participants in our studies to effortlessly articulate what they experienced when interacting with our prototypes?

As we discussed earlier, to understand the somaesthetic experience of someone else, you need to share it somehow. It requires an empathic engagement, a shared lifeworld. In the formative user studies we performed for the Soma Mat, one of our participants said: "The heat makes the feeling and the appearance of those areas change. So, the simple explanation is they get smaller and larger. So if the heat goes on, I could easily compare that, so yeah, now the space feels larger than on the other side, and vice versa." To us as designers in this project, this all makes sense and is helpful design input, but maybe it makes less sense to you as a reader who has not laid down on the Soma Mat and felt the heat under different parts of your body, slowly gaining insights about your own soma. How could you make sense of a statement that says that one side of your body feels larger than the other?

When working with the Feldenkrais sessions in our group, we always ended by discussing and sharing our experiences with each other. Every time, it was striking to see how much our descriptions differed from one another's despite the fact that we had been in the same lesson, listening to the same instructions, performing the same movements. Some experiences seem more easily expressed, such as pains in specific limbs or parts of the body. But beyond these spatially fixed and "ontologically clear" statements, there was a vast space of experiences that were not that easily captured and that were expressed using words and metaphors borrowed from other lived experiences, such as colors (blue, orange, or black), materials (rubbery), weight (light or heavy), or spatiality (elongated or compacted). Although our experiences were unique, it was still possible for us to relate to one another because we could use reference points from the lesson. If one of us said, "When she said we should make our hip and shoulder meet diagonally, I could not get my hip up from the floor, it was so heavy," then a minimal reference point we understand could be how all of us had attempted to raise our hip from the floor; we could empathetically simulate the heavy feeling.

It is quite different to be in a group of colleagues working together for a longer time period, sharing our experiences of Feldenkrais sessions and our prototype designs. When we brought in others to try out our systems, we could not be sure we would all share common reference points that would help them express their experiences or allow us to understand them. We tried a range of methods to elicit rich feedback that would help us further the design process.

For example, we asked the participants to sketch their experiences on a so-called body sheet before and after testing our designs. The body sheet has an outline of a human body that lets you scribble on top (see figure 7.1). We encouraged the participants to write words or draw pictures on top of the stylized body outline. We varied the body sheets, sometimes adding the option of reusing concepts that other participants had used. We also tried using the set of figurines in different shapes previously used in the sensual evaluation instrument (Isbister et al. 2006) as a resource for expressing affective experiences. In one variant, we provided participants

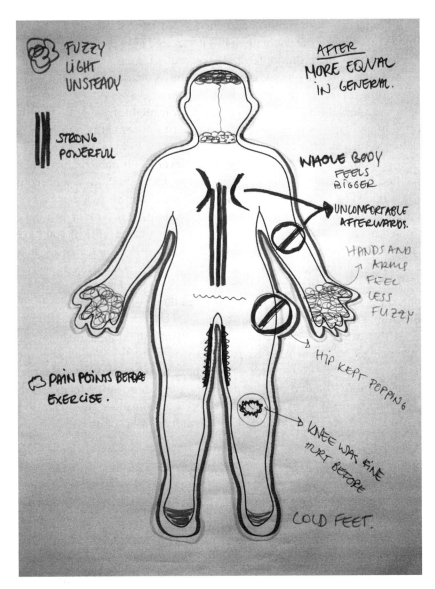

Figure 7.1
A body sheet from one of the participants

with lumps of soft, warm clay and encouraged them to shape the lumps into expressions of their somatic status before and after using our system.

No matter which form of feedback you request, user participation must be carefully crafted to provide genuinely useful feedback to the design team. Depending on what you are designing, it might make sense to let users live with your design for a longer time period. Or it might make sense to only bring in participants who are body-aware, with somaesthetics training and skill in verbalizing their experience.

Yet another method is a variant of Gaver's cultural commentators method (Gaver 2007). In the cultural commentators method, you bring in those skilled in judging a particular genre to critique your system. Gaver proposes that you can, for example, bring in a theater critic if you have created in an interactive theater performance or a comic critic if you have created some interactive comic strips. For somaesthetic experiences, it is a good idea to bring in participants who combine skills in body aware-ness with technological, designerly, and aesthetic competence: choreogra-phers, yoga instructors, elite sportspeople, or therapists could all be helpful, depending on the purpose of the design.

At the same time, my position is that somaesthetic design should be interesting to all—not only to a few experts in bodyworks. Ideally, the designs will be like skateboards or golf clubs: their somaesthetic potential is there already the first time we use them, but we can enjoy them also as experts after many years of use (as discussed in Tholander and Johansson 2010). Somaesthetic appreciation should not be an exclusive experience that only makes sense to highly skilled experts.

Comparison with HCI Methods

In the preface, I made some strong claims, insisting on the qualitative dif-ference between language-based, symbolic visual interaction and somaes-thetic design. To substantiate this claim, let us briefly analyze some of the methods and theories typically taught to engineers and industrial designers specializing in interaction design and compare them to the methods pro-posed here. This helps to clarify where the differences lie—and why they matter.

One of the most popular design approaches taught today is Stanford's articulation of design thinking ("Stanford D.school," n.d.). I have person-ally used many of the methods the school has included in its description with great success, and my aim here is not to critique this way of working. It has an important role in reaching out with design thinking to many contexts and different professionals. But an analysis of its descriptions quickly shows how fundamentally different somaesthetics-informed tactics are from the most common HCI methods.

Let us, for example, turn to the school's description of brainstorming and compare it with the tactics proposed in this book. In short, it proposes brainstorming for brief, fifteen- to thirty-minute sessions to maintain energy; writing down all ideas generated on a joint whiteboard, for everyone to see and share; repeatedly asking the question, "How might we?" during the session; and, if the energy of the room goes down or people slow down, adding constraints such as, "What if it had to be round?" or "What would superman do?" The overall aim is often to produce fifty ideas in twenty minutes. The space where the brainstorming takes place should be carefully chosen:

> SPACE—Be mindful about the space in which you conduct a brainstorm. Make sure that there is plenty of vertical writing area. This allows the group to generate a large number of potential solutions. Strike a balance between having a footprint that is big enough for everyone, but also is not so large that some people start to feel removed. A good rule of thumb is that all members of the group should be able to reach the board in two steps. Also, make sure each person has access to sticky notes and a marker so they can capture their own thoughts and add them to the board if the scribe cannot keep up with the pace. ("Stanford D-School—Facilitate a Brainstorm," n.d.)

Now, if we compare this to the slowstorming or embodied brainstorming we discussed previously, almost everything is different. A slowstorming session will only generate a few ideas, slowly, thoughtfully, in a setting in which you typically perform the acts you envision designing for, engaging bodily, emotionally, and socially. It takes days of involvement, and ideas have to be repeatedly acted out to know what they are, how they touch your soma, or what will be a compelling interaction in the long run. The process may take months. During the slowstorming, ideas might at some point be written down, but most importantly they have to be given shape and form to be properly felt and understood. Overall, throughout the description of the Stanford brainstorming session, the first-person perspective and felt experience are notably missing. The only reference to a somatic presence in the brainstorming description is the reference to "reach the board in two steps." Otherwise, the assumption is that people are sitting on chairs, talking, writing, engaging predominantly intellectually.

But there are of course overlaps between what the Stanford design thinking model argues and what we have argued here. For example, it recommends "prototyping for empathy" ("Stanford D-School—Prototype for

Empathy," n.d.). One of the examples matches precisely what a somaesthetic design tactic could be: "Simulate an aspect of what users are going
through to better understand it yourself (for example, if your users plant
seeds while carrying a baby, get a sling and carry ten pounds while planting
seeds)" (ibid.).

Another popular method to help you engage with your future users is
to create so-called personas (Cooper 2004). The idea is that by creating fic-
tional characters to represent the different user types that might use a site,
brand, or product in a similar way, the whole design team can make better
design decisions. The team gets help to design for people other than themselves. The path to constructing a persona is described as follows on the
usability.gov website:

> To ensure your personas are accurate representations of your users and have the
> support of your stakeholders throughout the process, you should:
>
> • **Conduct user research**: Answer the following questions: Who are your users
> and why are they using the system? What behaviors, assumptions, and expecta-
> tions color their view of the system?
> • **Condense the research**: Look for themes/characteristics that are specific,
> relevant, and universal to the system and its users.
> • **Brainstorm**: Organize elements into persona groups that represent your target
> users. Name or classify each group.
> • **Refine**: Combine and prioritize the rough personas. Separate them into pri-
> mary, secondary, and, if necessary, complementary categories. You should have
> roughly 3–5 personas and their identified characteristics.
> • **Make them realistic**: Develop the appropriate descriptions of each personas
> background, motivations, and expectations. Do not include a lot of personal in-
> formation. Be relevant and serious; humor is not appropriate. (US Department of
> Health and Human Services, Digital Communications Division, n.d.)

Again, creating personas is a great method that I have both used and
taught in classes, and it is especially helpful to drive home the idea that
not everybody will be the same and have the same needs as I do. But the
detached, third-person engagement with the end user stands in stark contrast to the first-person, subjective, somaesthetic engagement we have been
discussing.

In the persona method, we are asked to avoid a "lot of personal information" and to "be serious." In the somaesthetic design tactics, we are
instead engaging with our whole selves: living the design with our somatics, feeling the interaction, letting movements, emotions and feelings take
a front-row seat. This engagement is key both for the designers and later for
the participants engaging with our designs. Experiencing through humor,

thoughtfulness, pain, lust, exhilaration, sadness, or any other emotion, the movements of somatics, is not only a permissible strategy but the crucial path to somaesthetic design.

From Symbols to Felt Engagements

It might feel as though the tactics/methods introduced in this chapter are proffered as a bag of goodies, a set of diverse techniques that, if loyally followed, will always generate good results. Unfortunately, this is not true. First, design methods can never guarantee success as the designer's competence and judgment in applying these tactics will determine the results. Second, the point of enumerating all these methods was not to give you a ready-made decontextualized toolbox for soma-based design. The point was to further the argument that soma-based design *entails a qualitative shift from a predominantly symbolic, language-oriented stance to an experiential, felt, aesthetic stance permeating the whole design and use cycle*, as I argued in the beginning of this book. Through drawing upon not only our own work but also some of the tactics used by others, we note, again and again, how the strong emphasis on the first-person perspective of the designer and on movement, emotion, and reasoning as a whole soma needs to be the basis for understanding and designing. These somaesthetic design tactics can help you train your aesthetic sensibility, your ability to appreciate and discern those interactions that touch us.

In my own experience, it was liberating to engage with a new body practice such as Feldenkrais, to be surprised and engaged in a new manner. It reminded me how many ways there are to discover and rediscover myself and thereby expand my design repertory. When stuck in a particular design style, in which certain experiences are more easily attainable, almost routine, it might be helpful to step outside our comfort zones and try a new somaesthetic experience or a novel way of defamiliarizing the everyday, the habitual: Try Feldenkrais. Try horseback riding. Try designing with a new material (such as heat or biomaterials), feeding off its affordances and somaesthetic potential. Try imagining the orchestration of the interactive gestalt in a novel manner. Such practices not only unlock new directions for design solutions but also help retain the novelty, spirit, and fun that drew so many of us to design.

8   Politics of the Body

It is notable how much human reasoning revolves around dichotomies to categorize the world: male-female, rational-irrational, emotion-thinking, body-mind, white-black, and so on. On the one hand, it is a very helpful way of reasoning, allowing us to divide the world into reasonable chunks that we can make sense of. The patterns become more obvious and we can orient ourselves in a world full of uncertainties and dynamic unfoldings.

At the same time, it leads our thinking astray in many ways. For example, the male-female dichotomy became associated with the thinking-emotion and mind-body dichotomies. This association cast females as emotional beings, anchored in their bodies, without ability to reason and think rationally. That particular division goes back all the way to the Greek philosophers and is still alive and kicking in our Western culture today (Hirdman 1988). In other cultures, other dichotomies have come to dominate thinking. For example, some cultures associate women with fire, because women would typically carry the coal that makes fire (Lakoff 2008). If fire is dangerous, then women are dangerous. In this way, categories and metaphors come to influence our thinking and reasoning. They become ubiquitous, as they are so deeply ingrained in our language, culture, and behaviors.

As we have discussed already, these associations in turn affect not just our thinking, but our behaviors, all the way to how we move, sit, run, and engage with others. For example, in some cultures, women are taught not to run, to walk in high heels, or to sit with their legs crossed in certain ways. As Elizabeth Grosz (1994) said, "Our bodies are completed by culture." Women, as well as men, need to adhere to and be cultivated into particular movement patterns to be accepted.

As argued earlier, technology is not innocent in shaping our categorizations and metaphors, as well as our physical bodies. It carries our conceptualizations, our prejudices, our ideas of what the world is and what it should be. It therefore becomes impossible for me to avoid discussing politics.

I hesitated for a long time before writing this chapter. The topics I address herein, about how soma design intertwines with the politics of the body, deserve a whole book. These are complex topics, and many other talented academics have done a much better job than I can in sorting out how to approach them. In the end, I have decided to simply offer brief meditations on each topic, hoping they will help you to explore and engage with these centuries-old controversies still so present in our society today. They are all highly intertwined with our design practice, so our stance toward each of these political issues will directly impact designs we can and want to imagine and build. Our choices, in turn, will have effects on our society, because the design and technologies we shape will in turn shape us.

The Ethics of Soma Design

In my conception of this book, and this chapter, I was inspired by Shusterman's insistence that somaesthetic engagement is an ethical project:

> In proposing "somaesthetics" as a field of theory and practice, I could appeal to ancient and non-Western traditions that cultivate the body as means of improving one's cognitive and ethical virtues as well as one's aesthetic dimension. While modernity's dominant ideology compartmentalizes and trivializes the aesthetic by sharply distinguishing it from more serious realms of knowledge and praxis (by identifying the aesthetic with mere prettiness, appearance, surface, form, play, fantasy, etc.), somaesthetics blends aesthesis, cognition, and praxis to address some of philosophy's most central aims: knowledge, self-knowledge, right action, happiness, and justice. (2003, 109)

Initially, I dismissed this side of the somaesthetics project. My viewpoint was that cultivating the body seemed like a selfish activity, directing attention to the self and thereby avoiding caring for society. But gradually I came to see how it enabled me to take a holistic stance on some of the horrible plagues we battle right now—misogyny, racism, privilege, and denial of climate change. Although somaesthetic design will not remedy those issues—they are far too complex for that—it offers me, as a design researcher, a path toward a form of activism.

In the sections that follow, I introduce four difficult and interrelated political issues: dualism, feminism, privilege, and the politics of algorithms. For each, I show its relevance to soma design work. I do not offer answers, but rather questions that offer the potential to guide an ethical design research agenda.

Dualism

I started this book with a discussion of dualism. In fact, the whole book has been an attempt to avoid working in a dualistic manner and to instead speak of the soma as the unity of body, emotion, thinking, sociality, and being in the world. A dualistic way of thinking assigns bodies and emotions a low status and the mind, as the seat of "higher facilities," a high status.

In chapter 2, I mentioned an interesting wave of research on the role of emotion, developed over the last decade or two. It redeemed emotion from its low status, linked to irrationality, and instead showed how rational decision making in fact relies on emotion. By assigning emotion this new role, as the basis of rational thinking, this line of thought almost automatically entailed giving emotion high status—as a subject of academic study, as well as part of human behavior at large. Because rationality is the higher-valued part of the dichotomy between rational and irrational, thinking and emotion—and emotions, it turns out, are parts of rational decision making—rationality's high status can now rub off on emotions. But this, in a sense, devalues other roles emotion takes in our lives. Emotion is not only the basis for abstracted rational thinking necessary for survival. It also gives color, meaning and value to our lives. It is a fundamental part of aesthetics, linking our thinking, bodies, sociality, and meaning-making processes together.

It is very difficult to unravel and disentangle the dualistic dichotomy from our reasoning and ways of approaching design. The metaphorical associations are very strong in our everyday language. Just imagine trying to ban expressions such as "putting our feelings aside" (Lakoff and Johnson 2008, 17) or a "grounding in our bodies" (as if the body was lower, more close to the ground, than other aspects of ourselves). In fact, even this book is filled with these kinds of metaphors, as it would have been almost impossible to reach any common understanding otherwise. A striking example is perhaps Dewey's use of "lower cognitive skills" when discussing capacities that allow us to experience beauty. Why would they be "lower"? What kind of status of our senses does this indicate relative to the "higher" cognitive skills?

As we discussed in chapter 2, just coming to a place where we can use the word *body* without, on the one hand, separating it from our thinking or surroundings or, on the other hand, indicating its lower status, is a struggle. In the end, I took a pragmatic stance toward the whole problem: let us name body parts, thinking, mind, emotion, and so on as they are used in our everyday daily lives, so long as we remember that they are interdependent.

But how easy will it be to keep that in mind when our whole culture, our metaphors, our languages, keep reinforcing a separation?

At the core of this book lies a question: Does dualism matter to design? Will a dualistic stance toward mind and body render design that reinforces a dualistic stance, and will that in turn negatively affect how people live their lives? Is it an ethical question?

I say yes, it matters.

First, as I argued earlier, every conceptualization matters to design because it opens the design space differently. Depending on which conceptual or theoretical lens we use to look at a design challenge, different solutions will occur to us. Take, for example, kinaesthetic mimicry (Isbister and DiMauro 2011) or the affective loops (Höök 2008; Sundström 2010) that we discussed previously. Both thrive on the idea that engagement arises in between bodily movement, affect, and strategizing to win a game or express yourself in interaction. They cannot be separated. Those designs would have been harder to imagine with a dualistic stance: not impossible, but harder.

Second, apart from the fact that dualism is a misconceived or limiting account of what it means to be human, therefore limiting our imagination when doing design, the next question we might ask is whether a dualistic stance can lead to oppressive designs, harming us or hindering our ability to move, experience, and think. We cannot claim that a dualistic stance will always create oppressive technology, but can we claim that a nondualistic position is more likely to generate less oppressive design?

As argued earlier, the human condition is such that we are always embodied, always engaging with our whole way of being. But some technologies demand more work to become an embodied part of us. A good example of the work involved in making a reductionist technology embodied with the self is given by Kaiton Williams (2015). As he was attempting to lose weight, he decided to use a range of tools, among them *Lose It!*, a weight-loss and calorie tracking application for the smartphone and web. The tool allowed him to take control: "I had a renewed awareness of my self and what I was eating; I was feeling less stressed now that I felt more in control; I was starting to use exact measures rather than estimating" (ibid., 125). But he continues to have an anxious alliance with these numbers and measurements. Intellectually, he knew that the value of counting calories was dubious. He doubted whether the tool could provide a proper account of the number of calories or of how his body would respond to them. Still, the numbers kept having a "mesmerising effect" on him (ibid.). Although he knew that the health industry and app creators have reasons to position their tools as being accurate and able to measure every calorie as if the body was a precise system, he became reliant on and embodied with these precise measurements. And he achieved his goals—he lost weight.

After using these systems for a long time, Williams notes how they have changed him. Even if he stops using them, there is no going back to a state before using them. These measurements and ways of understanding food and his body will always be a part of himself. His position is as follows: "Criticisms of these technologies show how they, or at least the imaginaries that give birth to them, promote and cement a division of mind and body, and work to establish a self-legible body that is always at risk yet best addressed through objective 'information.' ... At the same time, even as a prosthetic, that information system expanded my ability to make sense of the world and in doing so increased my sense of freedom" (Williams 2015, 127).

In a sense, your body is always there for you; if we were to follow the ideas in *Walden* (Thoreau [1854] 2016), we might aim not to put layers of tools/representations between ourselves and our experience. Instead, we would strip off all the distractions to enable us to get closer to ourselves. Shusterman (2013) takes a more balanced view of this: "First, no technological invention of virtual reality will negate the body's centrality as the focus of affective, perceptual experience through which we experience and engage the world. Second, cultivating better skills of body consciousness can provide us with enhanced powers of concentration to help us overcome problems of distraction and stress caused by the new media's superabundance of information and stimulation."

A nondualistic stance might render better systems, avoiding, for example, the simplified measurements in *Lose It!* that annoyed Williams. What the nondualistic soma design perspective brings to the table is careful integration of emotion, body, values, thinking, and aesthetics. A dualistic design stance, or aiming to enforce a third-person perspective on the body so that we see ourselves from the outside and bodies become objects or machinery that can be trimmed and fixed, may render equally useful but more utility-oriented designs. Therefore, yes, dualism can (though doesn't always) lead to oppressive designs because they can make us regard our bodies as machines, to be fed, trimmed, kept in order, irrespective of what we might feel our needs are.

Rather than asking what guarantees a good design—which is almost always impossible to answer as it depends on the skills of the design team, the setting, the resources given, the ecosystem in which the product enters, the production qualities, and so on—we might do better to ask: How do we open the design space in a good way to maximize the chances of designs that celebrate values we care for?

Feminism

Feminist theories are concerned with many different topics, some of which are relevant to interaction design. I encourage you to read Shaowen Bardzell's (2010) feminist HCI agenda for an introduction to how feminist theories can contribute to interaction design more generally.

Several of the feminist theories and conceptualizations Bardzell discusses are highly relevant to soma design. A couple of them stand out as particularly pertinent. One such theory is *pluralism*. Bardzell interprets the impact of pluralist theories as a call to deconstruct the idea that we are designing for some universal user and that it is possible to reach universal usability. A feminist stance will not assume that there is only one universal way of being human. Instead, a pluralist stance will recognize that the category of *human* is "too rich, too diverse, and too complex a category to bear a universal solution" (Bardzell 2010, 1306).

In the soma design methods discussed earlier in this book, we have emphasized that we cannot design without engaging with our own bodies, our own first-person perspectives, as well as engaging with intersubjectivity— empathy with others and their bodily presence. In a sense, in a somaesthetic design process, pluralism will be in your face the whole time, acutely present, as you always must go back to your own as well as others' felt experiences and their corporeal reality. When performing bodily exercises together or engaging/touching/feeling the design materials, you cannot avoid speaking of what different subjectivities bring to the table. All sorts of differences, such as body height or size, pains and aches, and visual, auditory, or haptic sensitivity, will keep popping up in your design discussions, but the discussion will not revolve solely around the surface of bodily differences. Deeper somatic differences will be on the table—emotions, attitudes, and beliefs, thought processes, a sense of the other and of the self and how it changes with the joint experience. I would not go as far as claiming that a somaesthetic design process will guarantee design pluralism, but there is a better chance that the discussion will arise.

To really engage with feminism with respect to soma design, most interesting are those theories that speak directly of our human corporeal reality. With a feminist perspective, there is no way of avoiding accounting for corporeal differences among male, female, and other bodies. Some do so by seeing gender as entirely socially constructed; others use biological differences as the basis of their feminist theory. The theories I found most useful are those that do not deny the role of our bodies in how we perceive the world while still they acknowledge how those bodies learn and engage in every moment, throughout socialization and cultural influences.

Elizabeth Grosz (1994) provides one such interesting account in what she names the *volatile body*—an attempt to create a corporeal feminism. Grosz's theories have firm roots in the realities of our bodies, our morphology, the way we move, learn, and engage through movement, but they do not assume that these roots determine our behavior and intelligence—similar to Sheets-Johnstone and Shusterman. At the same time, she does not see gender as solely socially constructed. Instead, she insists that the constitutions of our bodies—be they male or female, young or old—matter to how we learn and behave. By naming her project *volatile bodies*, she points to the idea I raised earlier, that "our bodies are completed by culture" (ibid.). Grosz shows that though our bodies come into the world with different biological realities, they are changed through the child's development and later through cultural notions conveyed by society: "A stabilised body image or imaginary anatomy, a consistent and abiding sense of self and bodily boundaries, requires and entails understanding one's position vis-à-vis others, one's place at the apex or organising point in the perception of space, as well as a set of clear-cut distinctions between the inside and the outside of the body, the active and passive positions, and, as we will see, a position as a sexually determinate subject" (ibid., 48). What does she mean by this account? In short, when we come into the world as newborns we cannot speak, rise, walk, talk, grasp objects; we do not know even know where our bodies end and other bodies, such as our mothers', or the rest of the world, begins. The developmental process toward a sense of self, toward a soma, requires stimuli of various forms: being touched, learning how to suckle, starting to organize all our perceptual inputs into patterns that single out different objects in our environment. Later, as we learn language, attaching words to these perceptual patterns, we start to develop consciousness. Through this development, we discover the inside and outside of our bodies. We learn where our bodies start and where they end.

Grosz speaks of how the *ego* is formed through the use of the body—in particular, its surface, the skin, which becomes a screen or a filter that helps us select and sort all the sensory information we actively seek through perception. The skin is what separates the body from the rest of the world, as well as being an important locus of exchange between the inside and the outside, a point of conversation: we touch and we can be touched through the same sense. Step by step, the ego emerges through a process of differentiation as our perception meets the reality around us. As Simone de Beauvoir (1949) pointed out, "One is not born a woman: one *becomes* a woman." That is human nature is malleable, and this process of being exposed to stimuli, engagement with others, language, and being introduced to practices, culture, and movements shapes our human bodies and ourselves. In this manner, our (nondualistic) somas are always constructed through meeting with our environment. In this equation, our perception is *active*, it seeks the world, it engages through movement to probe what is around.

To the project of deconstructing dualism, Grosz and other feminists add how cultural gender roles are strongly enforced by society and how this in turn shapes our egos, our consciousness, our behaviors, and even our physical bodies. If we are brought up in patriarchies, we are of course shaped by ideas and behavior patterns telling us what is right or wrong for a particular gender, to the extent that we will walk, talk, and sit in ways appropriate to our gender role.

What Grosz adds to this account is a reminder that this process happens through a particular corporeality—a body that is not the same for males and females. It is through a *particular* body, with menstruation, childbirth, male or female genitals, and so on, that we project ourselves onto the world and the world is projected onto our bodies. This is also true for bodies of different skin colors, able or disabled bodies, aging bodies, bodies with and without pain, and so on. We internalize views handed to us through culture, but we do so through the specifics of our own bodies.

Throughout the last century, the fact that the different male and female corporeality leads to different subjectivities was ignored. In most of the early literature on this subject, all of development was basically described from a male norm perspective. If anything, the lack of a penis was seen as a form of castration, a lack that women had to deal with as part of their development.

Now back to our soma design project: In what way do these different subjectivities matter to design? On the one hand, this idea repeats the implications derived from dissolving dualistic notions and instead working from an integrated soma, a subjectivity stance, as we discussed earlier. But in my view, it also adds a dimension to the pluralism agenda. If our subjective selves are shaped by and shape our corporeal realities, and if those in turn differ between female and male, able and disabled, or young and old bodies, in an intricate interplay among corporeal reality, culture, and development of the subjective self (the ego), then the design process and the resulting designs need to reflect this. It will not only be important to care about whether the body is tall, heavy, or fits other biological realities as those biological realities cannot be separated from the sense of self—from the soma. The whole soma will be different, but not different in a generalizable sense. We cannot claim that *female somas* will behave, feel, think, and engage in certain manners, while *male somas* will always act in other ways. Instead, the idea points to the unique engagement with design from each subjectivity. It will not be important solely to adjust the size of the Soma Mat to fit different body sizes. It will be a matter of gaining an intersubjective understanding across quite different somas—volatile, lived, male and female bodies and subjectivities. And as argued earlier, the resulting designs will in turn potentially alter our somas and culture, thus changing us.

As mentioned above, a first-person perspective creates a blindness to the ways in which our *lived bodies* are different and how these differences color our user experiences. One can imagine having a different body—being short or tall, skinny or obese—but one cannot *experience* being another body. The closest we get is through a second-person perspective on the body, in which the designer uses his or her body as an instrument for feeling the bodily aspects of the user experience of the other in codesign practices (even if there are attempts to step into the shoes of someone else; see, e.g., Beuthel and Wilde 2017).

Shusterman (2012, 32) points out that the norms for women reinforce gender oppression, such as to "speak softly, eat daintily, sit with closed legs, and walk with bowed heads and lowered eyes." Not only are these limiting bodily practices that hinder movement, they also often are taken for granted and so escape critical consciousness. As we filter our experiences through our own somas, we might not even be aware of these behavior and movement patterns. Their influence on how we behave, how we feel, and our attitudes are profound but entirely bundled up and therefore invisible. Only when we engage with our own somas, discerning different experiences, engaging with others intersubjectively, empathically, we can come to see these norms, which in turn means that they can be challenged and altered.

How to challenge and alter those somatic practices that we may find oppressive needs to be shaped against the specific context we are designing in. The only way I believe we can do this is through the same process discussed in chapters 6 and 7: through methods in which we learn to appreciate our own somas, discern our experiences, put words to them, discuss them, work on them, and share them in an immediate emphatic and intersubjective sense. It requires, in every instance, openness and a critical stance toward experience, culture, corporealities, empathy, and an ability to see and engage with what is there.

As an example, a somaesthetic design project with an explicit feminist stance is the Wo.Defy dress created by Schiphorst, Chung, and Ip (2013). The dress builds on the early suffragette movement in China, at the beginning of the last century, in which women protested arranged marriages and wanted emancipation. As a symbol of their struggle, they wore wedding dresses, symbolizing getting married to themselves rather than being forced into arranged marriages.

The Wo.Defy project took inspiration from those wedding dresses but shifted the ideas forward into our own time. The Wo.Defy dress establishes several explicit provocations to male/female garment conventions. For example, the direction of the collar is the male direction from a left-side closing to a right-side closing. The dress is white—a symbol of death in China. The dress is also interactive, with the aim to invite discussion and reflection. The dress responds interactively to your breathing, translated into contractions of the floral elements on the dress and the amplitude of LED lights sewn into the fabric. With Wo.Defy, Schiphorst and colleagues show how somaesthetic design can engage with "self as resistance."

Shusterman sees somaesthetics training as a path to empowerment. Once we become more body aware, allowing ourselves to move in novel ways—ways that may, for example, not rhyme with our gender—our culture comes into focus and we can start questioning it. If we are not even aware of how our gender limits our movements, in turn limiting our reach, beliefs, and attitudes, we cannot change these limits. And so long as we do not change with and through our bodies, others cannot either and will respond to us accordingly.

Only for the Privileged?

From empowerment and feminism, the step to considering class, privilege, and economic status is small. Rather than introducing theories of privilege and class, I am going to discuss the topic from a slightly different angle. Repeatedly I have noted that people (sometimes reviewers on papers I have written on this topic, sometimes audiences at talks I have given, sometimes even myself) are rubbed the wrong way by the mention of practices such as mindfulness or Feldenkrais technique. Not only do they have a whiff of spirituality, new age, and shallow interpretations of religious practices such as Buddhism, they also convey a sense of "well-off, cultured design researchers" only interested in dance, Feldenkrais, and other "soft," "female" practices.

Hopefully this book also has provided examples of entirely different practices, including sports or uncomfortable games. But still, the critique is interesting, and if we broaden it somewhat we might ask: Are we solely arguing for design that fits into a rich, middle-class lifestyle in a Western context? Is this book solely for a privileged class of designers who have the time and money to explore designs that might seem entirely esoteric or luxurious, far from the everyday life of most people around the globe?

I would like to tackle this challenge with two different arguments. First, I want to defend—fiercely—those esoteric, playful, artful designs. They are not frivolous add-ons to an already rich, cultural lifestyle only of relevance to the well-off; instead, as I will show, they constitute a basic human right of *freedom*. My second argument concerns soma design relevance to all sorts of settings and all sorts of design challenges—even the utilitarian ones.

A Freedom for All

One of my former colleagues, Pedro Ferreira (2015), argues that play or playfulness is a basic human freedom. Ferreira bases his argument on Nobel Laureate Amartya Sen's (1999) capability theory, a welfare-economics theory. He argues that development in third-world countries should focus on enhancing people's abilities to choose the lives they value—increasing their capability. Sen sees three different freedoms: political freedoms and transparency in relations between people; freedom of opportunity, including freedom to access credit; and economic protection from abject poverty, including through income supplements and unemployment relief. By enabling these freedoms for all, value is, according to Sen, increased in three different ways: first, enhancing these capabilities has a positive correlation with socioeconomic growth—an *instrumental* value; second, the freedoms have an *intrinsic* value, representing legitimate aspirations that we all have; and third, they have a *constructive* value in that they open up space for a more inclusive deliberation of joint values.

To the list of freedoms that Sen brought forth, Ferreira (as well as Nussbaum [2001]) adds the *freedom to play* (Ferreira 2015). How does play relate to instrumental, intrinsic, or constructive values? Turning to the literature, it is notable how often research has documented various instrumental values arising from play. Play in primates often is argued to be the basis for learning, as we practice behaviors through playing. In the digital realms, there are documented positive effects of playing video games, such as training your strategic thinking or your language skills. In fact, studies from the third world shows that a few years after introducing a technology, such as computers or mobile phones, the economic situation improves.

But these instrumental values do not explain why we play. We play because play has *intrinsic* value (Huizinga 1944). Brown and Juhlin (2015) argue that scholars are brought up to ignore this aspect. They argue that not only is play a less established part of our lives than work, but valuing play also is "tinged with doubt" (ibid.). It is notable how academics in HCI have avoided approaching topics such as games or sex (with a few notable exceptions).

A third reason play is important is its *constructive* role in our lives, engaging with practices and behaviors in our society. In any culture there will be boundaries deciding who is allowed to play and enjoy, when, and where. It is an enactment and manifestation of the culture. The boundaries reflect people's needs and values in the culture. But when we play, we can probe those boundaries. It might even be a reason to play: we are allowed to overstep limitations and taboos. Play becomes constructive and able to perform *boundary work*: to question categories, values, and norms in and through the play activity.

Returning to soma design, this provides us with parallel arguments for designs that allow us to dance, play, and engage in mindfulness or Feldenkrais exercises. Why would these be available only to the rich? We have a responsibility to defend this basic human freedom: the right to play, to enjoy your own body, to engage in both pleasurable and challenging movements, to be mirrored in technology in a manner that promotes whole somas. This right goes beyond instrumental goals. We need to stop devaluing intrinsic and constructive values. We are here to live our lives, not to be production units in a socioeconomic system.

Soma Design Relevance

Now, let us turn to privilege from the viewpoint of the second argument—that somaesthetics is important to all design, not only to designs featuring more playful, esoteric, or art-oriented interactions. If Shusterman's claim is true that we can live better lives through engaging somaesthetically, and my claim holds true that this in turn can help us shape better technologies and better interactions, then the relevance for *all* sorts of activities follows. All sorts of interactive systems that engage with people should be designed not only with ergonomics concerns in mind, but also with somaesthetic concerns in mind.

In my view, somaesthetic design concerns are relevant to the most utilitarian design challenges, such as the design of word processing, mobile devices, Internet of Things services, or the organization of workplaces such as factories or offices. Today, many work their whole lives in front of computers, limiting and even harming their somatics severely. We become "enslaved" in front of our computers, moving only a few muscles in our fingers and arms and shoulders, engaging mainly through our intellectual, rational, language-oriented capacities—not much through our subjective selves.

In turn, a lot of the innovations in our IT industry originate from these office environments, replicating the same limited engagements for all sorts of interactions: applications for dating, interactive machinery for household work, video games, interactive play, or social media. There is something disturbing about this development in its lack of bodily, emotional, aesthetic engagements. The designs are "small"—rarely moving outside small glass screens. The designs reflect the shape and social organization of those offices where the brainstorming and design thinking takes place. For fun, as part of the Soma project, we have bodystormed and slowstormed out in nature, in barns, and around campfires. It is striking how often this has led to quite different form factors—sometimes physically bigger systems, sometimes mimicking sounds or shapes from nature (Ståhl et al. 2017).

The Internet of Things is an especially interesting development from a somaesthetic perspective. Imagine a world in which any object that benefits from being connected to the Internet is connected, sending data and using data analytics to control its behavior and actuation in the world. This includes cars, buses, climate controls, dishwashers, chainsaws, and just about all sorts of activities we can imagine. Not only machines will be connected; we will also have services that thrive on many different data sources connecting to sensors measuring weather, temperature, movement, and other measurable processes. A positive development would be for all these connected devices to fit our lifeworlds, creating aesthetically appealing, humane experiences and connections. Interfaces to Internet of Things services may take new forms, with autonomous decision making fitting with and learning from our aggregate behavior in new ways. A negative development would be for the Internet of Things to become governed by a "small screen" focus, for the design work to be done in the same confined office spaces and with the same brainstorming methods as used elsewhere, without care for the range of possible experiences and the fundamentals of our human condition.

The Internet of Things could move interactions beyond the screen. Systems in this connected world could potentially deal more *implicitly* with our behaviors. They could be responding to our movements and behaviors in richer manners. There is an opportunity for more and better engagement with digitally enabled systems.

What if somaesthetic design practices could influence this Internet of Things world? In my view, we have an obligation to educate designers and engineers in these perspectives. Unless they know how to design for somatics and aesthetics, then there is no chance we can influence and change the development of new technologies, such as those in the Internet of Things era.

Instead of removing the opportunity for aesthetics in movement—as we have done with remote controls and other interactions, basically minimizing the need for movement—we would do well to design in a different manner this time, bringing in the aesthetic perspective, bringing in movements we enjoy, making the environments places for creative self-fashioning and engagements.

Even in work environments, the somaesthetic perspectives can play a strong role. Let me briefly make a brief detour and present a historical machine: the Jacquard loom—the predecessor of computers. The Jacquard loom is a weaving machine, operated by a human being standing and moving inside complex machinery controlled by punched cards. By standing inside the machine on pedals moving back and forth, up and down, the human operator drives the machine, in turn producing different fabric patterns. My colleagues Fernaeus, Jonsson, and Tholander (2012) performed an analysis of the Jacquard loom, a machine that is still in use, and were fascinated by how the human operator can work for many hours without getting tired. The machinery is adapted for whole-body engagement, performing repetitive but not tiring movements. Fernaeus and colleagues point out that the loom involves human weight, size, muscle strength, and cooperative action—all embodied in the machine. They also note how the machine itself has wonderful aesthetic qualities through its sheer size, especially when juxtaposed with the obsession with the small and handheld in HCI.

What if we could design all sorts of modern workplaces with similar ambitions as the Jacquard loom?

In the early days of participatory design (Ehn 1993) in Scandinavia, the idea was to create tools that would empower workers in factories. To support this, the Swedish Social Democrat Party created a law that would guarantee workers' rights to influence their workplace (the codetermination law). The argument was that workers should have some control over the design of tools used to perform work tasks. Today, with the slimming down of industry through automatization, the demand for fast profits, and the effects of globalization making industries move to where the workforce is cheap, this may all sound like a utopian dream. But designing a workplace based on the bodily, emotional, intellectual, and social needs of those working would indeed create a sustainable work life and, ultimately, sustainable companies.

In summary, soma design is not confined to a space of art, nor should it be solely for the privileged and rich, but should instead be an important strand of design thinking permeating and altering all sorts of settings across the globe, in the formation of the Internet of Things, in designing workplaces, and in shaping open-design processes. It may seem a somewhat naïve position and seem that the realities of capitalism and globalism are harsh. At the same time, we do have a strong development toward sustainable businesses. Sustainable businesses often have progressive environmental and human rights policies—not only because it is the right thing to do, but because it is profitable.

Furthermore, the more esoteric aspects of somaesthetics, contributing to mindfulness, enjoyment, play, and fun, should not be dismissed as frivolous and confined to the art world. Both utilitarian and intrinsically motivated values can and should be harbored under the same soma design umbrella (and should perhaps not be entirely divided purposes anyway, but rather end points on a scale). Dismissing somaesthetic design as not concerned with both realms denies the important role of our somas as always being there, always with us in every walk of life.

The Politics of Algorithms and Data

Data is often portrayed as the "new big oil" due to its potentially enormous value in modeling and predicting behavior. This in turn can be used to create various *actuations* in the world: controlling processes in industry, organizing logistics, handling so-called smart homes or smart cities, or even crafting augmentations to our bodies.

But data analytics and machine learning do not come without complications. We live in a society with a strong faith in the objectivity and neutrality of raw data. This "objective" data is supposed to guide anything from political decision making to the automatic management of a person/home/city/country. But nothing in a design process that relies on data is ever neutral or objective. Even the first step, choosing data sources, is a value-led design choice. And once we add algorithms and choice of machine learning strategies, the outcomes can become even more narrowly determined by certain values and not others.

Data analytics and design tools based on data offer challenges to soma design values in at least three ways: (1) the risk of objectifying human behavior and our bodily signs and signals, (2) the shift from carefully honed somaesthetic crafts training to data-driven automated design processes, and (3) the challenge of maintaining soma design values when particular soma designs enter ecologies of interactions and data streams.

Objectifying Bodies

Raw data makes little sense. Only when we find patterns in the data can we associate meaning with that data. This is where specialized tools building on data analytics, such as movement recognition, facial recognition, or biosensor data analysis, will play an important role. Using these specialized tools will foster certain functions, forms, and interactions. But these tools also pose a risk; by measuring human experience, they may in fact objectify it (Boehner et al. 2007). Many data-driven tools build on a science-based perspective on the human body and how to improve on it.

In particular, these tools often isolate one measurable unit from its overall context. For example, in our work with the Affective Diary and Affective Health, we measured arousal levels by measuring sweat levels with a GSR sensor. But arousal is a complex mechanism; sweat is one of the signs of arousal, but it is a crude measurement of what is going on. To really understand the qualitative experience of arousal, you need to account for the social context at hand; the sociocultural setting in which the event is taking place; other processes in the body, such as hormonal levels, muscle tensions, or organ engagement; and so on. Likewise, others have used facial expression to recognize emotion (Picard 1997) or used the movement of some body part to measure sports performance (Consolvo et al. 2008). The answer lies not in measuring more and more signs and signals to disambiguate meaning. The processes are themselves ambiguous, consisting of many interrelated processes, some speaking against each other. The idea that there is one single interpretation of what is happening misses the point of personal interpretation and coproduction of experience (Ståhl et al. 2009).

Let me make it clear here that of course we can use data and data analytics in our soma designs. It is not whether we measure some aspect of the body that will determine whether we will be able to craft a somaesthetic experience, however. It is in how we approach that data, how we understand it, how we make it part of our somatics that matters. The data sources and analytics tools should not be seen as "innocent" materials, arriving at the soma design scene without any values or political agendas associated with them. Historically, there is nothing new here. Tools and materials have always impacted form-giving and function. What is important for soma design is how we shape these tools to allow for interactions harmonizing with our somas.

Another way data analysis enters our soma design practice is through the data-driven tools we can use while designing. Design today is not done through sketching, building models, and engaging with a small design team. Instead, it is done with tools that feed off data—modeling human movements, hands, fingers—or through crowd design over the Internet, in loosely coupled maker cultures and networked companies (Lindtner, Hertz, and Dourish 2014). It is no longer the case that big companies have permanent staff in a design department creating products from start to end. Instead we get "networked" company models, in which you do not hire coworkers but instead engage consultants with certain competences when you need them (Yetis-Larsson, Teigland, and Dovbysh 2015). As Lindtner (2014) has shown with her studies in Shenzen in China, the maker culture is on the rise and is starting to define what can be seen as novel HCI paradigms, as well as novel company structures. Both Lindtner and Yetis-Larsson and colleagues point to a future in which we might see fewer hierarchically structured big companies with whole departments for design, marketing, production, or research, and more of these companies created as networks on the fly, involving people who know one another and engage locally with one another, or even rely on web services that will get parts of their work done for them through the intelligence of the crowd.

Is it perhaps time to start creating various design tools from a soma basis? Similar to how Arduino shaped embedded programming designs, might we want soma-based sketching tools, data analytics tools and methods, and crowd-design tools that in turn foster many soma-designed systems? Bogers et al. (2016) at Technical University Eindhoven have started forming such tools for their design students.

Crafts versus Automated Design

Beyond ways in which design practice needs to engage with data analytics and various tools that will support form-giving practices, the data-driven changes in design and manufacturing have a more far-reaching impact on design practice. When parts of a design can be "completed" automatically, we might start to ask how much the profession remains as a craft-based practice in which we can rely on the designer's somaesthetics training to ensure the kinds of dynamic gestalts and user experiences we want.

One current commercial development system relies on a designer to come up with an initial idea, which is then posted online for crowdfunding or crowd design, allowing others to shape the idea, change it, in effect adding data that determines how to turn a loose idea into a particular form. The soma design process outlined in this book relies on an entirely different design process: giving a designer or an interdisciplinary team total control over the whole design process, from idea to product, in a craft-based process.

Big companies like IKEA or Ericsson have latched on to the codesign movement and now form various partnerships in which they codesign in open collaborations instead of keeping their innovation processes secret and behind closed doors. Increasingly, design work is shifting away from multidisciplinary teams controlling the whole process, from initial idea to product and market entry, to a crowd-design endeavor. The blueprints can be modified and printed on 3-D printers, open designs will be completed by others, and so on. Furthermore, the design process is no longer a matter of sketching with paper and pens but is instead handled with various sketching tools via which data analytics can be used to support the design process.

This raises a question: Is there any way we can guarantee that somaesthetic qualities can be honed and maintained in a future in which design is partly done automatically or crowd designed—a future in which the design is not finished once and for all and put out in world for use, but is continually designed? Can we rely on those tools and practices not to destroy or trivialize the somaesthetic experience?

Ecologies of Systems

Another assumption throughout this book has been that soma design will produce singular designs, working independently from any other systems or data streams. But the Internet of Things world is instead a complex interplay of designs built on top of services provided by others, deriving data from various sources, built using tools and toolkits that foster certain form-giving processes—and, most importantly, together forming whole *ecologies of products and services*, intricately interdependent. Users sign up for whole ecologies of services. By choosing Google products, you get stuck in their world, their apps, their systems. By choosing Apple products, you get stuck in their world. By choosing independent, open-source solutions, you get stuck in that world.

In this chapter, I have raised many questions. The answers will only emerge through trial and error, through the incremental development of soma design over time. However, my hope is that if soma designers bear these issues and questions in mind as they approach their projects, and if they remember that soma design, like all design, is governed by politics, power, and resources, then we will move toward a design that improves the world.

9 A Soma Design Manifesto

When writing this book, my aim was to argue for a different design engagement, an engagement that starts from the human condition, in which mind-body-emotion-sociality are seen as a unity, inseparably communicating and influencing one another. By introducing some of Sheets-Johnstone's thinking, I discussed how meaning-making processes start in movement and bodily realities. That fact, in turn, has profound effects on design. If meaning can arise without any language or symbolism between us and the world, then interaction design has enormous potential to generate entirely new ways of interacting and engaging with technology.

I also wanted to put aesthetics centrally on the scene. Shusterman provokes us by claiming that there are *better* ways of living your life beyond educating your intellectual skills. You need to engage with and improve on your somatics—body, mind, emotion, empathy, intersubjectivity—and to do so you must train your somaesthetic appreciation skills. I took Shusterman's provocation even further by claiming that somaesthetic appreciation skills will improve design—for both end users and designers. Such a design ideal would redeem emotion and body from their low status in our design processes—and thereby in society, because our culture is intertwined with the technologies and tools we surround ourselves with. Interaction design would be guided by a design ideal that is entirely grounded in us, in our human morphology.

By introducing some techniques, some conceptualizations, some earlier designs, I have created the beginnings of a soma design program. But while we have been able to draw upon the works of many soma-oriented designers, we are still in the early days of this field. Much more remains to be done to fill the soma design program with experiments, examples, and probings of its strengths and limitations. Soma design is in many ways in its infancy. Let us outline what I see as three major challenges.

Creating a Safe Space for Soma Designers

Whenever a radically new theory and practice is introduced in academia, we should expect it to be examined and questioned. The strength of the ideas, the validity, replicability, and relevance to key problems all need to be probed. At the same time, when a novel perspective is in its infancy, it is easy to kill it, to shut it down before it has even been explored at all. Although many in the field of HCI are very interested in soma design, there is also a degree of skepticism—partly for good reasons.

Validation and Acceptance

In any academic endeavor, processes of validation, critical examination, peer review, and scrutiny are key. Throughout the history of science, critical examination has always become more difficult when we propose a shift from one paradigm to another (Kuhn 2012). The field of HCI has struggled with such shifts in a slightly different manner. The field has been built from a multidisciplinary mix: engineering, psychology, sociology, ethnography, industrial design, game design, and, lately, interactive art, just to name a few (Grudin 1990). There has never really been a clear core—not even a basic agreement on a set of problems that HCI should tackle. This makes the field unstable, and thus knowledge production does not follow the steps to a mature field that an academic discipline typically follows.

Instead, waves of HCI research tend to follow the invention of new technologies originating in other fields. HCI takes on the responsibility for shaping those new technologies to better fit with people's lives. New theories and disciplines are brought into the field as new challenges appear in the footsteps of those new technologies and their novel uses. As a result, very little core theory unique to HCI has been developed. Instead, HCI stays one step behind. Framed in more positive terms, the field remains open to new influences and new technologies, new disciplines are continuously integrated, and new topics are explored: it is a vibrant, young discipline, with a readiness to face change.

But this state of affairs not only presents a challenge to the development of an HCI core but also has made peer reviewing and critique very difficult. Often new ideas are dismissed because reviewers might be coming from an entirely different academic discipline, bringing different criteria than what we might expect from an academic contribution.

In the preface of this book, I touched on two of my own struggles when developing soma designs. The first concerned breaking free from the language-oriented, symbolic, hypothesis-rationalization-driven assumptions in design and research. The second, related struggle was to break free from the strong objectivist (and reductionist) ideals in engineering and design. Although any design researcher knows that a lot of design decisions are made not based on empirical evidence or user studies but instead on design judgment (Nelson and Stolterman 2003), the first-person perspective is still a problematic stance for most HCI academics. For years, they have fought to let end users have a say in the development of interactive tools and systems. User-centered design has been of key importance to help steer design processes. Shifting back to making the designer's first-person perspective the main filter through which we develop soma designs is problematic to many in the field. It risks putting designers back on their pedestals (Fallman 2003), as geniuses delivering ready-made artifacts, instead of sharing power with the end users over how technology can and should be integrated with our everyday practices (see Schuler and Namioka 1993).

To address this challenge, soma design needs to become much better documented and validated. We need ways of teaching and designing with our somas that have a basis in intersubjective empathy and ways of involving end users in our design processes. We might also need ways of evaluating the success of our work that go beyond traditional user studies.

Terminology and Articulation

Some of the work on somaesthetics is unfortunately associated with a range of dubious terminology, often associated with new-age developments: terms such as *mindfulness, holistic design, spirituality,* and so on. I do not want to defend using terminology without proper groundings, but I also have some sympathy for why such terminology is used. As discussed earlier in this book, putting words to somaesthetic experiences is difficult. The reality of the experience is unquestionably there, but it can be very hard to express it in precise terms. Instead, sweeping terms like *mindfulness* or *flow* sometimes are used. To those not experienced in soma design, such terms do not make sense and might even signal frivolous, nonscientific work. We risk outright dismissal of the whole design endeavor.

When we developed the Soma Mat and Breathing Light, I hid our work inside a project with completely different aims for a couple of years before showing any results publicly. We did not report on it to funders, industrial partners, or even our colleagues in the Mobile Life center to begin with. Our colleagues saw us doing bodily exercises in our office, of course, building the mat and trying out various materials, sensors, and actuators, but it was not until we had struggled through the first most difficult phases that we opened our process for others to partake. Even then, we only invited a select few people who we believed would be open to our design explorations. If we had exposed our project to scrutiny after a year, in all likelihood it would have been canceled or stymied. In fact, when we showed the Soma Mat to a group of visitors at an early stage, one of the visitors, a powerful professor in computer science, was quite upset by how "unscientific" this project was. He argued that this kind of work should not be allowed at a university. His position was not irrelevant. We could not, at that stage, defend or validate what we had done from a proper "scientific" perspective. It was not until later, when we had tested the Soma Mat and Breathing Light thoroughly, going through a couple of redesigns, that we could really articulate and defend our contribution. Thus, the problem I am trying to frame here does not lie with his question and whether we should be able to defend our work in a relevant manner. My worry concerns the effects of critique that comes too early in the development of an entirely novel design stance. Luckily, when this professor delivered his critique, we were in a stage of our project in which we could already see that we were on the right path, and thus we were less sensitive to his critique—but comments like that could otherwise easily have killed budding ideas.

This said, once we had established that we could build interesting applications and that the path to doing so was different from the more symbolic, language-oriented interface design we had engaged in, as researchers we felt a responsibility to not only communicate but also validate our work.

Articulating the experience might sometimes be better done through letting people try the technology themselves, getting a first-hand experience of it. We exhibited the Soma Mat and Breathing Light at the largest conference in the HCI field. Many who tried it came back to us with a sense of enlightenment. Before trying the systems, the descriptions in the accompanying paper had lacked experiential reality to them. But after trying it out, the vague and unfamiliar terms we used were filled with meaning.

I have argued elsewhere that the academic field of HCI needs to allow for many different forms of articulation of knowledge (Höök 2012). Some experiences are best described through interacting with the systems we build. Other experiences can be framed in videos or pictorials (Blevis, Hauser, and Odom 2015). Design knowledge is often articulated in other forms. As pointed out by Löwgren, "Design educations are based on canons, examples, and crits; professional designer networks communicate knowledge through portfolios, exhibitions, design competitions, and awards." (2013, 32). There are reasons that those articulation forms make more sense to designers. The tacit knowledge embodied in interactions with designs is hard to capture verbally.

Because soma design needs its experiential, somatic reality to make sense, finding forms of articulation becomes extra important. But this does not excuse the use of dubious terminology, with terms that are sweeping and broad in scope. Together, we need to develop a terminology with groundings in design exemplars, experiences, orchestrations, and methods. In particular, we need to bring out many successful (and less successful) design exemplars to populate the soma design program.

A Protective Belt of Knowledge

To address issues of validation and breaking with the current HCI paradigm, the soma design research field needs to develop a "protective belt" of knowledge—articulated in forms relevant to the expression of aesthetic experience and engagement. This protective belt of knowledge might include articulations in many different forms: first-person accounts of engaging with soma design exemplars, a canon of successful (as well as failed) designs, a terminology associated with those exemplars and experiences, design methods, and so on. New user study methods are needed to capture benefits of soma designs, as well as to pinpoint failures. In particular, more commercial designs would help legitimize soma design as a viable design approach.

There is currently a wave of research underway relating to compassion, emotion, and the connection to bodily processes or well-being. Let me provide a few examples. In psychotherapy, a variant of cognitive behavior therapy (CBT) named *compassion therapy* is gaining traction (Gilbert 2009). Similarly, in leadership training and management, compassion training is seen as a path to making companies and their management groups work better together. In neuroscience, studies of the vagus nerve system show the connection between compassion and the parasympathetic nervous system (Stellar et al. 2015). These are only a few of the available examples. The soma design research program should relate to and contribute to these developments, thereby building relevant theory to explain how and why these interactions work.

Together, these activities will fill the soma design program with content, as well as a better understanding of its potential and limitations. A well-defined terminology, properly published, together with a canon of design exemplars, will not only tidy up the terminology in the field, making it respectable, but also will make it clearer and easier for design researchers outside of the program to assess its benefits.

This said, as we strive toward making soma design respectable and properly validated, we must not compromise and "tidy up" what is and needs to be a creative, experiential craft. Tacit knowledge is and will continue to be part of the bodily, emotional, and subjective aesthetic experiences. Cultivating deep aesthetic skills and understandings of the sociodigital materials takes time and devotion. Peer review of soma design contributions will continue to be difficult for those lacking those skills and experiences (Gaver and Höök 2017).

Furthermore, the creation of a protective belt must not fossilize the soma design program. As discussed earlier, design—whether at the level of a single design, a program, or a whole paradigm—is always in a perpetual state of change. As we make use of new materials and add new designs, the program will change, the terminology will develop, and the design methods will change to meet new demands.

In summary, the first challenge is to make soma design respectable without compromising or tidying up what is and needs to be a creative, experiential, subjective craft, and to do so through putting a protective belt around soma design. This protective belt will shift soma design from a marginal practice to a flourishing, validated, well-documented, and useful approach.

Responsibility and Impact

Taking Responsibility

I argued earlier that interaction designers have a responsibility to shape the space of movements that the system invites, to increase aesthetic experiences that rhyme with our somas, and to create meaningful interactions with our lifeworlds. My argument has been that our bodies are completed by culture. Our practices shape our bodies. And interactive technologies are and will increasingly be intertwined with all our everyday practices. Soma designers need to step up to this challenge.

Watching someone walking down the street, we can immediately see age, gender, cultural belonging, or injuries. We can guess what physical activities that body has been subjected to—be they sports, work, or mainly sitting at a computer. Imagine putting a mobile phone in the hands of a person walking down that street: it becomes immediately apparent how that piece of technology changes everything from the person's way of walking and use of his or her dominant hand and arm to his or her engagement with the surroundings, perceptually as well as socially (Ferreira and Höök 2011). Although mobile phones have brought amazing opportunities to all sorts of contexts all over the world, they are not always optimally fitted to those contexts and practices. We might speculate that a soma design approach could change the form factors or placement of the mobile phone on the body, or introduce new apps or sensor-based interactions that connect more strongly to the surroundings at hand. Perhaps those soma-based design processes would render a mobile phone form factor less reliant on symbolic interactions on the screen. Perhaps we would see applications more strongly weaving together the local context with that context that is virtually accessible.

Unfortunately, redesigning the mobile phone might be beyond our powers given its de facto standard form and widespread use. But soma design might impact other upcoming interactive technologies, such as those in Internet of Things developments, wearables, interactive textiles, and so on. In fact, I would like to claim that we have a responsibility to engage with that development as it will have profound effects on our everyday practices, social interactions, and even the most intimate of our bodily engagements (Bardzell and Bardzell 2011). How can we give soma design a voice in those developments? One path is to engage with commercial development, spreading our design approach to the big companies in our field. Another path is through integrating soma design with the HCI curriculum taught at universities across the globe.

Spreading Soma Design

To have real impact, soma design should be taught at technical universities, as well at design schools. But teaching soma design is nontrivial. In design and art schools, soma design will most probably fit nicely with the curriculum. In technical universities, we might expect a clash with the prevailing positivist viewpoints and their emphasis on logic, mathematics, and intellectual achievements.

Usually, computer-engineering programs will have at least one course in HCI. The syllabus for HCI courses should include soma design alongside learning about personas, task analysis, or user-centered design. It should become a tool in the design toolbox taught to engineers. But learning soma design requires a form of subjective engagement that stands in stark contrast to the prevailing positivist design approaches otherwise taught in engineering schools. How do we best introduce soma design in this setting? There is not yet a curriculum for teaching soma design, nor are there (software or hardware) tools and methods that may scaffold and support a design process. The design methods are often directed at those who have a background as dancers, artists, or industrial designers.

In summary, the second challenge is to take seriously our responsibility as soma design researchers and practitioners. Design of interactive technology should rhyme with our somas, expanding on our capacity to enjoy and appreciate. We need to make sure we have impact—spreading our insights academically, as well as commercially.

Addressing the Existential Crisis in HCI

Some argue that HCI is undergoing an existential crisis. Previously, HCI was "about interfaces and their design" (Janlert and Stolterman 2017), but now interactions are moving away from the screen, into our everyday practices, creating complex interactions based on ecologies of systems and diverse infrastructures from a whole range of shifting contexts. The HCI focus on an explicit dialogue with one device, through a screen with one clear interface, will not be as relevant going forward.

Scale Up

As Professor Brown, Professor Bödker, and I argue, though HCI had a massive impact on the world through streamlining and enabling millions of interfaces on billions of devices, current developments require that we scale up (Brown, Bödker, and Höök 2017). By *scale*, we mean adapt to the way technology is used in large networks of interconnected systems, with billions of users across diverse contexts (ibid.). These scales can be framed broadly as four difference scaling challenges, all currently increasing in complexity: technologies and devices are used in an increasing number of *different settings*; the *number of users* is growing; our methods address *one technology at a time* instead of ecologies of artifacts and practices; and we increasingly face *layers of systems* instead of monolithic systems. Technologies and devices often travel between contexts; the mobile phone, for instance, is used everywhere, blending contexts such as work and leisure. Interactive systems are constructed as layers of interconnected systems, residing in the cloud or in many different devices. It is no longer clear where this "interface" that HCI focused on will be. Sometimes, the interface will no longer happen through a screen but instead through faceless interfaces (Janlert and Stolterman 2015) or implicit interactions (Ju 2015; Ju and Leifer 2008), relying on data gathered from our devices and from tracking our behaviors via sensors. Those interactions will respond to our behaviors without involving us in any explicit dialogue. Sometimes they will behave in mysterious ways, with some activity we performed months earlier suddenly influencing the behavior of the system in the moment.

As we discussed in the previous chapter, the soma design tactics introduced here unfortunately are focused on the design of one system at a time, rather than large, interrelated, and complex relationships with a whole range of systems, designed by many different companies and other designers. The soma designs we imagined would have one clear interface aimed for one clearly defined setting. Although the interface might often take the form of an implicit interaction, the assumption is that we can control the interaction context. We assume that we know who the users are, when and why they use the system, and that we are creating one, singular system through which the interaction happens. We are not designing whole practices relying on ecologies of devices, layers of systems, or interactions happening outside of those technologies.

But this single-user, single-interface, single-system approach will not hold much longer. An interesting challenge would be to design a whole range of soma-based Internet of Things designs, all fitting together like puzzle pieces, but in which we can pick and choose which part of the puzzle we want. No matter what combinations the end users pick, the look and feel would aesthetically fit together, making a whole. Even more challenging would be to engage with already existing ecologies of systems, adding somatic engagement. This is the kind of thinking soma designers will be called upon very soon to engage in, to ensure that future designs enhance human enjoyment and thriving, as well as productivity.

Ideals

Another way of framing the existential crisis of HCI is as a lack of guiding ideals agreed upon by the field.

Interactive technologies already reach into our most intimate spheres. This is why HCI has had to find a way to address user experience rather than usability (Fallman 2011). Although work tasks had to be supported by usable interfaces, interactions with games, social media, and so on require more than a usable interface.

In this new, complex world in which digital interactions are mixed into every walk of life, it is no longer clear what distinguishes a *user* experience from any other experience, and even more difficult to determine what constitutes a *good* experience (Fallman 2011). As I mentioned earlier, interaction design is no longer limited to a controlled interaction between one user and one system; we must design tools and interactions that support whole practices. The digital becomes infused and intertwined with every aspect of those practices. We must search for *ideals* that can guide our design processes—a set of core values (Cockton 2004). HCI must prove that it can provide relevant knowledge to support the shaping of practices—now in settings in which technology is but one component.

The existential crisis also concerns the role HCI can play in facing the grand challenges of our time. Recently, Light, Powell, and Shklovski called for action as "right-wing populism sweeps through politics; climate predictions worsen; mass migration (within/across countries) escalates refugee numbers; new classes of automation threaten workers' jobs and austerity policies destabilize society" (2017, 722). Again, like Fallman (2011) and Cockton (2004), Light, Powell, and Shklovski ask for ideals that can help guide our design work, helping us to lead fulfilling lives together, in a functioning society. They argue that HCI researchers and practitioners should be designing "tools that focus on meaning, purpose and fulfillment in difficult, unstable and rapidly changing times" (ibid., 728).

Soma design carries strong ideals: empathy, compassion, a path to living *better* lives through connecting with ourselves. Whether those ideals in turn will let us address the grand challenges of our times is a different issue. In summary, the third, perhaps most crucial, challenge is to make soma design step up to face the existential crisis of HCI, addressing two interrelated design challenges. First, interaction will no longer be confined to a clearly identified interface between a user and a device, but instead will spread and intertwine with all our practices. Second, because digital communication and data are now integrated with all practices of our society— media, politics, work, leisure—we have a great responsibility in responding to the big challenges of our time.

Articulating a Soma Design Manifesto

Will soma design be able to scale up and address any aspect of these three challenges? To do so, we need to be clear about what values a turn to soma design would bring. To make them explicit, I have decided to articulate these values as a manifesto.

Manifestos can serve many different roles: They can be an aggressive call for action. They can declare artistic interests. They can set agendas for human rights. With this soma design manifesto, my aim is to set boundaries, creating a safe space in which we can jointly cultivate and expand our soma design knowledge. This safe space should be guided and guarded by a joint commitment to certain values.

Reflecting on what has been introduced in this book, the soma design manifesto makes the following declarations:

#1: We design for living better lives—not for dying.
#2: We design to move the passions in others and ourselves.
#3: We are movement, through and through.
#4: We design with ourselves—through empathy and compassion.
#5: We design slowly.
#6: We cultivate our aesthetic appreciation.
#7: We disrupt the habitual and engage with the familiar.

Where We Stand—What We Do

Given the de facto standards for digital interaction—on computers, on mobile phones, and through other screens—is there really an opportunity to change interaction design as dramatically as proposed here?

Let us just for a moment remind ourselves that interaction design has a very short history. Compared to all the other manmade tools and technologies—for cooking, transportation, farming our lands, seafaring, or constructing the homes in which we live—interactive technologies appear as a short blip in human history. The field had a good start, with roots in long-standing traditions such as ergonomics, caring about how workers move and interact to create a sustainable work life. The early work via the desktop metaphor continued along this path, letting movement (even if confined mainly to small movements of the hand and arm) be the starting point for design. Throughout the years, the academic field has included several strong voices arguing for value-based design (Friedman 1996), empowerment (as in the participatory design movement; Schuler and Namioka 1993), embodied interactions as a path to integrating technology with our fluid social acts (Dourish 2001), and a range of critical design pointing to the risk of reductionist positions (e.g., Boehner et al. 2007; Gaver 2012). But with the extremely rapid development of the Internet and the commercial success of computers and mobile phones in settings outside the regulated workplace, the commercial world has pressured the field to find the cheap solutions, the addictive interactions that speak only to a limited part of what it means to be human.

If interaction design so far is just a blip in history, there is still time to restart our field—perhaps even restart it several times. We can look to movements such as Bauhaus or the history of architecture to find inspiring examples of how to rethink the foundations of what we do. To make such change happen, we should take advantage of the disruptions about to happen with the introduction of new hybrid, digital-physical technologies, shifting interactions beyond the glass screen. As new technologies enter the scene, we can finally rectify the lopsided focus on our language-oriented skills: interactions that are overwhelming in their demands on the reasoning, intellectual side of the human intellect and underwhelming regarding their lack of care for bodies and perception. We should gather our resources, hone our aesthetic abilities, and educate our young designers and engineers to design. Even better, interaction design can become a richer practice, aiming to improve aesthetic appreciation—for all.

Notes

1   Why We Need Soma Design

1. Although *materials* usually refers to physical matter, such as wood, plastic, or clay, I am using the term in a metaphorical sense here. By the term *digital materials* I refer to all those materials used to shape interactive systems: algorithms, data, sensors, actuators, wireless communication, Internet infrastructure, and so on. This is inspired by Petra Sundström's work in my research group (Fernaeus and Sundström 2012; Solsona Belenguer et al. 2012; Sundström and Höök 2010), as well as some of the discussions of the material turn in HCI (Giaccardi and Karana 2015; Kuutti and Bannon 2014).

2   Theoretical Backdrop

1. As designers, we cannot prescribe that some particular aesthetic experience will take place. Users will bring their own understandings, moods, needs, and prior experiences to the interaction. They may choose not to engage, or to engage in a manner quite different from what we intended. All we can do is set the scene to make certain experiences more probable. That said, the form and shape of the design and its dynamic gestalt helps shape our lifeworlds.

2. I still remember vividly the confusion and grief of one of the horses in the stables (where I spent years of my childhood) when her best friend died. She spent days standing still, looking far away, neighing as if calling for her friend, interleaved with running around in the patch of field where she and her friend would spend most of their days together, externalizing her anxiety and worry about her lost friend.

3. Although controversial, I have always found Dunbar's (1998) arguments about why humans developed language intriguing. He claims that language is a shortcut for social grooming—the act of cleaning the fur or skin of your friend and at the same time forming a close relationship. Grooming is an important part of keeping a group of primates together, forming bonds and friendships. By keeping the group tightly knit with many strong relationships between its members, we are safer, we

get help, and we can get protection from enemies. A group of primates has a better chance of survival because it can act together against attack. But being in a group also creates tensions: we must share food and keep peace. This is when grooming becomes a tool to stay calm and remain friends (because it leads to the release of hormones such as oxytocin, which relax us). Dunbar claims that the larger the group is, the more time we need to spend on maintaining relations; otherwise, the group falls into parts. This is when language comes in handy—as a shortcut to maintaining good relations with many without spending hours grooming each other's fur. A short phrase of acknowledgment or seemingly empty chitchat about the weather can help us maintain good relations.

4. *Logos* here is taken to mean *word*, *reason*, and *ratio*.

5. See Ingold (2011) discussing Uexkull's theories on *umwelt*—the subjective world of a perceiving and acting animal—and, similarly, Gibson's (2014a) theories on affordances.

6. The term *qualia* refers to how we cannot know what someone else's experience might be (Is my experience of the color red the same as yours?). It is ineffable, as discussed by, among others, Daniel Dennett (1988).

7. The golden ration is a number approximately equal to 1.618. In arts, it has been used to construct, for example, harmonious balance between the whole and its parts, subdividing space 1 to 1.618 to create a feeling of balance.

8. As expressed by John Thackara, critiquing Don Norman's (2007) emotional design.

3   Showing, Not Telling

1. Burning Man is an annual gathering in the Western United States, near Reno. It is an art festival during which radical experiments of self-expression and participation are encouraged.

2. A theremin is a musical instrument played without physical contact with the instrument. The instrument consists of two antennas connected to oscillators, creating an electro-magnetic circuit. As he human body has a certain natural capacitance (ability to hold electrical charge) raising your hand in front of the antennas, you will be raising the capacitance in the circuit, in turn lowering the frequency of the oscillator. That in turn interferes with a second oscillator. The difference generates sounds. When played it looks as if the musician is playing in thin air. In Mediated Body, the mediator becomes the antenna.

3. Galvanic skin response picks up on sweat, which is an indication of emotional arousal.

4   Soma Mat, Breathing Light, and Sarka

1. The team consisted of an interdisciplinary group of researchers from the Mobile Life center: Anna Ståhl, industrial designer; Martin Jonsson, computer scientist; Johanna Mercurio, cognitive scientist; Ilias Bergström, musician and computer scientist (working on Sarka); me; and students, on and off. From IKEA Future Homes, Eva-Carin Banka Johnson was involved. From the design firm Boris Design, Anna Karlsson, industrial designer, was involved. We also had regular engagements with a Feldenkrais practitioner, Kristina Strohmayer.

2. We brought Soma Mat and Breathing Light prototypes to the ACM SIGCHI conference in San José in 2016. More than three thousand participants attended the conference. The exhibition hall was a large space in a conference center, with a concrete floor, no windows, and a high ceiling. It was full of interactive demos. Ours was placed in a corner in a booth made of dark cloth, forming a small room.

3. Personal communication with the author, May 7, 2016.

4. Inspired by a music video for the Swedish artist Robyn. In the video, she wears tubes wrapped around her body. Inside the tubes, different colored water flows. Lucy McRae and colleagues made the costume. See https://vimeo.com/16376731.

5. A body scan asks you to focus your attention on one part of your body at a time, usually starting from the feet and going upward, via legs, pelvis, stomach, and so on through the whole body.

6. Haiku is a Japanese poetic form. A typical haiku is a three-line observation about a fleeting moment involving nature.

7. This was the basis for one of our early designs, Affective Diary, briefly mentioned in the preface. It gathered all sorts of data, in a form of life-logging, and then let users rearrange and scribble on top of that data, letting users engage in this process of *change* (Ståhl et al. 2009).

5   Soma Design Theory

1. This statement is inspired by https://www.senatehouseevents.co.uk/features/exploring-art-deco-architecture-london.

2. Eric Satie (1866–1925) was a French composer.

3. As stated by Petersen et al. (2004): "Pragmatist aesthetics insists on their interdependencies in the aesthetic experience. In a pragmatist perspective, aesthetic experience is closely linked not only to the analytic mind nor solely to the bodily experience; aesthetic experience speaks to both."

6 Training Somaesthetic Skills

1. Personal communication with the author, May 7, 2016.

2. *Body Weather* is a training and performance practice, evolved in the early 1980s in Japan from collaboration between dancer/choreographer Min Tanaka and a group of dancers, actors, and performers. The group lived and worked on the Body Weather farm in the Japanese countryside, hence the name (Hug 2016).

3. *Proxemics* is the theory of how we indicate that we are open for dialogue (or not), often using our gaze and bodily orientation. For a full account, see, for example, Hall et al. 1968.

7 Soma Design Methods

1. The Lega system was one in a succession of systems through which we explored bodily expression between friends. The Lega is a touch-, motion-, and location-sensitive device that seeks to tap into bodily ways of expression and experience rather than falling back on text or visuals (Laaksolahti et al. 2011; Mentis, Laaksolahti, and Höök 2014). Shaking, squeezing, tapping, tickling, petting, and gesturing with the device in various ways creates expressions through bodily interaction to be shared with others but also lets one explore one's own bodily experiences. The shaking, squeezing, tapping, tickling, petting, and gesturing is translated into patterns of vibrations that a friend can experience through her own Lega device. When we were in the A-labs session, we did not know which material to cover the Lega device with. Cloth, fur, plastic: which one would be most inviting and relevant to the design context?

2. For an introduction to Bauhaus and what a modern, digital Bauhaus could be, turn to Binder, Löwgren, and Malmborg 2009.

References

Akner-Koler, Cheryl. 2007. "Form & Formlessness: Questioning Aesthetic Abstractions through Art Projects, Cross-Disciplinary Studies and Product Design Education." Unpublished thesis manuscript, Department of Architecture Chalmers University of Technology, Gothenburg, Sweden. http://publications.lib.chalmers.se/publication/45357-form-formlessness-questioning-aesthetic-abstractions-through-art-projects-cross-disciplinary-studies.

Andersson, Gerd, Kristina Höök, Dário Mourão, Ana Paiva, and Marco Costa. 2002. "Using a Wizard of Oz Study to Inform the Design of SenToy." In *Proceedings of the 4th Conference on Designing Interactive Systems: Processes, Practices, Methods, and Techniques*, ed. Bill Verplank, Alistair Sufcliffe, Wendy Mackay, Jonathan Arnowitz, and William Gaver, 349–355. New York: ACM. https://doi.org/10.1145/778712.778762.

Bardzell, Jeffrey, and Shaowen Bardzell. 2011. "Pleasure Is Your Birthright: Digitally Enabled Designer Sex Toys as a Case of Third-Wave HCI." In *Proceedings of the SIGCHI Conference on Human Factors in Computing Systems*, 257–266. New York: ACM. https://doi.org/10.1145/1978942.1978979.

Bardzell, Jeffrey, and Shaowen Bardzell. 2015. "Humanistic HCI." *Synthesis Lectures on Human-Centered Informatics* 8 (4): 1–185. https://doi.org/10.2200/S00664ED1V01Y201508HCI031.

Bardzell, Shaowen. 2010. "Feminist HCI: Taking Stock and Outlining an Agenda for Design." In *Proceedings of the SIGCHI Conference on Human Factors in Computing Systems*, 1301–1310. New York: ACM. https://doi.org/10.1145/1753326.1753521.

Barnes, Jonathan. 1984. *The Revised Oxford Translation, Vol. 1: The Complete Works of Aristotle*. Princeton, NJ: Princeton University Press.

Bell, Genevieve, Mark Blythe, and Phoebe Sengers. 2005. "Making by Making Strange: Defamiliarization and the Design of Domestic Technologies." *ACM Transactions on Computer-Human Interaction* 12 (2): 149–173. https://doi.org/10.1145/1067860.1067862.

Benford, Steve, Gabriella Giannachi, Boriana Koleva, and Tom Rodden. 2009. "From Interaction to Trajectories: Designing Coherent Journeys through User Experiences." In *Proceedings of the SIGCHI Conference on Human Factors in Computing Systems*, 709–718. New York: ACM. https://doi.org/10.1145/1518701.1518812.

Benford, Steve, Chris Greenhalgh, Gabriella Giannachi, Brendan Walker, Joe Marshall, and Tom Rodden. 2012. "Uncomfortable Interactions." In *Proceedings of the SIGCHI Conference on Human Factors in Computing Systems*, 2005–2014. New York: ACM. https://doi.org/10.1145/2207676.2208347.

Benford, Steve, Holger Schnädelbach, Boriana Koleva, Rob Anastasi, Chris Greenhalgh, Tom Rodden, Jonathan Green, et al. 2005. "Expected, Sensed, and Desired: A Framework for Designing Sensing-Based Interaction." *ACM Transactions on Computer-Human Interaction* 12 (1): 3–30. https://doi.org/10.1145/1057237.1057239.

Bergström, Ilias, and Martin Jonsson. 2016. "Sarka: Sonification and Somaesthetic Appreciation Design." In *Proceedings of the 3rd International Symposium on Movement and Computing*, 1–8. New York: ACM. https://doi.org/10.1145/2948910.2948922.

Beuthel, Janne Mascha, and Danielle Wilde. 2017. "Wear.X: Developing Wearables That Embody Felt Experience." In *Proceedings of the 2017 Conference on Designing Interactive Systems*, 915–927. New York: ACM. https://doi.org/10.1145/3064663 .3064799.

Binder, Thomas, Jonas Löwgren, and Lone Malmborg. 2009. *(Re)Searching the Digital Bauhaus*. London: Springer-Verlag.

Blevis, Eli, Sabrina Hauser, and William Odom. 2015. "Sharing the Hidden Treasure in Pictorials." *Interactions* 22 (3): 32–43. https://doi.org/10.1145/2755534.

Bødker, Susanne. 2006. "When Second Wave HCI Meets Third Wave Challenges." In *Proceedings of the 4th Nordic Conference on Human-Computer Interaction: Changing Roles*, 1–8. New York: ACM. https://doi.org/10.1145/1182475.1182476.

Boehner, Kirsten, Rogério DePaula, Paul Dourish, and Phoebe Sengers. 2007. "How Emotion Is Made and Measured." *International Journal of Human-Computer Studies* 65 (4): 275–291. https://doi.org/10.1016/j.ijhcs.2006.11.016.

Bogers, Sander, Joep Frens, Janne van Kollenburg, Eva Deckers, and Caroline Hummels. 2016. "Connected Baby Bottle: A Design Case Study towards a Framework for Data-Enabled Design." In *Proceedings of the 2016 ACM Conference on Designing Interactive Systems*, 301–311. New York: ACM. https://doi.org/10.1145/2901790 .2901855.

Brandslet, Steinar. 2015. "The Professor Who Misses His Tail." *Gemini Research News*, December 17, 2015. https://geminiresearchnews.com/2015/12/the-professor-who -misses-his-tail/.

Brown, Barry, Susanne Bødker, and Kristina Höök. 2017. "Does HCI Scale? Scale Hacking and the Relevance of HCI." *Interactions* 24 (5): 28–33. https://doi.org/10.1145/3125387.

Brown, Barry, and Oskar Juhlin. 2015. *Enjoying Machines.* Cambridge, MA: MIT Press.

Buchanan, Richard. 1992. "Wicked Problems in Design Thinking." *Design Issues* 8 (2): 5–21. https://doi.org/10.2307/1511637.

Burke, Edmund. 1998. *A Philosophical Enquiry into the Origin of our Ideas of the Sublime and Beautiful.* London: Penguin.

Cassell, Justine. 2000. *Embodied Conversational Agents.* Cambridge, MA: MIT Press.

Cockton, Gilbert. 2004. "Value-Centred HCI." In *Proceedings of the Third Nordic Conference on Human-Computer Interaction,* 149–160. New York: ACM. https://doi.org/10.1145/1028014.1028038.

Coelho, Marcelo, and Jamie Zigelbaum. 2011. "Shape-Changing Interfaces." *Personal and Ubiquitous Computing* 15 (2): 161–173. https://doi.org/10.1007/s00779-010-0311-y.

Consolvo, Sunny, David W. McDonald, Tammy Toscos, Mike Y. Chen, Jon Froehlich, Beverly Harrison, Predrag Klasnja, et al. 2008. "Activity Sensing in the Wild: A Field Trial of Ubifit Garden." In *Proceedings of the SIGCHI Conference on Human Factors in Computing Systems,* 1797–1806. New York: ACM. https://doi.org/10.1145/1357054.1357335.

Cooper, Alan. 2004. *Why High-Tech Products Drive Us Crazy and How to Restore the Sanity.* Indianapolis: Sams Publishing.

Corbellini, G., K. Aksit, S. Schmid, S. Mangold, and T. R. Gross. 2014. "Connecting Networks of Toys and Smartphones with Visible Light Communication." *IEEE Communications Magazine* 52 (7): 72–78. https://doi.org/10.1109/MCOM.2014.6852086.

Cross, Nigel. 1982. "Designerly Ways of Knowing." "Design Education." Special issue of *Design Studies* 3 (4): 221–227. https://doi.org/10.1016/0142-694X(82)90040-0.

Csikszentmihalyi, Mihaly. 1990. *Flow: The Psychology of Optimal Experience.* New York: Harper and Row.

Damasio, Antonio R. 1994. *Descartes' Error: Emotion, Rationality and the Human Brain.* New York: Putnam.

Darwin, Charles. 1965. *The Expression of the Emotions in Man and Animals.* Chicago: University of Chicago Press.

Davidson, Richard J., Klaus R. Sherer, and H. Hill Goldsmith. 2009. *Handbook of Affective Sciences.* Oxford: Oxford University Press.

Davies, Eden. 2006. *Beyond Dance: Laban's Legacy of Movement Analysis.* New York: Routledge.

De Beauvoir, Simone. [1949] 2014. *The Second Sex*. New York: Vintage.

Dennett, Daniel C. 1988. "Quining Qualia." In *Consciousness in Modern Science*, ed. A. Marcel and E. Bisiach. Oxford: Oxford University Press. http://cogprints.org/254/.

Dewey, John. [1934] 2005. *Art as Experience*. New York: Penguin.

Djajadiningrat, Tom, Ben Matthews, and Marcelle Stienstra. 2007. "Easy Doesn't Do It: Skill and Expression in Tangible Aesthetics." *Personal and Ubiquitous Computing* 11 (8): 657–676. https://doi.org/10.1007/s00779-006-0137-9.

Dourish, Paul. 2001. *Where the Action Is: The Foundations of Embodied Interaction*. Cambridge, MA: MIT Press.

Dunbar, Robin. 1998. *Grooming, Gossip, and the Evolution of Language*. Cambridge, MA: Harvard University Press.

Ehn, Pelle. 1993. "Scandinavian Design: On Participation and Skill." In *Participatory Design: Principles and Practices*, ed. Douglas Schuler and Aki Namioka, 41–77. Hillsdale, NJ: CRC Press.

Ekman, Paul. 1992. "An Argument for Basic Emotions." *Cognition and Emotion* 6 (3–4): 169–200. https://doi.org/10.1080/02699939208411068.

Ellis, Carolyn, Tony E. Adams, and Arthur P. Bochner. 2011. "Autoethnography: An Overview." *Forum Qualitative Sozialforschung/Forum: Qualitative Social Research* 12 (1): 273–290. http://www.qualitative-research.net/index.php/fqs/article/view/1589.

Fagerberg, Petra, Anna Ståhl, and Kristina Höök. 2004. "eMoto: Emotionally Engaging Interaction." *Personal and Ubiquitous Computing* 8 (5): 377–381. https://doi.org/10.1007/s00779-004-0301-z.

Fallman, Daniel. 2003. "Design-Oriented Human-Computer Interaction." In *Proceedings of the SIGCHI Conference on Human Factors in Computing Systems*, 225–232. New York: ACM. https://doi.org/10.1145/642611.642652.

Fallman, Daniel. 2011. "The New Good: Exploring the Potential of Philosophy of Technology to Contribute to Human-Computer Interaction." In *Proceedings of the SIGCHI Conference on Human Factors in Computing Systems*, 1051–1060. New York: ACM. https://doi.org/10.1145/1978942.1979099.

Feldenkrais, Moshe. [1972] 1977. *Awareness through Movement: Health Exercises for Personal Growth*. New York: Harper and Row.

Feltham, Frank, Loke Lian, Elise van den Hoven, Jeffrey Hannam, and Bert Bongers. 2013. "The Slow Floor: Increasing Creative Agency while Walking on an Interactive Surface." In *Proceedings of the 8th International Conference on Tangible, Embedded and Embodied Interaction*, 105–112. New York: ACM Press. https://doi.org/10.1145/2540930.2540974.

Fernaeus, Ylva, Martin Jonsson, and Jakob Tholander. 2012. "Revisiting the Jacquard Loom: Threads of History and Current Patterns in HCI." In *Proceedings of the SIGCHI Conference on Human Factors in Computing Systems*, 1593–1602. New York: ACM. https://doi.org/10.1145/2207676.2208280.

Fernaeus, Ylva, and Petra Sundström. 2012. "The Material Move: How Materials Matter in Interaction Design Research." In *Proceedings of the Designing Interactive Systems Conference*, 486–495. New York: ACM. https://doi.org/10.1145/2317956.2318029.

Ferreira, Pedro. 2015. "Play as Freedom: Implications for ICT4D." http://kth.diva -portal.org/smash/record.jsf?pid=diva2:813616.

Ferreira, Pedro, and Kristina Höök. 2011. "Bodily Orientations around Mobiles: Lessons Learnt in Vanuatu." In *Proceedings of the SIGCHI Conference on Human Factors in Computing Systems*, 277–286. New York: ACM. https://doi.org/10.1145/1978942 .1978981.

Fogtmann, Maiken Hillerup, Kaj Grønbæk, and Martin Kofod Ludvigsen. 2011. "Interaction Technology for Collective and Psychomotor Training in Sports." In *Proceedings of the 8th International Conference on Advances in Computer Entertainment Technology*, Article No. 13. New York: ACM Press. https://doi.org/10.1145/2071423 .2071440.

Forlizzi, Jodi, and Katja Battarbee. 2004. "Understanding Experience in Interactive Systems." In *Proceedings of the 5th Conference on Designing Interactive Systems: Processes, Practices, Methods, and Techniques*, 261–268. New York: ACM. https:// doi.org/10.1145/1013115.1013152.

Françoise, Jules, Sarah Fdili Alaoui, Thecla Schiphorst, and Frederic Bevilacqua. 2014. "Vocalizing Dance Movement for Interactive Sonification of Laban Effort Factors." In *Proceedings of the 2014 Conference on Designing Interactive Systems*, 1079–1082. New York: ACM. https://doi.org/10.1145/2598510.2598582.

Friedman, Batya. 1996. "Value-Sensitive Design." *Interactions* 3 (6): 16–23. https:// doi.org/10.1145/242485.242493.

Fuchs, Thomas, and Hanne De Jaegher. 2009. "Enactive Intersubjectivity: Participatory Sense-Making and Mutual Incorporation." *Phenomenology and the Cognitive Sciences* 8 (4): 465–486. https://doi.org/10.1007/s11097-009-9136-4.

Game, Ann. 2001. "Riding: Embodying the Centaur." *Body & Society* 7 (4): 1–12. https://doi.org/10.1177/1357034X01007004001.

Gaver, William. 2007. "Cultural Commentators: Non-native Interpretations as Resources for Polyphonic Assessment." *International Journal of Human-Computer Studies* 65 (4): 292–305. https://doi.org/10.1016/j.ijhcs.2006.11.014.

Gaver, William. 2009. "Designing for Emotion (among Other Things)." *Philosophical Transactions of the Royal Society of London: Series B, Biological Sciences* 364 (1535): 3597–3604. https://doi.org/10.1098/rstb.2009.0153.

Gaver, William. 2012. "What Should We Expect from Research through Design?" In *Proceedings of the SIGCHI Conference on Human Factors in Computing Systems*, 937–946. New York: ACM. https://doi.org/10.1145/2207676.2208538.

Gaver, William, and Kristina Höök. 2017. "What Makes a Good CHI Design Paper?" *Interactions* 24 (3): 20–21. https://doi.org/10.1145/3076255.

Giaccardi, Elisa, and Elvin Karana. 2015. "Foundations of Materials Experience: An Approach for HCI." In *Proceedings of the 33rd Annual ACM Conference on Human Factors in Computing Systems*, 2447–2456. New York: ACM. https://doi.org/10.1145/2702123.2702337.

Gibson, James J. 1966. *The Senses Considered as Perceptual Systems*. Oxford: Houghton Mifflin.

Gibson, James J. 2014a. *The Ecological Approach to Visual Perception*. New York: Psychology Press.

Gibson, James J. 2014b. "The Theory of Affordances." In *The People, Place, and Space Reader*, ed. Jen Jack Gieseking, William Mangold, Cindi Katz, Setha Low, and Susan Saegert, 56–60. New York: Routledge.

Gilbert, Paul. 2009. "Introducing Compassion-Focused Therapy." *Advances in Psychiatric Treatment* 15 (3): 199–208. https://doi.org/10.1192/apt.bp.107.005264.

Goodall, Jane van Lawick. 1972. "A Preliminary Report on Expressive Movements and Communication in the Gombe Streams Chimpanzees." In *Primate Patterns*, ed. Phyllis Dolhinow, 25–84. New York: Holt, Rinehart and Winston.

Grönvall, Erik, Sofie Kinch, Marianne Graves Petersen, and Majken K. Rasmussen. 2014. "Causing Commotion with a Shape-Changing Bench: Experiencing Shape-Changing Interfaces in Use." In *Proceedings of the 32nd Annual ACM Conference on Human Factors in Computing Systems*, 2559–2568. New York: ACM. https://doi.org/10.1145/2556288.2557360.

Gross, Shad, Jeffrey Bardzell, and Shaowen Bardzell. 2013. "Touch Style: Creativity in Tangible Experience Design." In *Proceedings of the 9th ACM Conference on Creativity & Cognition*, 281–290. New York: ACM. https://doi.org/10.1145/2466627.2466653.

Grosz, Elizabeth. 1994. *Volatile Bodies: Toward a Corporeal Feminism*. Bloomington: Indiana University Press.

Grudin, Jonathan. 1990. "The Computer Reaches Out: The Historical Continuity of Interface Design." In *Proceedings of the SIGCHI Conference on Human Factors in Computing Systems*, 261–268. New York: ACM. https://doi.org/10.1145/97243.97284.

Hadot, Pierre. 1995. *Philosophy as a Way of Life: Spiritual Exercises from Socrates to Foucault*. Malden, MA: Blackwell.

Hall, Edward Twitchell. 1966. *The Hidden Dimension*. New York: Anchor Books.

Hall, Edward Twitchell, Ray L. Birdwhistell, Bernhard Bock, Paul Bohannan, Marshall Durbin Diebold, Munro S. Edmonson, J. L. Fischer, et al. 1968. "Proxemics [and Comments and Replies]." *Current Anthropology* 9 (2/3): 83–108. https://doi.org/10.1086/200975.

Hallnäs, Lars, and Johan Redström. 2001. "Slow Technology—Designing for Reflection." *Personal and Ubiquitous Computing* 5 (3): 201–212. https://doi.org/10.1007/PL00000019.

Harper, Richard. 2006. *Inside the Smart Home.* London: Springer Science & Business Media.

Hatfield, Elaine, John T. Cacioppo, and Richard L. Rapson. 1993. "Emotional Contagion." *Current Directions in Psychological Science* 2 (3): 96–100. https://doi.org/10.1111/1467-8721.ep10770953.

Hirdman, Yvonne. 1988. "Genussystemet-Reflexioner Kring Kvinnors Sociala Underordning." *Tidskrift För Genusvetenskap* 3:1–49.

Hobye, Mads. 2014. *Designing for Homo Explorens: Open Social Play in Performative Frames.* Malmö: Malmö University.

Hobye, Mads, and Jonas Löwgren. 2011. "Touching a Stranger: Designing for Engaging Experience in Embodied Interaction." *International Journal of Design* 5 (3): 31–48. http://www.ijdesign.org/index.php/IJDesign/article/view/976.

Höök, Kristina. 2008. "Affective Loop Experiences—What Are They?" In *Persuasive Technology,* ed. Harri Oinas-Kukkonen, Per Hasle, Marja Harjumaa, Katarina Segerståhl, and Peter Øhrstrøm, 1–12. Lecture Notes in Computer Science, vol. 5033. Berlin: Springer. http://link.springer.com/10.1007/978-3-540-68504-3_1.

Höök, Kristina. 2010. "Transferring Qualities from Horseback Riding to Design." In *Proceedings of the 6th Nordic Conference on Human-Computer Interaction: Extending Boundaries,* 226–235. New York: ACM. https://doi.org/10.1145/1868914.1868943.

Höök, Kristina. 2012. "A Cry for More Tech at CHI!" *Interactions* 19 (2): 10–11. https://doi.org/10.1145/2090150.2090154.

Höök, Kristina, Adrian Bullock, Ana Paiva, Marco Vala, Ricardo Chaves, and Rui Prada. 2003. "FantasyA and SenToy." In *CHI '03 Extended Abstracts on Human Factors in Computing Systems,* 804–805. New York: ACM. https://doi.org/10.1145/765891.766002.

Höök, Kristina, Martin P. Jonsson, Anna Ståhl, and Johanna Mercurio. 2016. "Somaesthetic Appreciation Design." In *Proceedings of the 2016 CHI Conference on Human Factors in Computing Systems,* 3131–3142. New York: ACM. https://doi.org/10.1145/2858036.2858583.

Höök, Kristina, Martin Jonsson, Anna Ståhl, Jakob Tholander, Toni Robertson, Patrizia Marti, Dag Svanaes, et al. 2016. "Move to Be Moved." In *Proceedings of the*

2016 CHI Conference Extended Abstracts on Human Factors in Computing Systems, 3301–3308. New York: ACM. https://doi.org/10.1145/2851581.2856470.

Höök, Kristina, and Jonas Löwgren. 2012. "Strong Concepts: Intermediate-Level Knowledge in Interaction Design Research." *ACM Transactions on Computer-Human Interaction* 19 (3): 23:1–23:18. https://doi.org/10.1145/2362364.2362371.

Höök, Kristina, Phoebe Sengers, and Gerd Andersson. 2003. "Sense and Sensibility: Evaluation and Interactive Art." In *Proceedings of the SIGCHI Conference on Human Factors in Computing Systems*, 241–248. New York: ACM. https://doi.org/10.1145/642611.642654.

Höök, Kristina, Anna Ståhl, Martin Jonsson, Johanna Mercurio, Anna Karlsson, and Eva-Carin Banka Johnson. 2015. "COVER STORY: Somaesthetic Design." *Interactions* 22 (4): 26–33. https://doi.org/10.1145/2770888.

Hug, Joa. 2016. "Writing with Practice: Body Weather Performance Training Becomes a Medium of Artistic Research." *Theatre, Dance and Performance Training* 7 (2): 168–189. http://www.tandfonline.com/doi/full/10.1080/19443927.2016.1175371.

Huizinga, J. [1944] 2003. *Homo Ludens*. London: Routledge.

Hummels, Caroline. 2015. "Embodied Sensemaking to Explore Possible Futures during Engaging Encounters." *Making and Thinking*, 1.8. http://sliperiet.umu.se/en/making-and-thinking-start/18/.

Hummels, Caroline. 2016. "Embodied Encounters Studio: A Tangible Platform for Sensemaking." In *Proceedings of the 2016 CHI Conference Extended Abstracts on Human Factors in Computing Systems*, 3691–3694. New York: ACM. https://doi.org/10.1145/2851581.2890272.

Hummels, Caroline, Kees C. J. Overbeeke, and Sietske Klooster. 2006. "Move to Get Moved: A Search for Methods, Tools and Knowledge to Design for Expressive and Rich Movement-Based Interaction." *Personal and Ubiquitous Computing* 11 (8): 677–690. https://doi.org/10.1007/s00779-006-0135-y.

Ingold, Tim. 2006. "Walking the Plank: Meditations on a Process of Skill." In *Defining Technological Literacy: Towards an Epistemological Framework*, ed. John Dakers, 65–80. New York: Palgrave Macmillan. https://doi.org/10.1057/9781403983053_6.

Ingold, Tim. 2011. *Being Alive: Essays on Movement, Knowledge and Description*. Abingdon, UK: Routledge.

Ingold, Tim. 2013. *Making: Anthropology, Archaeology, Art and Architecture*. Abingdon, UK: Routledge.

Ingold, Tim. 2017. "On Human Correspondence." *Journal of the Royal Anthropological Institute* 23 (1): 9–27. https://doi.org/10.1111/1467-9655.12541.

Isbister, Katherine, and Christopher DiMauro. 2011. "Waggling the Form Baton: Analyzing Body-Movement-Based Design Patterns in Nintendo Wii Games, toward Innovation of New Possibilities for Social and Emotional Experience." In *Whole Body Interaction*, ed. David England, 63–73. Human-Computer Interaction Series. London: Springer. https://doi.org/10.1007/978-0-85729-433-3_6.

Isbister, Katherine, and Kristina Höök. 2009. "On Being Supple: In Search of Rigor without Rigidity in Meeting New Design and Evaluation Challenges for HCI Practitioners." In *Proceedings of the SIGCHI Conference on Human Factors in Computing Systems*, 2233–2242. New York: ACM. https://doi.org/10.1145/1518701.1519042.

Isbister, Katherine, Kristina Höök, Michael Sharp, and Jarmo Laaksolahti. 2006. "The Sensual Evaluation Instrument: Developing an Affective Evaluation Tool." In *Proceedings of the SIGCHI Conference on Human Factors in Computing Systems*, 1163–1172. New York: ACM. https://doi.org/10.1145/1124772.1124946.

James, William. 1884. "What Is an Emotion?" *Mind* 9 (34): 188–205.

James, William. [1890] 1981. *The Principles of Psychology, Vol. 2.* New York: Dover.

James, William. 1905. "The Experience of Activity." *Psychological Review* 12 (1): 1–17. https://doi.org/10.1037/h0070340.

Janlert, Lars-Erik, and Erik Stolterman. 2015. "Faceless Interaction—A Conceptual Examination of the Notion of Interface: Past, Present, and Future." *Human-Computer Interaction* 30 (6): 507–539. https://doi.org/10.1080/07370024.2014.944313.

Janlert, Lars-Erik, and Erik Stolterman. 2017. *Things That Keep Us Busy: The Elements of Interaction.* Cambridge, MA: MIT Press.

Jenson, Scott. 2014. "The Physical Web." In *CHI '14 Extended Abstracts on Human Factors in Computing Systems*, 15–16. New York: ACM. https://doi.org/10.1145/2559206.2580095.

Johnson, Don. 1995. *Bone, Breath & Gesture: Practices of Embodiment.* Berkeley, CA: North Atlantic Books.

Johnson, Eric Arthur. 1967. "Touch Displays: A Programmed Man-Machine Interface." *Ergonomics* 10 (2): 271–277.

Jonsson, Martin, Anna Ståhl, Johanna Mercurio, Anna Karlsson, Naveen Ramani, and Kristina Höök. 2016. "The Aesthetics of Heat: Guiding Awareness with Thermal Stimuli." In *Proceedings of Tenth International Conference on Tangible, Embedded, and Embodied Interaction*, 109–117. New York: ACM. https://doi.org/10.1145/2839462.2839487.

Ju, Wendy. 2015. "The Design of Implicit Interactions." *Synthesis Lectures on Human-Centered Informatics* 8 (2): 1–93. https://doi.org/10.2200/S00619ED1V01Y201412HCI028.

Ju, Wendy, and Larry Leifer. 2008. "The Design of Implicit Interactions: Making Interactive Systems Less Obnoxious." *Design Issues* 24 (3): 72–84.

Juhlin, Oskar, Yanqing Zhang, Cristine Sundbom, and Ylva Fernaeus. 2013. "Fashionable Shape Switching: Explorations in Outfit-Centric Design." In *Proceedings of the SIGCHI Conference on Human Factors in Computing Systems*, 1353–1362. New York: ACM. https://doi.org/10.1145/2470654.2466178.

Katz, Jack. 2001. *How Emotions Work*. Chicago: University of Chicago Press.

Kay, Alan. 1987. "Doing with Images Makes Symbols Pt 1." University Video Communications. Video, 46 min. https://archive.org/details/AlanKeyD1987.

Khut, George P. 2006. "Development and Evaluation of Participant-Centred Biofeedback Artworks." Unpublished thesis manuscript, School of Communication Arts, University of Western Sydney, Australia. http://researchdirect.westernsydney.edu.au/islandora/object/uws%3A2425/.

Khut, George P. 2016. "Designing Biofeedback Artworks for Relaxation." In *Proceedings of the 2016 CHI Conference Extended Abstracts on Human Factors in Computing Systems*, 3859–3862. New York: ACM. https://doi.org/10.1145/2851581.2891089.

Khut, George P, Angie Morrow, and Melissa Yogui Watanbe. 2011. "The Bright-Hearts Project: A New Approach to the Management of Procedure-Related Paediatric Anxiety." In *Workshop Program at OzCHI*, 10–13. Canberra: ACM SIGCHI.

Kohler, Chris. 2007. "A Glimpse into Harmonix's Punk-Rock Design Process." *WIRED*, September 14, 2007. https://www.wired.com/2007/09/mf-harmonix-sb/.

Kosmack Vaara, Elsa. 2017. "Exploring the Aesthetics of Felt Time." http://kth.diva-portal.org/smash/record.jsf?pid=diva2:1057437.

Kuhn, Thomas S. 2012. *The Structure of Scientific Revolutions: 50th Anniversary Edition*. Chicago: University of Chicago Press.

Kuutti, Kari, and Liam J. Bannon. 2014. "The Turn to Practice in HCI: Towards a Research Agenda." In *Proceedings of the 32nd Annual ACM Conference on Human Factors in Computing Systems*, 3543–3552. New York: ACM. https://doi.org/10.1145/2556288.2557111.

Laaksolahti, Jarmo, Jakob Tholander, Marcus Lundén, Jordi Solsona Belenguer, Anna Karlsson, and Tove Jaensson. 2011. "The Lega: A Device for Leaving and Finding Tactile Traces." In *Proceedings of the Fifth International Conference on Tangible, Embedded, and Embodied Interaction*, 193–196. New York: ACM. https://doi.org/10.1145/1935701.1935739.

Lakoff, George. 2008. *Women, Fire, and Dangerous Things*. Chicago: University of Chicago Press.

Lakoff, George, and Mark Johnson. 2008. *Metaphors We Live By*. Chicago: University of Chicago Press.

Ledoux, Joseph. 2015. *The Emotional Brain: The Mysterious Underpinnings of Emotional Life*. New York: Simon and Schuster.

Lee, Wonjun, Lim Youn-kyung, and Richard Shusterman. 2014. "Practicing Somaesthetics: Exploring Its Impact on Interactive Product Design Ideation." In *Proceedings of the 2014 Conference on Designing Interactive Systems*, 1055–1064. New York: ACM. https://doi.org/10.1145/2598510.2598561.

Levisohn, Aaron, and Thecla Schiphorst. 2011. "Embodied Engagement: Supporting Movement Awareness in Ubiquitous Computing Systems." *Ubiquitous Learning: An International Journal* 3 (January): 97–112.

Light, Ann, Alison Powell, and Irina Shklovski. 2017. "Design for Existential Crisis." In *Proceedings of the 2017 CHI Conference Extended Abstracts on Human Factors in Computing Systems (CHI EA '17)*, 722–734. New York: ACM. https://doi.org/10.1145/3027063.3052760.

Lim, Youn-kyung, Erik Stolterman, Heekyoung Jung, and Justin Donaldson. 2007. "Interaction Gestalt and the Design of Aesthetic Interactions." In *Proceedings of the 2007 Conference on Designing Pleasurable Products and Interfaces*, 239–254. New York: ACM. https://doi.org/10.1145/1314161.1314183.

Lindtner, Silvia. 2014. "Hackerspaces and the Internet of Things in China: How Makers Are Reinventing Industrial Production, Innovation, and the Self." *China Information* 28 (2): 145–167. https://doi.org/10.1177/0920203X14529881.

Lindtner, Silvia, Garnet D. Hertz, and Paul Dourish. 2014. "Emerging Sites of HCI Innovation: Hackerspaces, Hardware Startups & Incubators." In *Proceedings of the SIGCHI Conference on Human Factors in Computing Systems*, 439–448. New York: ACM. https://doi.org/10.1145/2556288.2557132.

Ljungblad, Sara, and Lars Erik Holmquist. 2007. "Transfer Scenarios: Grounding Innovation with Marginal Practices." In *Proceedings of the SIGCHI Conference on Human Factors in Computing Systems*, 737–746. New York: ACM. https://doi.org/10.1145/1240624.1240738.

Loke, Lian, George Poonkhin Khut, and A. Baki Kocaballi. 2012. "Bodily Experience and Imagination: Designing Ritual Interactions for Participatory Live-Art Contexts." In *Proceedings of the Designing Interactive Systems Conference*, 779–788. New York: ACM. https://doi.org/10.1145/2317956.2318073.

Loke, Lian, Astrid T. Larssen, and Toni Robertson. 2005. "Labanotation for Design of Movement-Based Interaction." In *Proceedings of the Second Australasian Conference on Interactive Entertainment*, 113–120. Sydney: Creativity & Cognition Studios Press. http://dl.acm.org/citation.cfm?id=1109180.1109197.

Löwgren, Jonas. 2007. "Pliability as an Experiential Quality: Exploring the Aesthetics of Interaction Design." *Artifact* 1 (2): 85–95. https://doi.org/10.1080/17493460600976165.

Löwgren, Jonas. 2009. "Toward an Articulation of Interaction Esthetics." *New Review of Hypermedia and Multimedia* 15 (2): 129–146. http://www.tandfonline.com/doi/abs/10.1080/13614560903117822.

Löwgren, Jonas. 2013. "Annotated Portfolios and Other Forms of Intermediate-Level Knowledge." *Interactions* 20 (1): 30–34. https://doi.org/10.1145/2405716.2405725.

Löwgren, Jonas, and Erik Stolterman. 2004. *Thoughtful Interaction Design: A Design Perspective on Information Technology*. Cambridge, MA: MIT Press.

Lutz, Catherine. 1988. *Unnatural Emotions: Everyday Sentiments on a Micronesian Atoll and Their Challenge to Western Theory*. Chicago: University of Chicago Press.

Lutz, Catherine, and Geoffrey White. 2003. "The Anthropology of Emotion." *Annual Review of Anthropology* 15 (1): 405–436. https://doi.org/10.1146/annurev.an.15.100186.002201.

Mailvaganam, Attalan, and Miguel Bruns Alonso. 2015. "Haptic Beats: Designing for Rich Haptic Interaction in a Music Controller." Paper presented at the 9th International Conference on Design and Semantics of Form and Movement (DeSForM), Politecnico di Milano, Milan, Italy, October 13–17.

Márquez Segura, Elena. 2015. "Co-creating Embodied Sketches: Playing as a Method to Design with Children." In *Proceedings of the 12th International Conference on Advances in Computer Entertainment Technology*, Article No. 18. New York: ACM. https://doi.org/10.1145/2832932.2832975.

Márquez Segura, Elena. 2016. "Embodied Core Mechanics: Designing for Movement-Based Co-located Play." Unpublished thesis manuscript, Disciplinary Domain of Humanities and Social Sciences, Faculty of Social Sciences, Department of Informatics and Media, Uppsala University, Sweden. https://uu.diva-portal.org/smash/get/diva2:920694/FULLTEXT01.pdf.

Márquez Segura, Elena, and Katherine Isbister. 2015. "Enabling Co-located Physical Social Play: A Framework for Design and Evaluation." In *Game User Experience Evaluation*, ed. Regina Bernhaupt, 209–238. Human–Computer Interaction Series. Cham, Switzerland: Springer. https://doi.org/10.1007/978-3-319-15985-0_10.

Márquez Segura, Elena, Laia Turmo Vidal, Asreen Rostami, and Annika Waern. 2016. "Embodied Sketching." In *Proceedings of the 2016 CHI Conference on Human Factors in Computing Systems*, 6014–6027. New York: ACM. https://doi.org/10.1145/2858036.2858486.

McCarthy, John, and Peter Wright. 2004a. *Technology as Experience*. Cambridge, MA: MIT Press.

McCarthy, John, and Peter Wright. 2004b. "Technology as Experience." *Interactions* 11 (5): 42–43. https://doi.org/10.1145/1015530.1015549.

Mentis, Helena M., Jarmo Laaksolahti, and Kristina Höök. 2014. "My Self and You: Tension in Bodily Sharing of Experience." *ACM Transactions on Computer-Human Interaction* 21 (4): Article No. 20. https://doi.org/10.1145/2617945.

Merleau-Ponty, Maurice. 2002. *Phenomenology of Perception*. London: Routledge.

Myers, Brad A. 1998. "A Brief History of Human-Computer Interaction Technology." *Interactions* 5 (2): 44–54.

Nelson, Harold G., and Erik Stolterman. 2003. "Design Judgement: Decision-Making in the 'Real' World." *Design Journal* 6 (March): 23–31. https://doi.org/10.2752/146069203790219344.

Neustaedter, Carman, and Phoebe Sengers. 2012. "Autobiographical Design in HCI Research: Designing and Learning through Use-It-Yourself." In *Proceedings of the Designing Interactive Systems Conference*, 514–523. New York: ACM. https://doi.org/10.1145/2317956.2318034.

Norman, Donald A. 1999. "Affordance, Conventions, and Design." *Interactions* 6 (3): 38–43. https://doi.org/10.1145/301153.301168.

Norman, Donald A. 2007. *Emotional Design: Why We Love (or Hate) Everyday Things*. London: Hachette UK.

Norman, Donald A. 2010. "Natural User Interfaces Are Not Natural." *Interactions* 17 (3): 6–10. https://doi.org/10.1145/1744161.1744163.

Nussbaum, Martha C. 2001. *Women and Human Development: The Capabilities Approach*. Cambridge: Cambridge University Press.

Ong, Boon Lay. 2012. "Warming Up to Heat." *Senses and Society* 7 (1): 5–21. https://doi.org/10.2752/174589312X13173255801969.

Oulasvirta, Antti, Esko Kurvinen, and Tomi Kankainen. 2003. "Understanding Contexts by Being There: Case Studies in Bodystorming." *Personal and Ubiquitous Computing* 7 (2): 125–134. https://doi.org/10.1007/s00779-003-0238-7.

Paiva, Ana, Gerd Andersson, Kristina Höök, Dário Mourão, Marco Costa, and Carlos Martinho. 2002. "SenToy in FantasyA: Designing an Affective Sympathetic Interface to a Computer Game." *Personal and Ubiquitous Computing* 6 (5–6): 378–389. https://doi.org/10.1007/s007790200043.

Papert, Seymour. 1980. *Mindstorms: Children, Computers, and Powerful Ideas*. New York: Basic Books.

Parkinson, Brian. 1996. "Emotions Are Social." *British Journal of Psychology* 87 (4): 663–683. https://doi.org/10.1111/j.2044-8295.1996.tb02615.x.

Parviainen, Jaana. 2002. "Bodily Knowledge: Epistemological Reflections on Dance." *Dance Research Journal* 34 (1): 11–26. https://doi.org/10.2307/1478130.

Petersen, Marianne Graves, Ole Sejer Iversen, Peter Gall Krogh, and Martin Ludvigsen. 2004. "Aesthetic Interaction: A Pragmatist's Aesthetics of Interactive Systems." In *Proceedings of the 5th Conference on Designing Interactive Systems: Processes, Practices, Methods, and Techniques*, 269–276. New York: ACM. https://doi.org/10.1145/1013115.1013153.

Picard, Rosalind W. 1997. *Affective Computing*. Cambridge, MA: MIT Press.

Purpura, Stephen, Victoria Schwanda, Kaiton Williams, William Stubler, and Phoebe Sengers. 2011. "Fit4life: The Design of a Persuasive Technology Promoting Healthy Behavior and Ideal Weight." In *Proceedings of the SIGCHI Conference on Human Factors in Computing Systems*, 423–432. New York: ACM.

Rasmussen, Majken K., Giovanni M. Troiano, Marianne G. Petersen, Jakob G. Simonsen, and Kasper Hornbæk. 2016. "Sketching Shape-Changing Interfaces: Exploring Vocabulary, Metaphors Use, and Affordances." In *Proceedings of the 2016 CHI Conference on Human Factors in Computing Systems*, 2740–2751. New York: ACM. https://doi.org/10.1145/2858036.2858183.

Redström, Johan. 2017. *Making Design Theory*. Cambridge, MA: MIT Press.

Rinman, Marie-Louise, Anders Friberg, Bendik Bendiksen, Demian Cirotteau, Sofia Dahl, Ivar Kjellmo, Barbara Mazzarino, and Antonio Camurri. 2004. "Ghost in the Cave—An Interactive Collaborative Game Using Non-Verbal Communication." In *Gesture-Based Communication in Human-Computer Interaction*, ed. Antonio Camurri and Gualtiero Volpe, 549–556. Berlin: Springer Berlin Heidelberg. http://link .springer.com/10.1007/978-3-540-24598-8_51.

Rogers, Yvonne, Helen Sharp, and Jenny Preece. 2011. *Interaction Design: Beyond Human-Computer Interaction*. Chichester, UK: John Wiley & Sons.

Rose, David. 2014. *Enchanted Objects: Design, Human Desire, and the Internet of Things*. New York: Scribner.

Sanches, Pedro, Kristina Höök, Elsa Vaara, Claus Weymann, Markus Bylund, Pedro Ferreira, Nathalie Peira, and Marie Sjölinder. 2010. "Mind the Body! Designing a Mobile Stress Management Application Encouraging Personal Reflection." In *Proceedings of the 8th ACM Conference on Designing Interactive Systems*, 47–56. New York: ACM. https://doi.org/10.1145/1858171.1858182.

Schiphorst, Thecla. 2007. "Really, Really Small: The Palpability of the Invisible." In *Proceedings of the 6th ACM SIGCHI Conference on Creativity & Cognition*, 7–16. New York: ACM. https://doi.org/10.1145/1254960.1254962.

Schiphorst, Thecla. 2009a. "Soft(n): Toward a Somaesthetics of Touch." In *CHI '09 Extended Abstracts on Human Factors in Computing Systems*, 2427–2438. New York: ACM. https://doi.org/10.1145/1520340.1520345.

Schiphorst, Thecla. 2009b. "The Varieties of User Experience: Bridging Embodied Methodologies from Somatics and Performance to Human Computer Interaction." Unpublished thesis manuscript, Faculty of Science and Technology, University of Plymouth, UK. https://pearl.plymouth.ac.uk//handle/10026.1/2177.

Schiphorst, Thecla. 2011. "Self-Evidence: Applying Somatic Connoisseurship to Experience Design." In *CHI '11 Extended Abstracts on Human Factors in Computing Systems*, 145–160. New York: ACM. https://doi.org/10.1145/1979742.1979640.

Schiphorst, Thecla, Wynnie (Wing Yi) Chung, and Emily Ip. 2013. "Wo.Defy: Wearable Interaction Design Inspired by a Chinese 19th Century Suffragette Movement." In *Proceedings of the 7th International Conference on Tangible, Embedded and Embodied Interaction*, 319–322. New York: ACM. https://doi.org/10.1145/2460625.2460679.

Schon, Donald A. 1984. *The Reflective Practitioner: How Professionals Think in Action.* New York: Basic Books.

Schuler, Douglas, and Aki Namioka. 1993. *Participatory Design: Principles and Practices.* Hillsdale, NJ: Lawrence Erlbaum.

Schutz, Alfred. 1967. *The Phenomenology of the Social World.* Evanston, IL: Northwestern University Press.

Sen, Amartya. 1999. *Development as Freedom.* Oxford: Oxford University Press.

Sheets-Johnstone, Maxine. 1998. "Consciousness: A Natural History." *Journal of Consciousness Studies* 5 (3): 260–294.

Sheets-Johnstone, Maxine. 1999. "Emotion and Movement: A Beginning Empirical-Phenomenological Analysis of Their Relationship." *Journal of Consciousness Studies* 6 (11–12): 259–277.

Sheets-Johnstone, Maxine. 2011. *The Primacy of Movement.* Expanded 2nd ed. Amsterdam: John Benjamins Publishing.

Sheets-Johnstone, Maxine. 2012. "From Movement to Dance." *Phenomenology and the Cognitive Sciences* 11 (1): 39–57. https://doi.org/10.1007/s11097-011-9200-8.

Sheets-Johnstone, Maxine. 2015. *The Corporeal Turn: An Interdisciplinary Reader.* Bedsfordshire: Andrews UK Limited.

Shusterman, Richard. 2000a. *Pragmatist Aesthetics: Living Beauty, Rethinking Art.* Lanham, MD: Rowman & Littlefield Publishers.

Shusterman, Richard. 2000b. "Somaesthetics and Care of the Self: The Case of Foucault." *Monist* 83 (4): 530–551.

Shusterman, Richard. 2003. "Somaesthetics and *The Second Sex*: A Pragmatist Reading of a Feminist Classic." *Hypatia* 18 (4): 106–136. https://doi.org/10.1111/j.1527-2001.2003.tb01415.x.

Shusterman, Richard. 2005. "Somaesthetics and Burke's Sublime." *British Journal of Aesthetics* 45 (4): 323–341. https://doi.org/10.1093/aesthj/ayi047.

Shusterman, Richard. 2008. *Body Consciousness: A Philosophy of Mindfulness and Somaesthetics.* Cambridge: Cambridge University Press.

Shusterman, Richard. 2012. *Thinking through the Body: Essays in Somaesthetics.* Cambridge: Cambridge University Press.

Shusterman, Richard. 2013. "Somaesthetics." In *The Encyclopedia of Human-Computer Interaction*, 2nd ed., ed. Mads Soegaard and Rikke Friis. Aarbus, Denmark: Interaction Design Foundation. https://www.interaction-design.org/literature/book/the-encyclopedia-of-human-computer-interaction-2nd-ed/somaesthetics.

Šimbelis, Vygandas. n.d. "Metaphone Project." Accessed October 20, 2017. http://www.simbelis.com/project/metaphone/.

Šimbelis, Vygandas, Anders Lundström, Kristina Höök, Jordi Solsona Belenguer, and Vincent Lewandowski. 2014. "Metaphone: Machine Aesthetics Meets Interaction Design." In *Proceedings of the SIGCHI Conference on Human Factors in Computing Systems*, 1–10. New York: ACM. https://doi.org/10.1145/2556288.2557152.

Solsona Belenguer, Jordi. 2015. "*Engineering through Designerly Conversations with the Digital Material: The Approach, the Tools and the Design Space.*" Unpublished thesis manuscript, Media Technology and Interaction Design (MID), KTH Royal Institute of Technology, Sweden. http://kth.diva-portal.org/smash/record.jsf?pid=diva2%3A8 75831&dswid=-4001.

Solsona Belenguer, Jordi, Marcus Lundén, Jarmo Laaksolhati, and Petra Sundström. 2012. "Immaterial Materials: Designing with Radio." In *Proceedings of the Sixth International Conference on Tangible, Embedded and Embodied Interaction*, 205–212. New York: ACM. https://doi.org/10.1145/2148131.2148177.

Ståhl, Anna, Kristina Höök, Martin Svensson, Alex S. Taylor, and Marco Combetto. 2009. "Experiencing the Affective Diary." *Personal and Ubiquitous Computing* 13 (5): 365–378. https://doi.org/10.1007/s00779-008-0202-7.

Ståhl, Anna, Jonas Löwgren, and Kristina Höök. 2014. "Evocative Balance: Designing for Interactional Empowerment." *International Journal of Design* 8 (1): 43–57. https://www.questia.com/library/journal/1P3-3304502821/evocative-balance-designing-for-interactional-empowerment.

Ståhl, Anna, Jakob Tholander, Jarmo Laaksolahti, and Elsa Kosmack-Vaara. 2017. "Being, Bringing and Bridging: Three Aspects of Sketching with Nature." In

Proceedings of the 2017 Conference on Designing Interactive Systems, 1309–1320. New York: ACM. https://doi.org/10.1145/3064663.3064764.

"Stanford D.school." n.d. Accessed October 25, 2017. https://dschool.stanford.edu/.

"Stanford D-School—Facilitate a Brainstorm." n.d. "Facilitate a Brainstorm." Accessed October 25, 2017. https://dschool-old.stanford.edu/wp-content/themes/dschool/method-cards/facilitate-a-brainstorm.pdf.

"Stanford D-School—Prototype for Empathy." n.d. Accessed October 25, 2017. https://dschool-old.stanford.edu/wp-content/themes/dschool/method-cards/prototype-for-empathy.pdf.

Stanislavski, Konstantin. [1938] 2017. *An Actor's Work.* Abingdon, UK: Routledge.

Starner, T. 2014. "How Wearables Worked Their Way into the Mainstream." *IEEE Pervasive Computing* 13 (4): 10–15. https://doi.org/10.1109/MPRV.2014.66.

Stellar, J. E., A. Cohen, C. Oveis, and D. Keltner. 2015. "Affective and Physiological Responses to the Suffering of Others: Compassion and Vagal Activity." *Journal of Personality and Social Psychology* 108 (4): 572–585. https://doi.org/10.1037/pspi0000010.

Stolterman, Erik. 2008. "The Nature of Design Practice and Implications for Interaction Design Research." *International Journal of Design* 2 (1): 55–65.

Suchman, Lucy A. 1987. *Plans and Situated Actions: The Problem of Human-Machine Communication.* Cambridge: Cambridge University Press.

Suchman, Lucy A. 1997. "From Interactions to Integrations." In *Human-Computer Interaction: INTERACT '97,* ed. S. Howard, J. Hammond, and G. Lindgaard, 3. Boston: Springer. https://doi.org/10.1007/978-0-387-35175-9_1.

Suchman, Lucy. 2007. *Human-Machine Reconfigurations: Plans and Situated Actions.* Cambridge: Cambridge University Press.

Sundström, Petra. 2005. "Exploring the Affective Loop." Licentiate thesis, Stockholm University. http://eprints.sics.se/98/.

Sundström, Petra. 2010. *Designing Affective Loop Experiences.* Unpublished thesis manuscript. Stockholm: Department of Computer and Systems Sciences, Stockholm University. http://su.diva-portal.org/smash/get/diva2:356101/FULLTEXT01.pdf.

Sundström, Petra, and Kristina Höök. 2010. "Hand in Hand with the Material: Designing for Suppleness." In *Proceedings of the SIGCHI Conference on Human Factors in Computing Systems,* 463–472. New York: ACM. https://doi.org/10.1145/1753326.1753396.

Sundström, Petra, Alex Taylor, Katja Grufberg, Niklas Wirström, Jordi Solsona Belenguer, and Marcus Lundén. 2011. "Inspirational Bits: Towards a Shared

Understanding of the Digital Material." In *Proceedings of the SIGCHI Conference on Human Factors in Computing Systems*, 1561–1570. New York: ACM. https://doi.org/10.1145/1978942.1979170.

Sundström, Petra, Alex S. Taylor, and Kenton O'Hara. 2011. "Sketching in Software and Hardware: Bluetooth as a Design Material." In *Proceedings of the 13th International Conference on Human Computer Interaction with Mobile Devices and Services*, 405–414. New York: ACM. https://doi.org/10.1145/2037373.2037434.

Svanæs, Dag. 2013. "Interaction Design for and with the Lived Body: Some Implications of Merleau-Ponty's Phenomenology." *ACM Transactions on Computer-Human Interaction* 20 (1): 8:1–8:30. https://doi.org/10.1145/2442106.2442114.

Svanæs, Dag, and Martin Solheim. 2016. "Wag Your Tail and Flap Your Ears: The Kinesthetic User Experience of Extending Your Body." In *Proceedings of the 2016 CHI Conference Extended Abstracts on Human Factors in Computing Systems*, 3778–3779. New York: ACM. https://doi.org/10.1145/2851581.2890268.

Svensson, Martin, Kristina Höök, and Rickard Cöster. 2005. "Designing and Evaluating Kalas: A Social Navigation System for Food Recipes." *ACM Transactions on Computer-Human Interaction* 12 (3): 374–400. https://doi.org/10.1145/1096737.1096739.

Svensson, Martin, Kristina Höök, Jarmo Laaksolahti, and Annika Waern. 2001. "Social Navigation of Food Recipes." In *Proceedings of the SIGCHI Conference on Human Factors in Computing Systems*, 341–348. New York: ACM. https://doi.org/10.1145/365024.365130.

Taylor, Alex S., Richard Harper, Laurel Swan, Shahram Izadi, Abigail Sellen, and Mark Perry. 2007. "Homes That Make Us Smart." *Personal and Ubiquitous Computing* 11 (5): 383–393. https://doi.org/10.1007/s00779-006-0076-5.

Tholander, Jakob, and Carolina Johansson. 2010. "Design Qualities for Whole Body Interaction: Learning from Golf, Skateboarding and BodyBugging." In *Proceedings of the 6th Nordic Conference on Human-Computer Interaction: Extending Boundaries*, 493–502. New York: ACM. https://doi.org/10.1145/1868914.1868970.

Tholander, Jakob, and Stina Nylander. 2015. "Snot, Sweat, Pain, Mud, and Snow: Performance and Experience in the Use of Sports Watches." In *Proceedings of the 33rd Annual ACM Conference on Human Factors in Computing Systems*, 2913–2922. New York: ACM. https://doi.org/10.1145/2702123.2702482.

Thoreau, Henry David. [1854] 2016. *Walden*. London: Macmillan Collector's Library.

Tinbergen, Niko. [1968] 2017. *Curious Naturalists*. Garden City, NY: Doubleday.

US Department of Health and Human Services, Digital Communications Division. n.d. "Personas." Accessed October 25, 2017. https://www.usability.gov/how-to-and-tools/methods/personas.html.

Vallgårda, Anna. 2014. "The Dress Room: Responsive Spaces and Embodied Interaction." In *Proceedings of the 8th Nordic Conference on Human-Computer Interaction: Fun, Fast, Foundational*, 618–627. New York: ACM. https://doi.org/10.1145/2639189 .2639254.

Vallgårda, Anna, and Johan Redström. 2007. "Computational Composites." In *Proceedings of the SIGCHI Conference on Human Factors in Computing Systems*, 513–522. New York: ACM. https://doi.org/10.1145/1240624.1240706.

Varela, Francisco J., Evan Thompson, and Eleanor Rosch. 2017. *The Embodied Mind: Cognitive Science and Human Experience*. Cambridge, MA: MIT Press.

Varshney, Ambuj, Andreas Soleiman, Luca Mottola, and Thiemo Voigt. 2017. "Battery-Free Visible Light Sensing." In *Proceedings of the 4th ACM Workshop on Visible Light Communication Systems*, 3–8. New York: ACM. https://doi.org/10.1145/ 3129881.3129890.

Verbeek, Peter-Paul. 2015. "COVER STORY: Beyond Interaction: A Short Introduction to Mediation Theory." *Interactions* 22 (3): 26–31. https://doi.org/10.1145/ 2751314.

Vidyarthi, Jay, Bernhard E. Riecke, and Diane Gromala. 2012. "Sonic Cradle: Designing for an Immersive Experience of Meditation by Connecting Respiration to Music." In *Proceedings of the Designing Interactive Systems Conference*, 408–417. New York: ACM. https://doi.org/10.1145/2317956.2318017.

Weilenmann, Alexandra. 2003. "Doing Mobility." Unpublished thesis manuscript, School of Business, Economics and Law, Gothenburg University, Sweden. https:// gupea.ub.gu.se/handle/2077/910.

Weiser, Mark. 1991. "The Computer for the 21st Century." *Scientific American* 265 (3): 94–105.

Weiser, Mark, and John Seely Brown. 1997. "The Coming Age of Calm Technology." In *Beyond Calculation: The Next Fifty Years of Computing*, ed. Peter J. Denning and Robert M. Metcalfe, 75–85. New York: Springer. https://doi.org/10.1007/978-1-461 2-0685-9_6.

Westerlund, Bo. 2009. "Design Space Exploration: Co-operative Creation of Proposals for Desired Interactions with Future Artefacts." Unpublished thesis manuscript, Human-Machine Interaction, Royal Institute of Technology (KTH), Stockholm, Sweden. http:// kth.diva-portal.org/smash/record.jsf?pid=diva2%3A241661&dswid=-9892.

Wilde, Danielle, Anna Vallgårda, and Oscar Tomico. 2017. "Embodied Design Ideation Methods: Analysing the Power of Estrangement." In *Proceedings of the 2017 CHI Conference on Human Factors in Computing Systems*, 5158–5170. New York: ACM. https://doi.org/10.1145/3025453.3025873.

Williams, Kaiton. 2015. "An Anxious Alliance." In *Proceedings of the Fifth Decennial Aarhus Conference on Critical Alternatives*, 121–131. Aarhus, Denmark: Aarhus University Press. https://doi.org/10.7146/aahcc.v1i1.21146.

Windlin, Charles, and Jarmo Laaksolahti. 2017. "Unpacking Visible Light Communication as a Material for Design." In *Proceedings of the 2017 CHI Conference on Human Factors in Computing Systems*, 2019–2023. New York: ACM. https://doi.org/10.1145/3025453.3025862.

Yetis-Larsson, Zeynep, Robin Teigland, and Olga Dovbysh. 2015. "Networked Entrepreneurs: How Entrepreneurs Leverage Open Source Software Communities." *American Behavioral Scientist* 59 (4): 475–491. https://doi.org/10.1177/0002764214556809.

Zhao, Liwei, and Norman Badler. 2001. "Synthesis and Acquisition of Laban Movement Analysis Qualitative Parameters for Communicative Gestures." *Technical Reports (CIS)*, January. https://repository.upenn.edu/cis_reports/116.

Index